Nothing
Will Come of
Nothing

Other titles by M A Dershem

Hell Hath No Fury Series

Something Wicked

Nothing
Will Come of
Nothing

A Hell Hath No Fury Mystery (2)

M A Dershem

Copyright

Dedication

To all the strong women throughout my life who
encouraged me to disturb the universe.

Dramatis Personæ

Mustardseed Productions Cast and Crew

The Kindley Family
Guppy, a witch, mother of the furies, and head of *Mustardseed Productions*
Alec, oldest, fury of moral failings
Meg, middle, fury of jealousy
Tisi, youngest, fury of vengeance

Troupe Members
Saumia, nagini or snake shifter
Cole, mountain lion shifter, older brother to Derek
Derek, mountain lion shifter
Eliava, a fairy
Bre, a banshee
Richard, a ghost
Carlos, oldest member of the troupe
Asher, lead of the tech crew
Mike, tech crew

Returning Characters from **Something Wicked**
Ethan Larkes, police officer stationed in Salida
Sherlock, Larkes' puppy, training in search and rescue

Prologue

The sun had long since set over the Flatirons, draining the last light out of the sky much the same way Laurel Monroe drained the last of the thirty year old Scotch out of one of her father's favorite tulip-shaped glasses.

"The shape helps funnel the aroma upward while you drink," he had explained once when she was younger, still in middle school, but always ready to learn anything about her parents' businesses.

She poured another dram, knowing she shouldn't, but not really caring at the moment. She missed them, her parents, taken from her in a pointless car accident only eight months ago. Flagstaff Road could be dangerous at night or in the winter with icy patches or if drunks were traveling on it. But none of those conditions had been present. No one had been at fault. The investigation found no foul play or signs of inebriation, only some skid marks from slamming on the brakes and a crushed trail of foliage leading to a large tree which had borne the brunt of the impact. She had lost both of them at the start of her senior year at the University of Colorado, and now, two days after graduating, she found herself lost and alone and missing them terribly.

The year had been tough. Besides having to finish her classes so she could graduate, she suddenly was in charge of her parents' estate, including the three restaurants they had established over the years since moving to the ever-growing edge-of-the-Rockies town. Not that she wasn't prepared for it. The Business Management degree was really just a formality on top of all the on-the-job training her parents had instilled in her. She had grown up in the tiny office of the first business, the quaint little coffee shop located between the campus and Pearl Street and would play with her stuffed black cat Ember while her mom helped work the counter, filling a growing niche long before the larger coffee chains started vying for customers.

The mid-price-range Italian restaurant was their second endeavor, and the first one they started from scratch; in middle school she would help dust off the imported classic espresso machine proudly displayed in the host area and would roll silverware into the red linen napkins so the wait staff could spend more time with their customers and still go home at a decent hour. In high school, Laurel and all of her friends had worked at both places at one time or another, and by the time she was a college freshman, she was running the coffee shop on the weekends with very little supervision from either parent or the general manager. Mostly this was because the third restaurant, the one several miles up the winding mountain road, that served only dinner and received several awards and Michelin Stars over the years, kept both her mom and dad busy. And that winding road had eventually killed them.

Laurel stretched out her arm and poured another dram into her glass, remembering the times she had worked at the "fancy place" as she and her coffee shop pals referred to it. Mostly she had just filled in when the staff was short-handed for bussers or hosts. The views were spectacular, the food exquisite, and the wine cellar unmatched. Working there wasn't an after school / pay-for-college type of job; it was a career where the waiters could make upwards of 500 dollars in tips in one night. It was her parents' pride and joy, and they had poured the majority of their energy into it to get it successfully up and running.

Now, all three places were hers, as was the giant restored Victorian mansion on Mapleton Avenue, and it was really just too much to think about, hence the evenings she spent drinking her father's favorite Scotch, or on other nights, her mother's favorite reds.

The first rumbles of thunder reached her ears as she finished off another glass of Scotch. Tomorrow was going to be busy considering she, with the family lawyer, had a meeting with the three restaurants' managers to make some decisions about what to do moving forward. Her parents had split the overseeing of the establishments between them; they were busy, but they made it work. Laurel knew that alone, she couldn't keep up with the constant demands. Also, as one of the managers really didn't like taking orders or suggestions from a "spoiled princess," she knew conflict awaited her, and she hated conflict. Her parents were naturally comfortable with their various employees and had their age, reputation, and knowledge of the industry backing up their authority; this skill was something she was working on, but it would never come intuitively. And as a new graduate, she lacked both the professional reputation and the years of experience of her parents; it was no wonder she wasn't taken seriously sometimes.

However, the other managers were more understanding of the situation and had, so far, not tried to take advantage of the sudden and unexpected change in the managerial hierarchy. But, she knew, she had mostly the lawyer to thank for that. With the king and queen gone, the last eight months had been a strange dance of people jockeying for positions as the new kingdom took shape around them.

Lightning flashed in the distance as Laurel set her now empty glass into the sink and filled it with water. She debated washing it—her mother made it a habit to never leave dishes in the sink overnight—but she was tired and more than a little woozy.

"As Dad would say, 'It will still be there in the morning,'" she said to herself, turning out lights as she headed for her third floor bedroom, wondering if she would ever want to move downstairs, or more liberating, move completely out and start fresh somewhere new, somewhere she wouldn't be seen as a Monroe first and Laurel second.

Gripping the railing of the narrow stairs, the young woman shook her head, trying to clear the fog that was beginning to settle over her.

"Guess I drank a little too much," she said to no one, finally making it to the top of the steps.

But someone was there to hear, "I guess so."

Laurel jerked her head up from watching her feet in time to see a gloved hand reach out and shove her viciously backward. She lost her grip on the railing and felt her feet tangle as she fought to regain her balance, but the hand shoved her again, sending her crashing down the stairs, finally coming to rest at the bottom, her body at an unnatural angle, blood beginning to pool around her head.

Slow steps worked their way down the stairs, carefully stepping over the broken form of the young woman, avoiding the blood, and heading toward the kitchen and the back door. Once outside and the door locked, the figure slipped through the rain and into the dark, leaving behind a broken body, no trace of another person's presence, and a mystery.

Chapter 1

"This is the excellent foppery of the world, that when we are sick in fortune (often the surfeits of our own behavior) we make guilty of our disasters the sun, the moon, and stars, as if we were villains on necessity; fools by heavenly compulsion; knaves, thieves, and treachers by spherical predominance; drunkards, liars, and adulterers by an enforced obedience of planetary influence; and all that we are evil in, by a divine thrusting on. An admirable evasion of whoremaster man, to lay his goatish disposition on the charge of a star!"

Derek finished delivering the conniving brother Edmund's soliloquy with the perfect levels of disdain and humor as my sisters and I, our entire troupe, and a small, mixed audience of high school and college students observed from the first few rows of the house.

Back in October, we had been invited by Guppy's old college roommate to be part of a local two week theatre camp the University of Boulder was hosting. So here we sat, introducing the characters of our chosen vehicle–*King Lear*–to the participants so they could finalize what character they might want to audition for and prepare that piece for performance the next day. *King Lear* boasts a large cast, and these same students would take over the acting portion of the production for two matinees at the end of the second week. We would each have an understudy once the students had auditioned, which can be fun if everyone involved is ready to work.

Two weeks is a short time to prepare a piece, especially one as long as *Lear*, but that's what the camp promised, and we were getting paid both for our shows and our part in running the workshop. Dr. K had already chosen the audition pieces for each role, and the students had received all those passages before the camp started so they could get a jump on preparation. We had done the same thing for the extras we would need to put on *King Lear*, and Dr. K had delivered those as well as a video of our production so our added cast would be familiar with how we staged this particular play. Of course, if it became necessary, there was always a little magic that could be done as well; we have a reputation to uphold, after all.

All eyes were on Derek as he finished the rest of the speech. The students, as they had for Carlos who had delivered Lear's "men of stones" moment from Act V, applauded wildly. Edmund is a fun character to play–smarmy, deceptive, funny, throws the word bastard around like confetti; I already knew we would have more tryouts for Edmund than either Lear or Edgar, the nice brother. No one ever wants to be the nice characters, not that the King is nice, but whatever.

From the corner of my eye, I could see Guppy and her former roommate, Dr. Ikeolua Kikelomo, (Dr. K to her students, Ike to her friends), discussing which of the wanna-bes watching should be trying out for this part, just as they had for Lear, and for every other character we had introduced on this first morning session of the workshop. It was a great way to introduce both ourselves and our profession to eager students hoping to maybe become professional actors someday.

I checked the time on my phone and looked to my left; Kit perched on the unfolded seat next to me, not heavy enough to weigh it down. Occasionally, she still popped images into my head, but more and more I was beginning to 'hear' her thoughts in my own language. And for the past 15 minutes, she had been asking when we were going to eat lunch as she was hungry.

"You're lucky Dr. K even okayed it for you to be in here," I reminded her quietly. "I could have left you back in the residence hall."

She rolled her eyes at me, a mannerism she had picked up from me or my sisters probably, and refocused her attention on the stage even as her stomach gurgled and an image of a clock running backward flashed into my head

Dr. Kikelomo had arranged for us to stay in one of the dormitories on campus not too far from the theatre building, just like the student participants and other adult helpers if they so wanted, and most of them did. Our caravan of vehicles was taking up most of the parking lot near our accommodations, although the tech crew had been taking some in for preventative maintenance and cleaning. While the rooms were tiny, we weren't spending the majority of our time there, so it wasn't a big deal. Most of us weren't even doubled up, but for some reason, Kit had chosen to be my roomie, maybe because I was the only one she could 'talk' to or maybe because the gift of removing rotten souls from the land of the living is not something everyone has in common.

I could feel my own stomach starting to rumble as Kit reminded me for the hundredth time that she wanted to eat, very soon, preferably now. My sisters and Saumia had already introduced Lear's daughters, and I had taken care of the Fool, so I wasn't needed for a while. We could probably slip out undetected for a quick bite.

Part of that intro had involved discussing how, if short of cast members as we usually are for a play like *Lear*, the roles of Cordelia and the Fool can be performed by the same actor, which is a neat trick because both of them speak the truth to the King, but only one gets away with it. Usually when we start discussing casting choices and tricks, people will tune out; the camp participants, however, ate it up. Dr. K had chosen her students wisely.

Alec glanced over to me as I slid my phone back in my bag. "Just take her and go," she whispered, nudging me with her elbow gently.

I didn't need to be told twice as the clock Kit was projecting into my brain was spinning like crazy, and I knew she would become more vocal as more time passed. Grabbing my stuff, I rose quietly and headed out of the auditorium, trying to make as little noise as possible. Kit quickly followed as Dr. K's co-teacher for the workshop, Dr. Mathew Galloway, was just beginning Kent's abuse of Oswald at the beginning of Act II as I closed the door behind us.

Before we could make our way out of the theatre building and decide on a place to go, Guppy slipped out and stopped us.

"You okay?" she asked, setting her hand on my arm.

I nodded. I had spent quite a bit of time with snakes for hair in Salida, and it would take a little while before I had my mind back all to myself.

I suppose I'm getting ahead of myself, as usual. While performing in Salida during an arts festival, my family's theatre troupe, *Mustardseed Productions*, had been caught up in a mystery involving a woman, Melanie Connors, who disappeared while out for her morning run. My sisters and I are witches, and more precisely Furies, like the classical figures who seek to bring justice down on the heads of those who cross certain boundaries, so this type of situation was right up our alley. Eventually, we resolved the issue, but not before I progressed through several changes that happen if I can't mete out justice in a timely manner. Some of those changes are more noticeable than others, especially the Gorgon-like snakes that twist through my hair. Once justice has been served, the snakes disappear, as do the other changes, but it takes a while for me to feel like myself again.

Which made this "return to normal" a little more difficult now because of being on a college campus.

The fun thing about universities is that many people become themselves while attending (or not) classes, meeting new people, and living as almost-adults with a large safety net around them. Some people meet the love of their lives or find a new family in the friends they make. These same people return for reunions, or homecoming, or Parents Day should their kids attend their alma mater. Leaving college can be difficult for a great many students as the eventuality of adult life looms in front of them, filled with responsibilities and many times empty of the comfort the campus can offer. Some of these students just keep being students, either switching majors so they have to start all over or racking up degrees which many end up never using. I suppose this is natural in some way, an avoidance of growing up, but even with scholarships, it would be an expensive way to live.

So the problem with campuses, at least for me, is that when these people die, many times they return to where they first felt like they belonged, where they first found happiness or acceptance. They return to the safety and comfort of their lives when their lives were at their best or maybe the most carefree. I've not been to a campus yet that didn't have ghosts wandering around, sitting in on classes, watching the competition on the field or court, or searching the stacks for a beloved book. In fact, a ghost dressed like a flapper had watched our entire morning's work, sitting in the back of the theatre, and she seemed taken aback that I could see her. I was going to approach her, but she quietly vanished. Later, when I thought no one was watching me, I wandered back to where she had been and spoke softly in case she was still there, letting her know she was welcome and that I would leave her alone.

Lucky for me, usually these types of ghosts aren't looking for justice; they're just looking for the warmth and inclusion they felt while attending school. So far, the spirits I had encountered on this campus were all just reliving their glory days, maybe making good on promises made to friends to always be there for them, not realizing how strong a promise like that could actually be.

"Nothing out of the ordinary?" Guppy pressed, watching my face to see if I was telling the truth.

I shook my head. "Just the usual: campus ghosts and Kit's starving. Things seem quiet in comparison to Salida.

Guppy chewed her lower lip deep in thought, then pulled me over to a bench to sit down.

"You know when we handed out packets and name tags this morning that a couple participants weren't here."

This absenteeism wasn't unusual; signing up in November for a workshop in June might have seemed like a good idea at the time, but then summer shows up and all bets are off.

She hurried on before I could voice that thought. "Ike knows why one of them isn't here, and I just can't get it out of my head that something's rotten in the city of Boulder."

I will be the first to admit that Guppy can overreact, but I will also be the first to admit that she is right more times than not.

Cutting off any comment I might make again, my mom continued.

"Laurel Monroe is one of the participants that didn't show, for obvious reasons."

I thought this over. I had seen a brief blurb in the *Rocky Mountain News* a few days before we left Salida and headed for Boulder, but hadn't given it a second thought because, well, snake-hair and such. This young woman had either attempted suicide or had been trying to drown her grief over the loss of her parents through booze and accidentally fell down some stairs in her house. Dr. K had informed Guppy that Laurel was currently still in the hospital in a medically induced coma. While the trajectory of her life was tragic, I hadn't really spent much time thinking about it; after all, everyday we are surrounded by people living out their own comedies and tragedies while we live out ours, neither one noticing the other as time marches by. Nothing drew me to this story beyond the normal human compassion and empathy, but again, I had been just a little bit preoccupied.

Guppy continued. "Apparently, Laurel, upon graduating, came into her inheritance, which, according to Ike, is a pretty big chunk of change and a successful restaurant empire worth millions. Had her parents not died back in September, she would have become a full partner with them; but with their demise, she now is the solitary owner."

I rolled that around in my head for a bit. Maybe it's just my nature, but my brain always seems to travel to the darkest possibilities in scenarios like this; maybe, it's because I see the aftermath of people's greed and ambition up close; maybe it's because I tuned into too many true crime podcasts or tv shows when I was younger. My first thought centered on Laurel and her part in the car wreck; I'm sure while investigating, the authorities focused on the daughter as well because of how much she had to gain. Money is always a giant incentive for murdering people, even people you love, especially people you love.

"But?" I asked, knowing Guppy had more to report from her conversation with Dr. K by the way she was looking at me.

"But with her in limbo, so to speak, no major decisions can be made about the businesses or the fortune currently being made from them."

I could see where Guppy's reasoning was taking us. "And if she was involved in the car accident and was days away from reaping her reward, why attempt suicide? Unless her guilt caught up to her and she couldn't deal with it any more." As I said this I was picturing the husk of Keith Connors, Melanie's husband and killer, in my head, broken and left nearly soulless after being confronted with the guilt of his own actions; all Kit and I had left him with was that guilt, a constant cold presence that would never let him go. It may sound ghoulish, but I was looking forward to seeing pictures of him once the trial started.

"So," I continued, "maybe the whole scenario is just one cruel trick of the Fates taking first the parents and then the daughter. They've done worse."

Before Guppy could respond, the door to the theatre opened, and Dr. K walked out to join us, followed closely by Alec and Meg. Both my mom and I looked up from our conversation as she began to speak.

"Ladies," she started, her rich voice laced with the slightest of accents, accents she could change at the drop of a hat from Scottish to Nigerian to French to Texan and everything in between. She had trained with the Royal Shakespeare Company after finishing her college degrees, toured for a while, and then returned to CU to teach theatre to the next generation of actors. When I was little, I wanted to grow up and be Dr. Kikelomo; in my high school theatre classes, the only way I made it through auditions and performances my first two years was to pretend I was her, with her beautiful voice and unshakable confidence. I had to pretend to be someone else who was pretending to be someone else, like mirrors in a funhouse.

"We are breaking for lunch; let me treat you to some of the finest Italian cuisine in the city: Cesare's. You will love it. And they have a patio, so Kit can join us."

With that said, she motioned for us to follow her, and we did, no questions asked.

Chapter 2

The walk from the campus to Pearl Street Mall was lovely; the day's temperatures were hovering in the low eighties, and we strolled along comfortably, talking about the students in the workshop and how to design the set for the outdoor theatre. As we crossed the bridge over Boulder Creek, Kit scrambled up my leg and onto my shoulder, peering nervously down at the water below. However, the image she pressed into my head wasn't of her falling in, but of her wearing a silly hat and walking around on her hind legs.

"The Fool should have a cat?" I asked, hoping I was translating this right and not mistaking the image for some desire to become human. Flowers started raining down on the Kit in the image. Here we go; I think I've mentioned that the little cait sith was becoming a bit of a diva by the end of our time in Salida.

"Hey Moms," I called out, speeding up a little now that I didn't have to walk as slowly so Kit could keep up with us. "Kit wants to be the Fool's cat."Both Guppy and Dr. K threw glances back at us; one of my sisters snorted–probably Meg–but said nothing.

"I think that is a wonderful idea," Dr. K smiled as she spoke. "But will she work with your understudy during the student performances?"

The flowers stopped falling in the image. What replaced it was a larger image of Kit standing in front of a tiny person.

"Ummm," I wasn't sure how to translate this image to anyone. "I think we'll have to work on that."

Before I could address Kit's delusion of grandeur, we arrived at Cesare's. Dr. K went in to arrange seating for us on the patio, which was not packed even though the day was gorgeous.

"I think we beat the lunch crowd," Alec stated, smiling as a host appeared with Dr. K and led us to a nice table for six.

"And could we have a booster seat for Kit?" Guppy asked. The host raised an eyebrow at the request, but returned with one shortly. Kit leapt gracefully into the seat and waited for me to push the chair closer to the table.

Once we were settled, the talk quickly turned to Laurel Monroe while we drooled over the menus.

"I don't believe for a second she tried to harm herself," Dr. K insisted. "She has taken several of my theatre classes as electives over the years, both as a way to keep up her grade points and relieve the stress from her business management courses. She is a head strong young woman, and while the death of her parents hit her hard, she never showed signs of desperation or hopelessness. Of course she was devastated, but I believe she trusts me well enough to have told me if she were feeling those things. All the times we did speak, her future ideas and what she wanted to do with the businesses were the center of the conversation; she was planning on being here to bring those ideas to fruition. I am probably not making much sense, but I just feel that something is off."

She paused as the waiter came back to take our order, glancing at his name tag briefly.

"First, Jeremy, we must start with the arancini appetizer—make that two of them—and a bottle of Lambrusco. Then give us a few moments more to decide on lunch."

Guppy spoke as the waiter left. "I understand what you are saying; something isn't sitting right with me either, and I don't even know Ms. Monroe."

The two old friends and former college roommates looked at each other before looking over to me and my sisters.

"I'm getting no murder vibes," I said simply. "If someone tried to kill her, I can't tell since they didn't succeed."

"And there isn't any more or less anger or jealousy than any other place we go; everything seems like business as usual, minus murder," Alec added, Meg nodding in agreement.

Dr. K leaned back and sighed. "I guess I just don't want to believe she would harm herself. She is a wonderful person, as were her parents."

We were all silent for a moment as Jeremy set down our appetizers and opened the bottle of wine, pouring us each a glass, except for Kit, of course. She flattened her ears a bit at being left out, so I held my glass over to her to let her sniff it.

"Wine at lunch; Ike, you are spoiling my girls," Guppy laughed, taking a sip of the slightly fizzy red. The bubbles must have gotten to Kit because she chose that moment to sneeze, thankfully turning away from my glass before she did so.

Dr. K laughed. "Well let me spoil them; I am their guide-mother after all."

"Are you ready to order?" Jeremy finally broke in, pen poised over his order tablet.

We all ordered, Meg and I going last, finally deciding to split a margherita pizza. Jeremy double-checked to make sure he had everything correct, then disappeared back into the depths of Cesare's.

"Tell us more about the car wreck," Alec stated quietly, nibbling on an arancini.

Dr. K sighed deeply. "Such a tragic moment. The investigation led to nothing; it was apparently just an accident. The going theory is that something jumped out in front of the car—a deer perhaps—and Paul Monroe swerved too zealously to miss it and wound up losing control. I guess they came to that conclusion based on the tire marks and the fact no one witnessed the wreck."

She paused for a moment, motioning to the restaurant itself as she resumed speaking. "Cesare's is their most popular business, and is well known for hosting events for the local schools; it is named after Lucia Monroe's grandfather. When the theatre department holds banquets off campus, we always have them cater—the food is excellent and the price is reasonable. Of course, while Laurel was a student, we would get an even bigger discount," she smiled sadly as she spoke. "The Monroes will be greatly missed; they did so many things for the community in general, but especially the theatre department even before Laurel enrolled. They were great supporters of the arts."

"What about Laurel? What happened there?" I asked, cutting up an arancini for Kit before starting to eat my own.

"And that is also unresolved, as I have said. Laurel was found at the bottom of a wooden staircase, badly battered from the fall; she had been drinking, but according to some inside information or maybe just rumors, there were also traces of a sedative in her blood. This is what is confusing people, if it is true. Laurel had no prescription for the medicine and none was found in the house, and yet it was in her blood. So no one is sure if she procured the drug to take her own life or to help her sleep, and then maybe overdid it and just fell down the stairs. There was no note, no sign of forced entry, and the house was locked up tight for the night. The family lawyer found her the next morning when she swung by to pick Laurel up for a meeting they had with the restaurants' general managers."

"That must have been awful," Meg said, leaning back as Jeremy arrived with our food.

"Who had the side of grilled chicken?" he asked, and as I pointed to Kit, she meowed loudly. "Right, I'm sorry; I'm a bit muddled today." He set the plate down slowly; it was obvious to me he wanted to say more, but didn't know how to start. I glanced at Alec and knew immediately she had spun one of her tongue-loosening spells with the intent of gathering the most information possible without having to ask weird questions. When cast properly, people just opened up to us like we were old friends catching up on things.

Dr. K sensed it as well. "Jeremy, do you know Laurel Monroe? Do you have any news of her condition?"

The young man sighed, glanced behind him toward the door. "Our manager told us the doctors are going to bring her out of the coma, but she still may not wake up. She really whacked her head during the fall." He threw another glance toward the restaurant, his nervousness apparent to all of us.

Before he could leave, Alec asked, "Did you know her, Jeremy?" I could tell that she was reading him, hoping he would open up and give us some more insight into this young woman.

He sighed again before speaking. "She would come in sometimes with her mom, sometimes with her dad, and then of course alone, just to check on things. Sometimes before she left, she would ask the chef to make the staff something fun to eat at the end of our shifts, and she would pay for it, just like Mr. Monroe used to do. When I first started here, I was a little down on my luck–law school is expensive, and she would come in and order dinner to go, and then pretend like she forgot she had other plans and ask me if I wanted it. I knew what she was doing, but I played along. She just cared about people, but it would drive Mr. Garrett nuts." He flinched when he caught the door opening out of the corner of his eye.

"Jeremy, you have other tables waiting on you," the man called out sharply.

Guppy jumped into the conversation immediately. "Sorry, that's our fault; we just wanted him to let the chef know that our lunch is simply fabulous!"

Jeremy threw a grateful smile at Guppy, then took this opportunity to escape back to his duties; the man came over to us, suddenly all happiness and sunshine except for the small twitch at the corner of his mouth when he realized a cat was sitting at our table.

"I'll be sure to let Chef know," he smarmed with his smarmy voice grating on every last one of my nerves, and some of them twice. "All the recipes are authentic Italian dishes with one or two tweaks when Chef sees fit."

Kit growled softly; she didn't like this guy either.

"Are you the owner," Meg asked far too sweetly, her tone revealing to me he had set her off on a fury level, which was probably why my nerves were fraying so rapidly and Kit was low-key growling under her breath.

"No; well not yet anyway; I'm Cal Garrett, the general manager."

Before anyone could question him further, a loud crash from inside made everyone on the patio jump, except Mr. Garrett, whose face flushed purple as he spun around and hurried off to check the damage.

"Charming," Alec muttered, then glanced at Meg who was still watching the door the man had stormed through. "Meg?"

"So full of artless jealousy is guilt," she uttered, without turning her eyes from the door. For a moment we all followed her gaze, waiting for Meg to order her thoughts and give us the skinny on Mr. Garrett.

"Jealous of what? Or of whom?" Dr. K questioned.

Meg blinked a few times, clearing the darkness that had started forming in her eyes.

"Everything. Everyone. Jeremy because he is young; Laurel because she owns what he considers his restaurant; the people dining here, including us, because we have the time to dine out and enjoy ourselves and, shock and horror, have wine in the afternoon. Geez this dude is wound so tight I'm surprised he hasn't blasted into orbit yet."

Alec swallowed a mouthful of her pasta with pesto before speaking, "Let me just throw in that he has some serious anger issues as well. Jealousy and anger are never a good mix."

I wished I could add to the conversation, but this guy had murdered no one; of course that didn't mean he hadn't tried. I said as much to the table.

We had cleaned our plates and drained our glasses by the time Jeremy returned to give us the check, which Guppy and Dr. K fought over for a brief moment with Dr. K eventually the victor.

"I'll get the tip," my mom said, pulling cash from her purse and folding it as small as possible. When Jeremy returned for the payment, Guppy slipped him the money, telling him to just put it in his pocket. He glanced quickly at the door, then did as he was told.

"When we get back to the theatre, you should talk with Madison Drake; she and Laurel are good friends," Dr. K paused, seeing Jeremy returning with her card and receipt. After signing, she continued. "In fact, I think Madison would make a very competent Fool; and she loves cats," she added, throwing a glance at Kit, who stretched luxuriously, still smacking her lips over her chicken.

With the meal done and paid for, our group left the patio, heading back to the campus and an afternoon of preparing the camp participants for their tryouts tomorrow. These two weeks would fly by, especially once we started performing.

Chapter 3

When we reached the theatre after leaving Cesare's, the camp's participants had mostly filed in and were sitting in small groups chatting about the roles they wanted and which roles they thought their peers should attempt. Their chatter dropped to a low buzz before falling silent completely when Dr. K took the stage and began the second half of the day.

"Thank you for returning from lunch," she smiled as she spoke, her tone light as she glanced around the audience. "Sometimes not everyone makes it back, especially when the weather is so beautiful." Her smile widened as some of the students started laughing, looking around to see if anyone was missing, and upon catching sight of Dr. Galloway trying to sneak in without being seen, began laughing all over again.

Dr. K let the chuckling die down before continuing. "My plan for this afternoon is to figure out who is interested in which parts. Tomorrow, you may try out for more than one, which might be wise, as setting your heart on one might lead to it breaking if you do not get that part. We will try to get everyone their first choice, but that may not be possible in all cases." She motioned to our troupe, all sitting together in chairs behind her on the stage. "Please take some time and talk to our actors about the roles they introduced. Ask questions, learn as much as you can. Once you have done that, sign up sheets for the characters will be on the tables, stage right."

As she finished and the students rose to join us on stage, we pulled our chairs farther apart and into clusters of "like" characters. My sisters sat together as Lear's older daughters Goneril and Regan; nearby, Kit and I partnered up with Saumia, as Cordelia, who as I mentioned earlier, is often double cast as the Fool. Cole and Derek were together as the sons of Gloucester, as were the older characters Lear, Gloucester, and Kent. The husbands and would-be husbands of the daughters were in a group that also had the minor / walk on roles. As I said before, *King Lear* has a big cast, and when we perform it, we rely heavily on local talent to help us. Bre and Eliava were helping Guppy with the various other minor roles that could be double or even triple cast.

Not everyone who attends a camp like this wants to be a lead actor or have a large role; some people gravitate towards picking up the minor roles, using the opportunity to try out different voices, mannerisms, anything that makes it hard to tell the characters are being played by the same person. I know this because that's how I was my first couple of years in high school theatre. Even as an upperclassman, I was more interested in being a supporting role and not a lead, especially in musicals as my singing voice is, simply put, non-existent, which actually lends itself to more comedic characters anyway.

Dr. K strolled among the groups, pulling people out occasionally to speak with them before moving to the next station. They gazed at her intently when she spoke with them, nodding vigorously and some even taking notes. When she finally reached our group, we had finished our introductions and had answered several questions about our lives on the road as a traveling troupe, and were in the middle of tossing out ideas on how to work Kit into the play as a role not listed in the Dramatis Personae–the Fool's Cat.

"Sorry to interrupt," Dr. K's voice was warm, her hand resting on the back of Saumia's chair. "I wanted to bring Ms. Drake into your group. She wasn't sure where she belonged. I would also like to steal Mr. Gallegos for a few moments to try convincing him to think about being Edgar."

Our group was small: two women who were both interested in Cordelia, and a young man, Jaime, who liked the idea of being the Fool, but also maybe just wanted to be near Saumia and the two Cordy wanna-be's. He reluctantly followed Dr. K, already engaged in a discussion about what it meant to be the older, legitimate son of Gloucester.

"I'm Tisi." I smiled at our new arrival, and, motioning at the Nagi, our snake shape-shifter, "This is Saumia. Did Dr. K have you in mind as a Cordelia or a Fool?"

"I'm not sure whether I should be insulted or not, but she seems to think I would make a good Fool," the young woman grinned back at me, but the smile didn't quite reach her eyes. "I'm Madison, Madi for short."

So here was Laurel's friend, and suddenly the dullness in her eyes and the hesitancy to pick a group or show interest in a role made sense. And very slightly, under the cloak of sadness draped over her like a dark shroud, I could taste her guilt: guilt at not being there the night her friend fell down the stairs; guilt for having two living parents supporting her as she graduated and entered a new phase of her life; and, strongest of all, a guilt for being the one that was attending the acting camp, alone, instead of being the one in the hospital. This was not snake-inducing guilt—she hadn't murdered anyone even if she did feel responsible in some way for Laurel being hospitalized—and it tasted differently, aimless and salty, like tears.

I wasn't sure how to enter into this conversation without seeming like I was nosing around for information, which is exactly what I was attempting. So I chuckled at her comment and decided to run with the Dr. K angle. "Don't be insulted; she was mentioning you at lunch today, and I believe her exact words were 'competent fool' which sounds worse in some way. She also may have let slip that you like cats, and we were just sitting here discussing how to work Kit into the production as the Fool's cat." I let my gaze travel over to Kit, sending her an image of being nice to Madi.

The cait sith narrowed her eyes at me, rolling them ever so slightly, then lightly hopped down from her chair. As she made her way past me, she almost brushed her head on my leg, but faked me out, turning at the last moment to stride over to Madi and rub her leg instead, casting a quick glance back to me before leaping onto the young woman's lap. Again, the image of flowers cascading down on Kit while she stood front and center on stage invaded my head.

"She's so sweet," Madison's eyes brightened a little more as she hesitantly held her hand over Kit's fur. "Is it okay that I pet her?"

"Knock yourself out; she's taken a shine to you it seems," as I spoke, the image in my head now included a man in a tuxedo presenting Kit with a giant trophy of some sort. This was getting out of hand.

I'm not sure how long we sat in our group and discussed the play and motivations of both Cordelia and the Fool, but before I knew it, Dr. K was back over and redirecting us into the Lear group. Because neither the Fool nor the youngest daughter have long soliloquies, it makes sense to have them run lines with Lear for the auditions. Carlos welcomed us warmly and more introductions were made. He then pulled me to my feet, and we began a section from Act I, Scene iv where the Fool tries to tell Lear he's an idiot but Lear refuses to listen—this is basically their entire relationship in a nutshell. Our larger group listened intently, watching the dynamic Carlos and I constructed, with Lear a little confuddled and the Fool being a petulant smart ass because he misses Cordelia and is able to get away with it because he's a fool.

Other groups around us had also reached this point, and snippets of *King Lear* rang throughout the theatre. I love this part of production; an energy starts buzzing around the room and grows as people begin to fall into their lines, growing more comfortable with them and with the other characters. I could tell from watching Madison that she was enjoying herself, maybe finally getting out of her own head, even if only for a little while.

The rest of the first day of camp galloped along as we helped the students prepare for auditions the following day. Dr. K finally called for silence, clapping to gain everyone's attention.

"I know not all of you are staying at Baker Hall, but please come join us for dinner. I'm having all kinds of pizza delivered. If you can't join us, we will see you all bright and early tomorrow morning!" And with another clap of her hands, we were dismissed.

The walk back to our temporary residence went quickly since we were all still chatting about what we accomplished in the workshop, and we were also realizing that it had been a while since lunch and were looking forward to the pizza Dr. K had promised. Madison and I walked together, Kit strolling along between us, and we slowly fell back from the main group to accommodate Kit's shorter stride.

I knew I needed to start a conversation about Laurel, but I wasn't sure how to start it without just getting to the point. Subtly has never been my strongest trait; my anxiety often makes me just blurt out whatever it is that is on my mind, and that tends to lead to some very awkward silences and follow up situations. Even now, the continued silence was beginning to make me feel like an idiot, like I should be saying something, and as the silence stretched, that feeling just got stronger.

When Kit suddenly yowled, I nearly jumped out of my skin. We both turned to look at her: the little diva was sitting, one forepaw raised, ears drooping, eyes wide and sad. When she saw she had our attention, she took a step forward, and nearly collapsed on her face.

Before I could move, Madi scooped her up. "Oh Kit! It's so far to walk. Let me carry you." She arranged Kit so that the cait sith was looking over her shoulder, directly at me. In my head, the Kit on stage was now receiving a standing ovation and another trophy, larger than the previous one. I was opening my mouth to call her out, when Madi turned, her arms tightening around Kit.

"My best friend loves cats, black cats especially," her eyes were filled with genuine pain, not the manufactured pain Kit had whipped up for what I first thought was just a free ride, but now realized she did it to create an opening for me.

"Your friend Laurel? Dr. K mentioned her at lunch as well."

Madi nodded, squishing Kit a little tighter. "When we were little, we wanted to go to a magic academy–like the ones in movies–learn spells, and do all those magical things. One time when I was spending the night, Laurel's mom hid a couple plushies for us to discover when she sent us on a magical quest to find something for her. Laurel's was a black cat with a white spot on her chest, just like Kit's. Mine was a spotted green frog wearing a purple bow tie; I love frogs, by the way, and Mrs. Monroe knew that." She took a deep breath, her mind focusing on a time when life was easier and sorrow had not yet cast its heavy cloak over her friend. "Ember and Frodo; they were our familiars."

She fell silent as we continued strolling along. Kit's image was now signing autographs in my head. I thanked her silently. "She sounds like a great mom," I said aloud, hoping Madi would continue.

"Yeah, she was cool. There's a butler's pantry off their kitchen, and she bought an old apothecary and put it in there, filling the drawers with stale spices, dried flowers, and other odds and ends. Laurel and I used to pretend that was our elixir classroom. I know she was trying to keep us out of trouble and out from underfoot, but it was so fun to be over there with them; they were like second parents to me. And now Laurel is really hurt, and I can't do anything except sit and talk with her. I don't even know if she can hear me." She sighed deeply, the sadness returning and settling into her eyes again, deeper as the realization she had been happy during the workshop gave way to more guilt, this time for that happiness.

"Well it can't hurt," I offered. "She may not understand what you're saying, but I bet she can hear your voice. You're probably doing more good than you realize."

We had reached the residence hall. She handed me Kit after hugging her tightly one more time. "I'm going to go see her right now and talk about making elixirs with Ember and Frodo. Will you let Dr. K know? I don't want her to worry. Thank you for listening to me; I guess I really needed to get that out." And with that said, she trotted back up the steps and off into the growing darkness.

After she disappeared into the night, I turned, still holding Kit, to make my way inside.

Alec met me at the door. "Hurry up and eat, Fool; we're about to start a mahjong tournament to end all tournaments."

Chapter 4

When my alarm went off the next morning, I really didn't want to get out of bed. I had set it to go off long before I needed to get up, mainly because I didn't want the shared common bathroom to be full when I went to get ready for the day. For starters, I like to stand in the shower as long as I can because it relaxes me and helps me think, and when you're sharing facilities, that doesn't go over well; and secondly, I don't really like groups of people in confined spaces. In fact, I don't really like groups of people anywhere, and I like them much less if I'm in the middle of them. I probably wouldn't have chosen acting as a profession if it wasn't a family organization. And don't get me wrong, I do enjoy being on stage, but mostly that's because I don't have to be me on the stage; I get to be a Fool, or a Weird Sister, or a Second Murderer, basically anyone who doesn't wind up with snakes in her hair if the right conditions arise. Maybe 'wrong conditions' would be a better way of putting that.

Kit was curled up on her bed in the tiniest circle of a kitten she could become. Because we were staying inside, I had bought a litter box and supplies for her, but I think she was mortified by them. I grabbed my shower kit and headed out, hoping the bathroom would be empty, and I wouldn't have to make small talk. I can make small talk; I know how to engage in polite conversation. I'm just not really good at it, at least in my own head.

Before the door could shut, Kit shot out of the closing gap and followed me down the hall and into the community bathroom.

"Taking a shower this morning?" I asked. See, I can do polite speech; but really, what a dumb question.

She yawned, waiting for me to open the door which was too heavy for her to push. Once inside, she went into one of the stalls and politely suggested in her own Kit way that I hold the door closed for her. Still in a bit of a sleep stupor, I did so. When she jumped off the toilet, the automatic flusher went off, and she slipped out under the gap.

"Who taught you that?"

Her response was to roll her eyes at me, an image of detailed schematics registered in my head. "Not rocket science? Well, good to know," was all I could think to reply–another brilliant example of my conversational skills–and hurried into a shower stall. I had been spaced out for a while under the water, thinking of ways to investigate, when I heard someone else enter the room.

"Did you get stuck in here?" I heard Guppy ask.

"She's with me," I called out, finishing up and drying off so I could slip into my clothes.

Guppy was quiet for a moment. I guessed she was checking to make sure it was just us before speaking.

"Did you learn anything last night from Madison?" With the water not running, she didn't have to speak so loudly.

Now dressed, I quickly packed all my bathing accouterment into my basket and stepped out of the dressing area of the shower. "She and Laurel used to play Witch Academy when they were kids; Lucia Monroe sounds like she was a great mom; and Laurel has a black cat stuffie that looks like Kit."

Guppy chewed the inside of her cheek thoughtfully. "With what Ike told us yesterday, I'm just not sure who would want to kill the Monroes, so maybe that crash really was just an accident. Maybe you're right, and it's just the Fates," she sighed. "I was just so sure something wasn't right."

"That's because you worry about people," I smiled. "Laurel and the Monroes sound like a nice family who just had a crappy string of luck. But, if there is something hinky going on, maybe I should go visit the crash site. If the Monroes are still there because they're waiting for justice, I should be able to find them, even though it has been a while since they died." This idea struck me while I was in the shower; as I've said, water helps me think.

Guppy nodded as I spoke. "I wonder if Ike would be able to get us that information. You're going to sound like a ghoul asking to see a site where people died."

I shrugged. I was always the weird one anyway; it didn't really bother me anymore. Of course I didn't feel that way when I was in elementary school, or middle school for that matter. Before I could voice that being perceived as ghoulish was the least of my issues, Kit suddenly shoved the image of Sherlock talking into a telephone into my head.

I smiled at her, "Sherlock might be able to locate the site, but I think it would be easier if I just called Officer Larkes and asked him if he could access the information."

Guppy watched this exchange. "I take it your lines of communication are solidifying a bit?"

Both Kit and I nodded; I spoke: "She understands what I say, and she obviously understood your question, but she's still working on how to go from pictures to words for her thoughts to me. It would be super if I could speak Meowlish or Felinese."

When Guppy opened her mouth to respond, I cut her off. "And I'm not drinking another one of your potions, especially if you're going to whip it up in the bathroom."

She laughed as Kit and I made our way out the door and back to our own room. While I worked on my hair, Kit bathed. Then, catching sight of herself in the mirror fastened to the back of the door, she started striking different poses. The arched-back puffy-tail Halloween pose came first. She hopped sideways a couple times, growling. Next was the Fool's Cat pose she had put in my mind: up on her hind legs, hop-walking, head tilted to the side. Pleased with that one, she then rolled onto her side, ears-drooping, tongue sticking out of her mouth. A death scene: what actor doesn't want a good, dramatic death scene?

We've had the Fool die on stage before in productions of Lear; it's the easiest way to explain why he disappears after Act III scene vi. With Lear completely off his rocker and Poor Tom talking up a storm of gibberish, a third fool is superfluous.

"You really want a death scene?" I commented. Kit opened one eye at me, so many flowers falling in my head I couldn't see her through them.

"Noted," I said as a knock sounded at our door.

Kit sat up and licked some of her fur back in place as I let in our guest.

Meg smiled at us both. "I'm glad to see the two of you are up. We're going for coffee at Willow's Coffee, Tea, and Chakra Realignment."

When neither of us reacted, still trying to figure out if Meg was serious or making up a fictional shop, she continued. "It's the Monroe's coffee place. Some of the camp participants are going, and I think we should, too. Could be a good opportunity to pick up more scuttle about Laurel. Alec is already downstairs waiting on us."

And here I thought I had gotten up early. Grabbing my cross-body satchel which carried everything I might need for the day, including a passable service vest for Kit, and if necessary, Kit herself, I followed Meg and the cait sith, locking the door on the way out. As I pocketed the key, I wondered how many people had keys to the Monroe house. They were openly generous and may have trusted a great many people enough to allow them access to their home. I was sure Madison had a key; she mentioned during the workshop that she had been taking care of the place once the investigation into the fall had finished and been ruled an accident. They might have had a housekeeper as well, as busy as they were. Dr. K had also mentioned a family lawyer who had found Laurel after her fall; I assume she had a key to get in once Laurel didn't answer the door, but I suppose she could have called the police when no one answered.

As we entered the lobby area, I could see small groups of participants already heading out the doors.

Alec waved us over, and we followed the other students in the pilgrimage for our morning go-juice.

As we headed up the steps, I stopped for a second to pick up Kit. The handy thing about the satchel was that she fit right in and could arrange herself so she could see out or not be seen. The service cat ruse worked in most places, but sometimes secrecy was best. Kit tends to disagree with me on that; I think she enjoys the acting and the attention she gets for it. For now, she was sitting up, her head just poking out over the halfway closed zipper.

While we walked, I dialed Officer Larkes's number, hoping he wouldn't answer so I could just leave a message. I'm even more awkward on the phone because I can't see reactions to what I am saying to know if I have said something wrong and should shut up. I also can't text long strings of words while walking, or I would have just sent a message. I fell back from my sisters a little more to lengthen the space between us and the group of students who had left before we did.

After his "please leave a message" played, I spoke my piece: "Hey Officer Larkes, it's Tisi. I was hoping you might be able to help me with something in Boulder. Tisi Kindley, I mean. How many Tisis do you know? Haha. Right. Uhhh. Can you find out where the crash sight for a car accident was back in September? The Monroe accident, somewhere on Flagstaff Road? Just wondering. Hope you're doing well. Call me back if you can help. Or maybe just text. Whatever is easier for you. Okay? Okay. Bye."

That wasn't so bad, I thought, until I looked up and both of my sisters were looking back at me.

"'Just wondering'?" Alec questioned. "I thought the whole point in asking him was to avoid sounding like a ghoul.

Meg chimed in. "You know, he probably could get access to the whole report on the investigation, which could also come in handy. Call him back and leave another message."

I stuffed my phone back in my pocket. "I'll text that request once we get our brew." I was not calling again, especially with this many people around waiting to critique me.

"Good idea," Alec winked at me; "You don't want to sound desperate."

I could feel my face flush. Ever since I had invited the officer along for our last night in Salida shindig, I had faced constant ribbing from both my sisters. I was lucky I hadn't called him "Officer Hottie," which is what Saumia had dubbed him once the situation in Salida had been solved. Aside from my troupe and my quarries, no one had ever seen me in action, so to speak, with snakes for hair, a voice in triplicate, and eyes like black pools of nothingness. The fact that Larkes had witnessed this and still wanted to dine out with us that night told me two conflicting things: he was okay with it or he wanted to arrest all of us. I just couldn't think of a plausible in between position for him to be holding.

Our whole troupe and some of the people we had grown close to over our time in Salida had all gone out to celebrate after our last performance. I had found myself on a patio at one end of a large group of tables with Larkes across from me and Bre, the Banshee in our troupe, at the end–she hates being in the middle of crowds as much as I do. The three of us had spoken about what had happened with Keith Connors, and the officer had opened up about his ability to see ghosts, which he believed he inherited from his grandmother.

"I always thought she and I were the only ones," he had confessed, sipping his beer since he was off-duty. "It's nice to be able to talk to people who have the same ability."

Bre and I had both nodded, but the banshee spoke first. Is your grandmother a witch?"

Larkes shook his head. "No, Nanna wasn't a witch; she passed last year. I haven't seen her spirit, and I don't know if it is because she's avoiding me. She knew I was always a little uncomfortable with the ability."

I hadn't known how to respond to that then, and I still don't now. Mostly the spirits I deal with have a desperate need for justice which they desperately need me to provide. Occasionally they're just confused or mistaken as to what has happened to them and are calling out for verification, thinking they must have been wronged in some way. Most often, spirits like the flapper in the theatre or the young woman under the tree in Salida just exist, either not ready to move on or merely enjoying where they are at the moment.

Kit rustled around in my bag, bringing me out of my reverie. When I looked down at her, she had the service vest in her mouth, waiting for me to help her put it on. Still walking, I took the vest and scrunched it up so she could poke her head through the neck and I could smooth it down over her back. I guess we weren't going for secrecy today.

We had caught up to our camp participants, and we all passed through the door while Jaime Gallegos held it open. When he saw us, he smiled: "Poor Tom's a-stuck holding the door."

"So Dr. K talked you into Edgar, did she?" Meg grinned, and the young man's smile widened a little as my sister continued. "She can be very persuasive, but if she wants you to try for it, she knows you can do it."

We made a long line just by ourselves, but we weren't the only patrons that morning. I was reading off all the choices of coffees they had and styles to have them when I felt Kit tap my hand. She was growling, or trying to. I know that all growls are warnings, but she is so tiny the growl sounds anything but threatening. Looking down at her, I was about to ask her what she wanted, thinking she was miffed at being left out of the fun of morning coffee addiction, but I saw she was looking at a small table tucked back in the corner furthest from the door.

Mr. Garrett and a woman probably close to Guppy in age were having a conversation, which, from the gesticulating and furtive glances thrown around at times, suggested it was heated.

"Interesting," I said, nudging Alec and motioning with my head toward the far away table. Alec in turn nudged Meg. But Meg needed no nudging. She was already laser focused on Mr. Garrett, as she had been in Cesare's when he stormed away from our table.

"He's jealous of whoever that is, too," she hissed quietly so only we could hear.

Alec's eyes were also zeroed in on their table. "The anger is radiating off of both of them, but it's not a shared anger; he's pissed at the world, and she's pissed at him."

"Who wouldn't be," I quipped, thinking of our lunch yesterday, and how he had treated his staff. I had to give Meg a little push to get her refocused on the line and the fact that she was up to order.

"I've got this," she stated, blinking rapidly before facing the barista. "I'd like a cappuccino, a caffe latte, and an affogato; and could you put a little ice cream on the side?"

Alec and I traded glances.

"For Kit," Meg said, tapping her phone on the card reader. "Go find a table close to the action, but not so close that we look suspicious."

Because Mr. Garrett had his back to the door, we were able to sit relatively near them without him picking up on us. I wasn't really worried that he would recognize us, but service cats are not a dime a dozen. Alec had grabbed a booster seat on the way over and placed it in the fourth chair at our table. Kit immediately jumped from the bag to the seat, threw a glance at Garrett, growled for a second, and then started scoping out the rest of the crowd.

"I can't tell if she's mad at him or mad at being up so early," I said, also taking a look around.

The shop was definitely retro in its stylings; rainbow beaded curtains that separated the front of house from the back were held open by ceramic hands to avoid snarling every time a worker passed through. Each table had a hand-painted fortune wheel under a thick layer of bartop. The walls were decorated with various paintings, some sporting price tags, and in the middle of the feature wall, surrounded by other art work, was a chakra chart that looked like it had been in the store since the 60s. Though it was framed and behind glass, it was weathered as if it had spent decades out in the open, fading and aging.

As Meg approached with our drinks, Alec, who had also caught sight of the chart, wondered aloud if the owner actually did readings.

Meg shrugged, setting down the cups and one small dish of ice cream, which she put in front of Kit with a warning. "I would take it slow on that; you don't want to get brain freeze."

The cait sith sniffed the ice cream suspiciously before sticking her tongue out to try it. She jumped back immediately, surprised at the temperature, then cautiously took a second small lick. Her purr started up almost immediately after; the dish of ice cream was now being showered with flowers in my head.

"We aren't going to make this a habit," I cautioned. "I'm not sure you should even be eating that."

She threw a scathing glance at my affogato which had ice cream in it, then transferred that look to me.

"Hypocrite? Who taught you that word?" Before we could get started into a full on argument over the merits or dangers of ice cream, Alec put a hand up to shush us both.

"Can you two act casual for five seconds? I'm trying to eavesdrop on the conversation going on over there."

We both had the decency to look chastened. Kit flashed me an image of Alec with ice cream on her head, and I had the presence of mind to not reply back verbally: *Tell me about it.*

We all sat and sipped or licked our morning treat. I knew that the anger coming from the argument was affecting Alec; she rarely snaps at people, but something about the conversation was bothering her, even if she couldn't hear all of it. Meg's eyes, though still blue, were darker than usual. The proximity to Mr. Garrett was waking up the Furies in my sisters, and I knew we needed to leave. I'm not usually the responsible adult in this trio, but today I was.

"So," I began cautiously, "Kit looks finished; let's start making our way to the theatre." Neither of my sisters moved until I stood up, put Kit in my bag, grabbed both my drink and what was left of the ice cream, and bumped my chair back under the table. At the sliding noise of the chair, my sisters seemed to come out of their trances, both blinking several times while grabbing their coffees.

Before either could stand, Mr. Garrett rose so suddenly that his chair tipped over. He stormed by us, casting one scathing look at Kit when he caught sight of her as he made for the door and exited.

Meg moved quickly to the table he had just vacated and righted the chair before the woman was even out of her seat.

I threw a glance at Alec; her eyes were settling back into blue and her shoulders lowered as her tension released. She, too, stood and turned to face the table where Meg was now standing, hands on the back of the chair she had just pushed back in, and conversing with the woman.

"That's very kind of you, dear," the woman was saying, her cheeks still flushed with anger, the red slowly fading as she composed herself. "I'm sorry we disturbed you."

I could tell Meg was calculating what her response should be. Of the three of us, Meg is the best at improvising, so neither Alec nor I responded.

"Mr. Garrett can be a real . . ." Meg's voice trailed off.

"Horse's ass? Yes, yes he can," the woman finished for her. She looked us up and down briefly, her eyes, filled with something akin to worry, coming to rest on Kit's face, just visible over the edge of the satchel. "You're with that acting troupe, Mustardseed Productions, aren't you? I heard one of you had a service cat."

Alec broke in then abruptly. "Do you actually do chakra readings? That is so cool."

A smile finally appeared on the woman's face. "My mother did; she was all into that stuff back in the day. This is her shop, or was, until the Monroes bought it."

Her voice held no bitterness when she said this. I could see the changes in my sisters' postures. Whatever anger the woman had been feeling was dissipating in the wake of Garrett's exit.

Meg spoke again. "I guess you have to deal with him often, especially now. And you're right, we are with the troupe. I'm Meg, by the way; these are my sisters Alec and Tisi, and that little gremlin is Kit. We heard about a cool coffee place and had to try it out."

"Moira Amin," she said by way of introduction. "And I do have to deal with him more than I would like since the accident, well, both accidents I guess. Aside from the tension in the air, how was everything?"

We raved about the coffees we had tried and the vibes the decor provided. Her smile widened as we talked about her establishment, her pride in it obvious. "My mother and grandmother opened it back in the early 60s; Willow was my mother's nickname," her voice had taken on a tinge of sadness, her mind in the past, remembering how things were. "I grew up in this shop."

Before we could take the conversation further, the bell on the door sounded and another wave of people entered, seeking out the caffeine to start their days. Moira thanked us again for coming in and hurried off to bus the many tables that had been vacated. While most people had discarded their trash, she was intent on wiping each one down as we left, leaving it sparkling for the next guest.

We walked silently for a while.

"Anyone catch any resentment about the Monroes buying the place?" Alec finally asked.

Meg and I both shook our heads, but Meg spoke. "Nope, and no jealousy either."

Alec continued. "She was furious with Garrett, but when he left, all that anger just dissipated. I wish I knew what they had been discussing."

When we reached the theatre building, I let my sisters continue without me. Kit wanted to finish her ice cream, and I wanted to check my phone without having any cracks made about me and my inability to communicate like a normal person. I had a missed call with a message and a text from Officer Larkes. I went for the text first; it was short: *Is there trouble?*

Before listening to the message, I tapped in a reply: *I'm not certain; I need to find the site so I can make that decision.*

When Kit looked up from her now empty cardboard cup, she had ice cream on her nose and her whiskers, including the whiskers over her eyes which were half closed as she proceeded to lick off the traces, savoring the last bits to the end. The image of my phone with me talking to it came to rest in my head.

"I will," I said, "But for now, I think we need to get inside and get Madi ready for her audition. I'm sure Officer Larkes is busy and I don't need to bother him with this right now."

Kit's eyes narrowed; the image of chickens flapping around replaced the phone.

She was right, but I wasn't ready to concede just yet. "Let's get going," I stated instead, ignoring the increased flapping in my head and holding the door open so the cait sith could enter. I would call him, but right now I needed to focus on Madi's audition.

Chapter 5

Sometimes, on the second day of a camp like this, participants choose not to come. Either they didn't like the work of the first day, or they realized how much of their time was going to be consumed with memorizing their lines, practicing both with and without the blocking, remembering their verbal cues, and maybe hardest of all, listening to constructive criticism on how to make their performances the best possible. While the camp part can be fun, and the experience and exposure gives the students an idea of what this type of life entails, things don't always go as planned, and that's just life.

Our opening performance of Lear was Thursday night; the students wouldn't perform until the second weekend, so while they had time to get comfortable with the idea, they also were becoming aware of the demands that would be put on them. I was a little shocked when I walked in and saw that no one had bailed on us yet.

Aside from the student participants, several adults were standing around the stage as well. Because *King Lear* sports a large cast, Dr. K had recruited some of her fellow instructors, both from the high schools and the university. These people would flesh out our professional performances, allowing us to have more roles filled instead of doubling or tripling up on some. Dr. K had also invited a few of her favorite alumni to be part of the show as well. Some of these additional cast members were present on this second day to help get our students ready for auditions and for their own upcoming performances. I could already see that I wouldn't be missed if I went out searching for the Monroes once I had the info I needed. I took Kit out of my bag and set her on the stage near Alec. I was about to head to the upper seating area so I could either make a phone call or respond to texts when I realized someone was calling out to me.

"Tisi!" It was Madi; she had just come in the doors, a bit late, but then who am I to judge as I was late as well. She rushed over to me, and as she neared, I could see she was carrying a stuffed frog.

"Frodo, I presume?" I smiled at her; she looked happier today than she had yesterday.

"Laurel squeezed my hand! Or at least, I think she did. One of the nurses said it might have just been a twitch or something, but I felt it, and it was right after I finished talking about how much fun our 'elixir class' was and our adventure to find our familiars!"

Then she suddenly wrapped me in a hug, just as quickly letting go when she realized she might have overstepped her bounds.

I hurried to reassure her. "That's great news. Maybe she's on the road to recovery."

But something was bothering me. If Laurel had fallen accidentally, this was indeed great news; if someone had helped her fall, this could become a very dangerous time for her, especially as the fall had been written off as an accident. At least in the hospital she was somewhat protected if someone was after her; they might even have her on suicide watch, which would be an extra layer of protection.

Before she could rush off to tell everyone, I set my hand on her arm to stop her. "You might want to keep this under your hat for now; if it was just a twitch, you might get people's hopes up. The next couple of days should tell."

Madison looked at me for a second, mulling over what I suggested. "You're probably right; I don't want to get people excited for nothing—it might affect their performances, too." She started down to the stage before I could respond. I could tell she thought I cared more about the play than her friend, and that wasn't it at all. And with my exquisite conversational skills, I would probably just make it worse by trying to fix it. Suddenly, stuck between the Scylla and Charybdis, a phone conversation with Larkes seemed the lesser of my problems; at least it would be fact based versus foot-in-mouth based. I continued to the upper deck, already dialing.

Larkes picked up on the second ring. "Tisi, what's up?"

I told him about my concerns, throwing in my latest information—that Laurel might be waking up and why that troubled me. The other problem with phone conversations for me, besides not being able to see facial expressions, is that the audial clues you listen for sometimes register later than they do in person, if you catch them at all. I was so wrapped up in the information I wanted to pass on that I completely forgot to listen for them.

"So anyway, I asked her not to mention it, and now she probably thinks I care more about having crappy performances than her friend who may or may not have been shoved down the stairs or attempted suicide." As the words left my mouth, I realized I had been rambling. "Are you still there?"

Larkes chuckled a little. "Yes; and I'm sure you're reading into her reaction more than you should. A woman I went through the academy with works for Boulder PD, and she was happy to share details with me about both cases concerning the Monroes as neither one is considered an open investigation. I can text you the basics. I already sent you the coordinates of the accident. You should be able to find it; the closest place to park will be something called Halfway House."

I nodded my head, registering his directions, then finally remembered he couldn't see that and spoke. "Got it; I wondered about where to park." I hesitated a second. "Your friend wasn't curious about why you needed to know? Should I expect company up there? That could be awkward."

"Just cop talk between old friends," he replied. "She also mentioned that there have been several accidents on that particular stretch of road over the past few years, not all fatalities, but you might see more than one spirit, so be careful. I've got to get back to work; Sherlock has a performance test coming up, and he still needs some practice. Let me know what you find."

We exchanged goodbyes, and I switched to my text app to find the coordinates. After plugging them into the GPS, I stood up, tucked my phone into my pocket, and headed down to the front of the stage. Kit was sitting with Madi, and they looked like they were in deep conversation. Alec caught my eye as I approached, her unspoken question obvious to me. I flashed her a quick thumbs up, and she immediately called out.

"Tiss, Guppy wants you to take Kit and go find fabric for her Fool's costume; I'll work with Madi on her audition." As she finished speaking, she tossed me the keys to the Fiat which I managed to catch, almost like we had rehearsed this, which we had, many times, knowing there would be occasions I needed an excuse to leave. Kit was just a new prop for this scene.

The cait sith leapt gracefully into my arms after head-butting Madi's leg, and the two of us headed to the lot where the car was waiting.

Kit was flashing me images of the hat she wanted and a multi-pointed collar made out of various, clashing fabrics. Tiny bells adorned each garment. She did look cute in the costume she was imagining, I will admit.

"You wanna do that first or take care of the other business first?" I asked, pulling onto the road suggested by my Waze app.

Kit exhaled loudly through her nose. Was she picking up mannerisms from me and my sisters? It was such a human reaction to being reminded of obligations that I couldn't help smiling. In order, she flashed me first a damaged tree, then the costume, and finally a plate of bacon and eggs, her price for allowing me to check out the accident scene first.

"Check," I said. "Once we finish on Flagstaff, we can search for a fabric store and a good place for breakfast."

I turned right on Baseline Road and headed toward the Flatirons, the road's gradual rise becoming more obvious as we progressed. We traveled for a while in silence while I focused on the GPS directions and Kit stared out at the scenery. After some twists and turns, I saw parking on the left and pulled in. We would have to hoof it from here.

I shouldered my bag and reached for the cait sith; when she narrowed her eyes at me, I gestured at the world around us. "There's hardly a shoulder, and we already know several accidents that have occurred here and at least one that killed people. This is for your own safety and mine."

The plate of bacon and eggs resurfaced as she allowed me to put her in the satchel, and off we went, me staring at my feet, trying very hard not to slip or trip on the way. I didn't really notice the hairs on the back of my neck standing up until I heard Kit growling. When I glanced at her, I could see a few faint sparks jumping around her head.

"Well this just got interesting," I murmured, slowly letting my gaze travel over the road and the wilderness on each side.

Kit's growl intensified, her eyes fixed on some overgrown undergrowth twenty or so yards ahead of us. I peered intently, hoping it wasn't a bear and slowing my walking speed. Were there bears around here? Maybe I should have done more research before

I set out on this excursion. Slowly, as we drew nearer, a form began to take shape; it wasn't a bear.

A young woman was staring at me, and when she noticed I caught sight of her, she tried to fade back into her surroundings. I crossed the road, finding a new route on the high side that would take me directly to her. Kit continued to both growl and spark, but she made no move to leap out of the bag. As we closed in on the vegetation that sheltered the spirit, she finally stepped out to meet us, looking me up and down before speaking.

"This is my territory," she snapped, chomping on some gum like she wanted to grind it out of existence. I had never seen a spirit chew gum before, and if they all chewed like this one, I'd be happy to never see it again. When we were a few feet away from her, she suddenly realized we were alive. Her face immediately twisted into an angry snarl.

"Oh so you can see me. Big deal. Your hair looks stupid, by the way, Freak."

At that comment, Kit stopped growling and turned her face up to mine. An image of the spirit with birds tweeting around her head surfaced, but even though the thought was lighthearted, the cait sith's fur was sparking more wildly now.

"You know," the girl continued, "Most people carry purse dogs, not purse cats. What a dumbass; you're not special." She rolled her eyes, smacked her gum, and waited for me to respond. I wasn't sure what to say; it's been a hot minute since I've been bullied by mean girls in high school. I never knew what to say then, either.

On the other side of the road, another spirit wandered into view. "Would you please shut up and let us go?" When this ghost saw me and realized I could see him, he continued. "You can see she's not in a car; you can't make her crash. What are you going to do? Push her down the hill and hope it kills her?" He smiled at me. "I think your hair looks nice."

The smacking of the gum intensified, which while incredibly annoying, was completely harmless; more disconcertingly however, her eyes started to redden, the hate in them making the young man stop where he stood.

"A deer, perhaps," I said under my breath, echoing what Dr. K had told us about the Monroe's fatal accident.

"Do I look like a deer, Dimwit?" she snapped, motioning toward her body. "Deer don't have curves like this; deer don't get to be Prom Queen or date the hottest boys in school." She punctuated this statement by striking a pose, complete with duck lips and peace sign, like I was going to take her picture. When I didn't oblige her, she narrowed her eyes and continued ranting.

"Awwwww, are you gonna cwy? Did I hurt your feewings?" She pouted, pretending to rub her eyes like she was about to cry, all the time the red deepening, beginning a slow burning glow.

I tilted my head, feeling my eyes starting to itch, and not because I was about to weep. This creature had caused the death of the Monroe's, I was sure of it, and of the young man still standing on the other side of the road, trapped there by her malevolence. She was not quite a rusalka or siren—both creatures that feed on the essence others—yet, but she was well on her way. I was guessing she couldn't control more than a few spirits at a time, so Laurel's parents may have been able to escape her. But the longer she stayed here, the stronger she would become. Kit and I would have to settle this first, then we could go search.

My refusal to rise to her goading must have pissed her off, because she started up again, still smacking on her gum like a maniac.

"Are you deaf or just stupid?" she sniped, waiting for me to react.

"Paisleigh Cliffson," I said, as I dug the information out of her, enjoying the way her eyes widened, the anger flickering to doubt for just a second. Whatever had once been human in this creature resurfaced, resentment rolling off of the quivering form.

"I bet you were a band nerd in high school; that or a theatre geek," she finally managed to snarl.

I heard Kit snort, her version of laughter, at the theatre geek comment. I chose to ignore both of them.

How could she have mistaken me for a band nerd? Without speaking again, I crossed over to where the young man was still transfixed.

"What happened to you?" I asked, already knowing pretty much what his story would be.

My proximity to him allowed him to drag his gaze away from Paisleigh as he realized I was not just another would-be victim. I held his eyes with my own, which were rapidly darkening into lightless voids.

"I was coming home from a late hike with my girlfriend. Paisleigh over there jumped out in front of my car and I swerved and then, nothing. My girl survived, though," he smiled faintly as he said that, then dropped his voice so only I could hear. "Is her name really Paisleigh?"

I nodded. "Yes, spelled all fancy and everything; and you're Simon Crannick. Are there others trapped here?"

His smile returned, but it was wrapped in sadness. "Was Simon Crannick, anyway. And yeah, there are a few others." He motioned to the steep decline behind him. "Mostly we chill down there, away from the whackadoo. But we can't go very far, and she always finds us."

"I know you're talking about me," Paisleigh snapped out, her voice getting louder as she crossed the road to our side, her eyes flaming red and boring into Simon, who visibly began to fade as she fed.

"Right," I clapped my hands together, startling the rusalka wannabe out of her feast. She turned to face me as I set a sparking and growing Kit on the ground.

For a brief moment, Paisleigh almost looked worried, but she was too far down the road of malignancy to turn back now. She locked her eyes on mine, maybe thinking she could draw power from me like she did her victims.

In that assumption, she was sadly mistaken.

"What are you gonna do? I'm invincible; you're just a band nerd trying desperately to get attention with your pink hair and stupid purse kitten—'look at meeee; I'm not like the other girls. I'm speshulllll.'"

"Theatre geek, actually," I responded finally, the Kit void next to me now the size of a St. Bernard. "And my 'stupid purse kitten' would like a moment of your time."

Her gaze flicked over to Kit, and the anger intensified. There was no remorse for what she had done, no sign that she would stop hurting people on this road, but would instead continue to harm and feed, a continuous loop that would eventually turn her into a monster that would become the source of local legends, which I'm sure would make her immensely happy. Finally recognizing the threat, she turned her focus to the void, and the cait sith pounced, wrapping a shrieking Paisleigh in the sparking blackness.

Simon's eyes widened, his form gathering some substance again as Kit devoured the monster who had trapped him here.

As the shrieking from Paisleigh lessened, the other trapped spirits began appearing from the surrounding wilderness, already gaining a little freedom. There weren't many, and most seemed to be younger than the Monroes. They stood silently, watching as the horrific screams finally stopped, and the void that was Kit began to shrink down to a regulation-sized cat.

"Wow," one of them finally broke the ringing silence. "We're not next, are we?"

Kit burped for an answer, her eyes half closed; the soul eating part of her ready for a monster sized nap. I scooped her up and slipped her back in my bag. She immediately disappeared from view.

"Nope; you're all free to move on; but before you go, can I ask you some questions about a couple that died here back in September, maybe because of Paisleigh? An older couple, Lucia and Paul Monroe; they would have been in their 60s or so?"

"Paisleigh? Paisleigh Cliffson?" One of the spirits blurted out; "I hated her; she always picked on me in school, like since I was a kindergartener. I don't know what you and your cat did, but thanks, lady."

"What a dumb name," another added. "Who names their kid Paisleigh?"

"The Monroes?" I interrupted gently, hoping to guide the conversation back on track.

"The Monroes named their kid Paisleigh?"

I sighed. Spirits can be a little disoriented sometimes. I suppose it is a natural state, especially if they have been held against their will from moving on to the next stage of being while acting as a food source for the creature who killed them. "No. They named their kid Laurel. I'm looking for their spirits; they crashed around here as well."

The four ghosts appeared to think for a while. Finally Simon spoke. "I think I remember them. They stayed together, trying to avoid the . . . whatever she was. When I started pushing my boundaries, wandering up to the road, talking back, basically being the biggest pain in the ass I could be in this state, she started focusing more on me. The Monroes vanished around the time I started pushing back. You don't think she completely removed them, like your cat just did, do you?"

I smiled at the young man. "She didn't; she can't completely erase a spirit the way Kit can. But I think your aggression allowed them the opportunity to pass on."

Simon straightened up then, cracking his own smile. "Ha! Good. I'm glad I helped them escape; they seemed nice."

He reached out to shake my hand, realized he couldn't, and gave me two thumbs up instead. "Later, Pinks," he quipped, then shimmered out of this plane.

Once Simon disappeared, the other spirits realized they were actually free to move on, and did so, thanking me as they vanished to start the next phase of their existence.

I walked a little further down the hill, heading toward what I was sure was the spot the Monroe's car came to rest, the damage to the tree still glaringly visible. "Paul? Lucia?" I called out, but I sensed nothing. They had indeed escaped.

With no spirits to converse with here any longer, I turned and headed back to the Fiat, the faintest of snoring sounds coming from my bag. As Kit would be sleeping off her meal for a while, I skipped the other errands and headed directly back to the theatre. We could get started on the costume after lunch. While I had no further information to help me find out the truth behind Laurel's fall, I had found enough evidence to rule out foul play on her parents, just like the police had, though by different means.

I glanced briefly at my satchel; Kit was still inside, still sound asleep. I hoped she wouldn't be too angry about lunch.

Chapter 6

By the time all the auditions were over, we had full casts for both productions of King Lear. For the student production, the majority of the participants had successfully landed the roles they really wanted. The biggest conflict was between the two Cordelias; one had nailed her audition and had good rapport with the young man playing Lear. The other had frozen up during her audition and nearly bolted off the stage in tears before Dr. K could reach her and convince her to finish her piece.

Bolstered by the older woman's broad and confident smile, the nervous young woman finished, apologized for her breakdown, and volunteered to help with make-up, costuming, and anywhere else she could be useful. At that point, Guppy had swooped in and began consulting her about costume design ideas, and the day was saved.

My sisters and I sat in the upper deck of the house, Kit still asleep in my bag. I missed lunch, but removing a monster from the world kept me from really noticing how hungry I was. I filled them in on Paisleigh and the ghosts, finishing with the idea that the area should be a little less crashy in the future.

Meg performed a quick search on her phone and discovered that this particular monster-to-be had died in a wreck of her own making, and out of the five people in her car, she had been the only one who hadn't survived. That explained quite a bit of her behavior. I have encountered several spirits who hadn't come to grips yet with the fact they had, in fact, caused their own deaths. Mostly, it's always someone else's fault: someone ran the red light, someone was driving too slow, someone couldn't take a joke. Whatever the excuse, the spirit hangs on to it like a lifeline, thinking that surely since they didn't mean to die, they should get a do over, as if our lives are video games.

For Paisleigh, I'm sure the denial started her down the path of destruction, but it was really the fact that she died and no one else did that pushed her over the edge. Her self-absorption, main-character syndrome provoked her jealousy that her friends would continue to live and carry on with their lives without her. And that while the moment had been traumatic for them, they would eventually move past it emotionally, maybe only pulling it out when they were together or at a reunion of some sort. Most people when they die do not become envious of those who are still living; but when they do, we often wind up with problems like Paisleigh.

As the workshop wound down for the day, Dr. K took the students back to the residence hall where another communal dinner was being provided—all part of the workshop experience. They would spend the meal discussing ideas for staging and costumes, throwing out ideas and getting to know one another better, which would lead to a more cohesive production.

Guppy led our troupe and the people who would be filling out our cast over to the Mary Rippon Outdoor Theatre so we could start doing some design and practice of our own. Tomorrow, most of us would be here working on our show while the theatre teachers and newly minted cast started working on their own version. At some point, the students would be watching our production, but we wanted them to practice their blocking and delivery skills before being influenced by our choices. If you've ever seen Kenneth Brannaugh's *Henry V*, you know that every actor who has tackled that role since has channeled his performance. Don't get me wrong, it's a great interpretation worth copying, but no one can deliver it quite like he can. The longer the students work on their own, the more ownership they have of their work, and that ownership is where the first inkling of pride comes into the performance.

While our professional cast intermingled with the students, working through ideas, I sat with Kit in the back row, wondering when she would finally poke her head out of the bag and start berating me about her costume and her bacon and eggs, not necessarily in that order. A promise is a promise, after all, and Guppy did need to get started on her costume.

When Carlos sat down next to me, Kit finally popped up, stretching her mouth in a bone-cracking yawn, and leapt out of the bag to sit between us.

"Alec told me about the creature and that the Monroes were not at the site. Do you think they're back in their house?"

It was a valid question. They may very well have gone back to their home once Simon's rebellion allowed them to escape. Spirits do like to check in on their loved ones, especially when the family is close knit, which it seems the Monroes were.

"They could have; it would make sense to go check on Laurel and then move on. I wonder if Madi could tell me about any 'strange' happenings occurring at the house," I paused, trying to order my thoughts. "If all seemed well with Laurel, they may have felt satisfied with their check, and progressed. If they believed she was struggling, they may have stuck around longer, and could still be there."

Carlos nodded. "You need to get into the house."

Kit chose that moment to stand up on her hind legs and hop around in a circle, like she was dancing. In my head, she was wearing the costume, the little bells delicately jingling.

I smiled and described the image to Carlos, who also smiled before speaking.

"I think I have an idea on how to work Kit into the Fool scenes."

The cait sith immediately stopped hopping about and fixed a rapt gaze on Carlos, who I'm sure was fast becoming her new favorite person in the troupe.

"What if the first few times we speak, I address the lines to Kit, and you pretend to translate, but as we move further into the play, I speak to both of you but only you answer, not pretending to translate any more as the situation grows more dire?"

Kit fastened her gaze on me, the excitement in her eyes obvious. It was a good idea: speaking to the cat at the beginning would demonstrate that Lear is already a little off kilter. As the tragedy moves to the storm on the heath, even the Fool's wit can't keep up with Lear's accelerating descent into madness. Addressing his concerns to Kit would segue nicely to using objects to stand in for his daughters when he puts them on trial.

"I think we should give that a try," I agreed, much to Kit's delight. She hopped back into the bag, the image she shared was her costume again.

"We didn't get around to shopping, yet," I explained. "We also missed lunch. Do you know if we're doing anything for dinner?"

"Funny you should ask; Guppy wants to bring in Cesare's; she already put in the order, and I am charged with picking it up. Why don't the three of us go find fabric and then grab dinner on the way back. Two birds, one stone." He looked to Kit for confirmation, already getting into character.

The cait sith tipped her head first to one side, then the other, like she was debating this suggestion, then meowed loudly, looked up at me, and waited for me to tell Carlos.

"Sounds like a plan."

One might have thought that the fabric store would be the easy part and picking up all the food and putting it into the back of the Italian Job would be the pain in the butt part. But alas, I'm guessing most people have never gone shopping with a supernatural cat with dreams of becoming a Tony award winning actor.

She wanted satin, not cotton, even when I told her how heavy it would be. She wanted bright colors, not pastels; she wanted gold bells, not silver. And all this happened before we went down the aisle with the rhinestones and Bedazzler on it. Her eyes widened in wonder at the sparkling faux gems, and in a flash, all her previous demands switched to a black and white costume decked out in so many colorful rhinestones that the sun would have been put to shame.

I tactfully reminded her that the black part of her costume wouldn't pop so much because it matched her fur. She paused for the briefest of moments, and sent back the same costume only with red instead of black. I described this to Carlos, who when he responded spoke directly to Kit, all three of us already getting into character.

"Sounds smashing, New and Improved Fool," he declared, grabbing the Bedazzler kit and extra rhinestone sets, which immediately set the cait sith's purr going. While they continued looking at all the trimmings, I took the fabric to the cutting station and placed my order.

The woman glanced over to my companions. "Your grandfather is lucky to have you, taking him and his cat out for some shopping. What are you making?"

Instead of trying to correct her assumption of us which could have taken all day, I played along. "A jester costume for the cat. He says she's always wanted one."

"So sweet," she continued, cutting my fabric for me and writing the ticket, not really hearing what I had said or deciding that my grandfather had dementia and talked to his cat and I was a saint. Either way, it kept me from having to make idle chit chat.

I took the package and thanked her, motioning to Carlos that we were ready to roll. He scooped up Kit and put her in the basket with the trimmings, and we headed to the counter to check out.

Once our transaction was complete, we made our way back to the car to begin the second errand we needed to run. Kit sat in the back with the bags, gently stroking the satin with her paw. The image in my head shifted from the Fool costume to a princess dress.

"Not this time, Kit; I'm not sure the world is ready for one of the daughters to be a cat." I said it as seriously as I could, and from the corner of my eye saw Carlos's expression shift before he spoke.

"I had no idea you were so interested in acting, Kit," there was a smile in his tone, but also genuine interest. "We can work you into larger roles as you grow more comfortable with the stage. It is a demanding life."

Kit sighed loud enough for both of us to hear, then flashed a plate of arancini in my head.

"I'm pretty sure Guppy ordered those; if not, I'll add an order just for you," I reassured her.

Guppy had indeed ordered plenty of arancini for everyone, and several different pastas with sauces, garlic rolls, salad, and even some cannolis. Carlos had the order confirmation pulled up on his phone, and he and the host were going over items meticulously to make sure that nothing had been left out.

As my stomach started growling at the smell of the food, I realized I hadn't eaten much all day, which is rare for me. Kit was flashing non-stop images of food into my head, including one where she was swimming in a pool of noodles. From this, I gathered she, too, was starved, the meal of Paisleigh not satisfying the cat part of her.

Once the inventory had been finished, we started to gather up our bags, quickly realizing that it was going to take more than one trip. Before we could start on the first leg, Jeremy, our waiter from the afternoon before, popped out to the hostess stand and offered to help.

"You're not going to get in trouble for helping, are you?" I asked, genuinely concerned having seen his boss's temper in action the day prior.

Jeremy smiled a smile that almost reached his eyes this time. "He's at a dinner meeting with his 'attorney' about something."

He flashed the air quotes before grabbing several of the bags, but I could hear the sarcasm without the hand gesture. We trekked back to the car, my mind running over questions I would like to ask, but not sure how any of them would land. His sarcasm told me that he wanted to speak more about this meeting, but I was focused instead on Laurel, still needing information as to what was happening around her.

Before I could speak, Carlos threw out a question about the attorney. "Why the air quotes? Is she not really a lawyer?"

"Oh she is, but she hasn't been for very long. And the way she talks, you'd think she was about to take over the entire firm. She would come in with Ms. Faulkner sometimes to speak with Mr. or Mrs. Monroe. It's when she comes in by herself that's annoying."

"So she's a diva," Carlos smiled. "There's divas in every profession."

Jeremy laughed. "Yeah, she's something, alright. Snaps her fingers when she wants a server, that kind of crap. Mr. Garrett is a thousand times more likely to fly off the handle when she's around, too. Makes the nights she comes in a real joy. Fortunately for us, they're meeting elsewhere tonight."

"Any news about Laurel?" I finally threw out after a stretch of silence.

"I heard she may have woken up for a few moments, but went right back under. I'm not sure if that is normal, but no one seems to be panicking about it, so maybe it is," he responded as we neared the car.

I was panicking, but I didn't say that aloud. If rumors were starting to spread about Laurel possibly waking up, if someone had in fact pushed her, she was in danger. Trying to mask the growing anxiety in my voice, I asked: "Where did you get that information? Mr. Garrett?"

We had reached the Fiat by then, and after I popped the hatch, Jeremy answered me while he and Carlos began to stow our food inside.

"Yeah. He came into work, said he and the other managers heard from Ms. Faulkner that signs pointed to Laurel maybe waking up soon, and then told us he was meeting with his own lawyer during the dinner service. Believe me, we are all thrilled about Laurel, but even more thrilled he isn't at the restaurant tonight. You guys caught him on a good day."

My mind started clicking over this new information. The meeting could be about procuring ownership of Cesare's, but it could also be about anything under the sun that one has to talk to a lawyer about. It was the timing that made it seem suspicious. As I mulled this around, Carlos pulled out his wallet and gave Jeremy some bills for helping us get all the food in one trip.

Once we were safely on our way back to the amphitheatre loaded with food, Carlos ventured a question.

"What are you thinking, Tisi?"

I took a deep breath and slowly let it out while I tried to put my thoughts into coherent sentences.

"I think I'm stuck. With Laurel alive I can't tell if someone tried to kill her or not. The only way I would be able to discover that is if they tried it again and succeeded, and I don't want that. For all I know, she really did fall down the stairs of her own accord, and

I'm overreacting by getting paranoid that she is waking up. But if I'm not paranoid and she wakes up, someone might take a shot at her again. The first time we met him, Mr. Garrett let slip that he didn't own Cesare's 'yet', but that's hardly an admission of attempted murder. And Meg said his jealousy about everything and everyone is off the charts, and this meeting with his own lawyer so soon after receiving news about Laurel is nagging at me, like I'm missing something."

I paused for a moment, realizing I was talking Carlos's ear off; but like the others in the troupe, he knew I struggled with verbalizing my experiences.

He remained silent, waiting for me to continue if I needed to, which I did.

"I don't want anyone to die, but I'm really at a loss here. My gut is telling me something is off, but I have no idea what. And I'm hungry."

"Hangry even?" Carlos asked, and pulled from a bag he had taken out of our order a container with some arancini in it. He handed it to me, breaking off a small piece for Kit who had stuck her nose up between the seats when she saw what he had.

I took the food gratefully, popping the whole thing in my mouth in one bite. Kit also took her bite gently from his fingers. We were all quiet for a moment, chewing, each lost in our own thoughts.

"I think," Carlos finally broke the silence after swallowing, "You need to get in that house tonight; and if I might suggest it, take Meg with you. If she had such a strong reaction to this Garrett guy, she might be able to sense that vibe in the house even though some time has passed. Or maybe the Monroes are still there, and they'll be able to tell you something."

When he finished speaking, he pulled out his phone to text Guppy that we were nearly there with the food and we would need some extra hands to carry it all.

Carlos was right. Getting into the house was the best move to make next as it could provide us with some answers as to what really happened to Laurel. I could see Eliava and Cole waiting for us as we parked next to the big Vista. While Carlos divvied out the bags for carrying back to the waiting actors, I threw out my need to get into the Monroe house to Eliava, who I knew could get us in there without being seen. Fey walking is not my favorite thing to do as it can be a bit nauseating, but with all the cameras around these days, it would be a necessity.

The fairy was nodding along as I spoke, finally adding her two cents when I was done. "Absolutely we can do this. Now that I don't have to be five different characters for Lear to work, we shouldn't be missed. Are we taking Kit too, or just Meg?"

I glanced down at the cait sith's face; she had been listening to the entire plan. I didn't need her there, but I also didn't want to insult her by not inviting her along–we were becoming a team, after all. Before I could answer, Carlos jumped to my rescue.

"If you don't need her, Tisi, she could stand in for you while we block out some things and get more comfortable with the other characters we have scenes with; I'm sure Guppy would read your lines."

Kit sat up straighter in the bag. The idea definitely appealed to her. She sent me an image of Carlos, Guppy, and herself working together. "She's ready to work," I translated as we made it to the outdoor theatre and began setting out all the items for people to come grab. I took my plate over to where Guppy was eating with my sisters, and again explained my plan for the house visit, adding that Kit would be staying and working with Carlos. I also handed my mom the bag from the fabric store, describing the costume Kit had in mind.

"Check and check," she responded, smiling at Kit. "We've some work to do, little miss."

With everyone now aware of what would be taking place, I could finally start shoveling my food into my mouth. I needed to fuel up to make it through our excursion tonight. For the rest of the meal, our cast conversed about set ideas and performances in our pasts. When Guppy called for certain groups to start working on different scenes, I knew it was time to put my plan into action.

Chapter 7

The sun was sinking below the Flatirons as we made our way back to Pearl Street. Our plan was to park somewhere unobtrusive and walk the few blocks to Mapleton. Meg had the address locked in her phone, and was searching the map for a place that wouldn't get us noticed if we stayed too long. Even though it was only Tuesday, the street parking was full, so I started weaving up and down the side streets, trying to stay in reasonable proximity to the Monroe's house.

Meg tapped my shoulder. "There," she said, pointing at an old yellow Victorian that had been turned into a restaurant. "They only serve breakfast, so no one should really care if we park here."

In fact a few other cars were already in place in the spaces in front. I pulled in next to a Land Cruiser, and the three of us hopped out, scanning the area around us to see how many other folks were out and about.

After that short bit of recon, we headed off in the direction of the Monroe's, sticking to the sidewalk and talking about the show we would be putting on. There were not that many people about, but enough that we were waiting to pull our vanishing act when we could find some suitable cover.

The sun continued to drop, the shadows disappearing completely. As we approached a house on the corner of Pine and Broadway, Eliava reached out and took our hands. A cluster of cars, mostly larger SUVs outside a house where music was playing, offered the perfect moment, and as we wove through the vehicles, I could feel the shift happen.

The colors around me changed, and the edges of the cars, houses, and trees all began to blur and smear as the fairy took us into the Fey. If anyone had seen us during this transition, they would have questioned if they had seen anything at all. Fey walking is not disappearing, it's more like being out of focus for anyone not involved. The harder people might try to see what they thought they saw, the more they couldn't focus on it.

With our hands linked and Meg leading, we wove through the party cars and continued our way through the neighborhood slowly. We were silent; sound does not stay in the Fey, though it will bounce around and those outside can't discern where it originated. It's easier to just be silent and move as fluidly as possible.

People might see three women walking along, holding hands, but only out of the corners of their eyes. If they tried to look, to focus, we were gone. This was true to an extent inside the Fey, which is why I was clutching Eliava's hand in a death grip and walking with my eyes closed. I'm not sure if it's a relative of motion sickness or some other condition, but being in the Fey makes me queasy as my eyes try to focus on something that will never come into focus. When the fairy squeezed my hand, I would squint to see the obstacle I was supposed to avoid, and then resume moving blind.

Meg was focused on the map on her phone. Having something that didn't weave around as much helped her keep her stomach under control. Though the walk didn't last longer than fifteen minutes, I was ready to see again, and was relieved when Eliava squeezed my hand twice and spoke softly.

"We're here; we just need to get through the gate to the back yard."

I figured I could go a few steps with my eyes open without spewing up my dinner, and curled a bit around the fairy to hold the gate as we made our way through. Once in the back, I slowly closed it, making sure it latched, and then focused again on making it to the rear entrance and not revisiting my dinner.

Even though the backyard was thoroughly blocked from the neighbors' prying eyes by the large trees, the board on board fence, and the cover over the patio, we remained in the Fey while Meg worked a little magic on the door lock. Once in and the door shut behind us, Eliava dropped our hands, and everything snapped back into focus.

The back door led into a mudroom, complete with benches and coat hooks, a large wardrobe for storing other winter gear, and at the far end, a laundry area. The dust was just beginning to collect, which reminded me that I needed to find out if the Monroe's had a housekeeper they would have trusted with a key. Had someone broken in, the cover in the back would have shielded them from being seen, but the door had no evidence of being tampered with, according to the report I had.

I reopened the door, crouching to look for myself at the lock. The door showed no damage, but lock picks didn't leave damage. I quickly shut the door again and locked it for good measure. As we stepped into the kitchen, I pulled my phone out of my pocket, looking for the texts from Officer Larkes about the case, and read a few to help us find a direction.

"Neither entry showed signs of being forced. There were take out containers in the fridge from Cesare's and a receipt in her purse from earlier in the day. The dishwasher had been run and no plates or glasses were found in the sink or on the table."

"So either she took care of the dishes after eating or just ate out of the boxes," Eliava stated. "I do; then you don't have to do dishes."

Meg nodded in agreement, "Yeah, except we know she was drinking. She probably just shoved everything in and ran it. Let's scout about here; Tisi, try calling up the Monroes. I'm guessing they aren't here though or you would already be talking to them. Unless they're shy."

I moved away from the kitchen, taking note of the pantry door and opening it. The apothecary was still there. I was tempted to look in the drawers to see how much of the Elixir Class supplies still existed, wondering how sentimental Lucia Monroe had been about her only child.

I made my way up the stairs to the second floor. "Lucia? Paul?" I called out listening intently for any response. "You don't know me, but I'm here to help Laurel. A friend and I took care of the creature on the mountain road that caused your accident. She can't hurt anyone else."

The house was perfectly still except for the slight noises of rummaging going on below. I worked my way down the hall until I found the stairs heading up to Laurel's room. They were steep and narrow. I hesitated, waiting to see if I felt something left over from the event. The house continued to resonate stillness, the only noise that of Meg and Eliava coming up behind me.

"No Monroes?" Meg asked, and after acknowledging the shake of my head, she continued. "There is a slight residue of jealous anger here. Let's go on up; if she was pushed, it wouldn't have been from the bottom."

I started the steep climb. How must Laurel have felt every night, alone in this giant house? The second floor had a guest room, along with her parents' room, and two smaller offices—one which doubled as a work-out room according to the treadmill lined up to give a view of the Flatirons out the window. She could have slept down here, though maybe that would have been more strange, sleeping in a guest room in the house she grew up in, like a stranger just stopping by before moving on with her life.

The third floor was really just a glorified attic renovated into three rooms: a full bathroom straight off the head of the stairs, a roomy bedroom down a short hall to the left, and what had probably been a playroom at one point before becoming a young woman's study and hangout on the right. I had turned into this last room before I realized Meg was no longer behind me. I poked my head out and looked back to the top of the stairs.

Meg stood clutching the railing. From where I stood, she couldn't have seen me until I fully stepped out. I realized at that moment how easy it would be to give her a push and send her crashing down the stairs. A half drunk, self-medicated girl would never have seen what was coming.

"The jealousy is stronger here, but the anger is worse," she took a deep breath, launching herself off the stairs, nearly running over me. I didn't need to turn on lights to know that Meg's eyes were going black; my own were starting to itch in sympathy.

"Can you tell if it was Garrett?" Eliava asked from the foot of the steps.

"No, just anger, resentment really, hence the undertone of jealousy," she sighed deeply. "So maybe someone was here, and maybe someone pushed her; or maybe not."

I slipped back in the study room, Meg following. "It's strong here, too." She wandered around, looking at the book titles, the games—both table and computer—before heading toward the bedroom. "Not so strong here," she called out not realizing I had followed her, so when she turned around, she jumped.

"Geez, Tiss; warn me next time," she snapped, turning on her phone and using the ambient light it gave off to have a look around.

I wasn't surprised by the snapping. Again, I could tell the severity of situations concerning anger or jealousy by the way my sisters began to react to the world containing those sentiments. Both Meg and Alec had learned over the years how to tune the petty stuff out, or else they would be a couple of serious raging bitches day in and day out because of how common those two emotions are in our current world. Of the two, Alec probably had it easier because in our 'look at me' world right now, many people no longer try to control their anger; they just let it out, film it, and post it to stir up what they assume is righteous indignation, but is really just more negativity the universe has to absorb. Something we really don't need right now, or ever in fact. People still tried to hide their jealousy, so pockets of it, like the one Meg had encountered here, could linger for years where the jealous person had spent time. And while interesting, it didn't help me figure out if it was an accident or not.

Meg's voice broke the silence again, "Sorry. I'm a little frazzled. But look on the bed." She directed the light from her phone over to the queen bed. There, front and center, was Ember the stuffie familiar.

"She does look like Kit," I remarked, letting Meg know there were no hard feelings for her snapping at me.

"In fact," my sister continued, "totally off subject, but I think I'm going to start painting her on tiles in her costumes to sell as souvenirs."

"She's gonna love that idea; she might just get impossible to live with at some point," I joked.

"I'll make her cross eyed if she gets an ego about it," Meg replied, turning to face me, her eyes crossed and her tongue sticking out. "We'll see how she feels about that."

And because we had been in a forced silence for so long, we both started giggling to the point that we couldn't stop. "I'll have one with her all puffed up and sparking and cross eyed," Meg managed to gasp out between laughs we were trying to stifle which only made us laugh harder.

"Girls!" Eliava called out from the darkness. "We need to get back; the show must go on, and it won't if we don't get to rehearse."

As we navigated our way back down the stairs, I mused again on how easy it would be to shove someone down the steep steps. But I also realized that just because someone was pushed down the narrow stairs, that didn't guarantee they would be dead by the bottom. As far as a murder weapon went, the stairs were not as reliable as a gun or a knife. If I really wanted someone dead, I wouldn't rely on a fall to carry out the deed, unless it was from the top of a cliff. With no clearer idea on what had happened to Laurel than when we came in, I was starting to believe that either Laurel had tripped in her inebriated state or she had taken her cocktail of alcohol and sleep aids and tripped on her way up to fall into a sleep she didn't want to end.

As we slipped out the back, Meg relocking the door with a little more magic and Eliava reaching for our hands to return to the Fey, I was hoping that Laurel was indeed waking up and would survive. There were plenty of people in Boulder who loved her and wanted to help her; all she needed to do was return to the world of the living, and she could get the therapy she needed.

The return trip to the car was easier, and we uncloaked ourselves when we reached the party house, the party still in full swing and getting louder. By the time we made it back to campus, the moon was above and the actors were mid-scene—Goneril dismissing her father's men and Lear preparing to stomp off into the night. As Carlos turned to storm off, Kit hissed at Alec, and Alec aimed a kick at her, which Kit dodged, then fled off stage. Nice touch.

Once the scene was finished, the actors involved, including Kit, debriefed with Guppy, who glanced up and nodded at us to acknowledge we were back. Eliava headed to the stage while Meg and I wandered over to where the leftovers were. There wasn't much left, but we did find a couple cannolis and sat down in the audience to eat them.

As we sat there in silence enjoying the dessert and taking in the bustle that was rehearsal, we didn't notice Madi arrive until her bicycle crashed to the ground, her eyes frantically searching for someone. When her gaze finally found me, she ran over, her eyes wide and frightened.

"Madi, what's wrong," Meg and I asked at the same time, rising to meet the panicking young woman.

"Laurel woke up, for just a couple minutes; she was disoriented, wasn't sure where she was. I was trying to calm her down and when she heard my voice she started to speak. She was pushed! She said someone pushed her down the stairs."

Chapter 8

The sounds from the stage began to fade in my ears. The actors were still making noise, but it was just a blur in the background as I tried to focus again on Madi, not sure how to calm the panic in either of us.

Meg squeezed Madi's arm, threw a glance at me, and made her way to the stage and Guppy, who was wrapping up the scene notes with the actors. I turned back to the shaking form in front of me, hoping words would come to me on how to handle this situation, but I was two steps away from joining her panic party.

"What do I do? I told the nurse what Laurel said, but he told me not to worry, that when people wake up from comas they can be disoriented and say strange things. But what if she was pushed? Tisi, what if someone tried to kill her?"

The itching in my eyes which had started at the Monroe's house intensified, and it was all I could do to not start digging at them. Somewhere in my blood, the fury was slowly waking, scenting the surroundings, reaching out to find the guilty party. Madi's intense belief in an attempt on her friend's life was strong enough to set off the alarm, although I was trying my best to hit the snooze button until I had more proof.

"Madi," I said, looking the frightened young woman in the eyes hoping to calm her down and hoping mine hadn't already completely gone black. "What did she say exactly?"

She took a deep breath, trying to steady her nerves. "She said 'Too much to drink; someone pushed me'. I asked her who, but she drifted off before she could tell me, or maybe she couldn't see them. Tisi, someone tried to kill Laurel; I know it!" Her voice was rising, and I reached out, taking her ice cold hands in mine.

Out of the corner of my eye, I could see Guppy dismissing the rehearsal, and my brain flashed back to Lady Macbeth frantically telling her party goers to leave after Macbeth starts talking to Banquo's ghost. Guppy was a little less frantic, but no less adamant about people getting a move-on. Our crew started cleaning things up, taking their hint from Guppy's actions that something had changed. I could see Meg with Alec, both of them making their way toward me, concern and determination set on their faces.

"Madi, are visiting hours over?" I asked. "Can you go sit with her?"

For a brief spell, confusion washed over her face; I could see the exact moment when she realized why I was asking as her eyes grew wider and she pulled her hands from mine to cover her mouth.

"Oh no, I shouldn't have left! She could be in danger," she blurted out, already turning to rush back to the hospital.

Before she could ride off, Alec gently stopped her, which kept me from having to grab her hands and force her to stay. "Let me have your phone; I'll put Tisi's number in it. Call the police if you see anything strange. If they won't let you sit with her, sit outside her door. Let us know as well. Chances are she is perfectly safe, especially if no one else heard her; but you being there will be a little safety net, okay? We'll figure something out."

Madi did as she was told, nearly dropping her phone as her hands were shaking so badly.

Meg spoke up while Alec fussed with Madi's phone. "Do you want one of us to come with you?"

"No, that's okay," she said, taking her phone back and starting to type on it. "I'm going to text my boyfriend to meet me there when he gets off work. I'll be okay; I think I just freaked out. I'm sorry."

Alec smiled reassuringly, her hands weaving a small calming spell as she spoke. "Deep breath. It's going to be fine, Madi; keep us posted."

Madi nodded, sticking her phone in her backpack and heading back to her bike, unceremoniously lying on the ground where she left it.

Once she was out of earshot, Meg turned to both of us. "I have an idea. We need to go to the Vista and ask a little favor of Richard."

Alec and I both winced. Asking Richard to do a favor wasn't difficult; the aftermath once the favor was done, however, was nearly unbearable. While Kit might be a blossoming diva, Richard was a full on drama queen; everything was a life or death situation, which is kind of funny considering he's a ghost.

The campus was mostly deserted as we walked from the theatre to where our vehicles were parked, but I could hear voices coming from somewhere. As the sidewalk curved by some trees, the voices grew louder.

"Prithee, wenches, hast thou some sustenance? We needs must quell the pangs o' our hunger; perhaps thou wouldst give us some hazelnuts?"

I stopped dead in my tracks, my sisters continuing forward for a few steps before they realized I wasn't moving.

"Tiss?" Alec questioned my abrupt halt.

"Squirrels," I answered her. "They want something to eat. I kinda thought this would wear off." The potion Guppy had given me in Salida must have been stronger than either of us expected.

"Or we can feast upon your loveliness, growing stronger by what makes us longer." This last comment was followed by what I recognized as squirrel laughter.

Looking up, I spotted the three fluffy tailed rodents lounging around on separate branches, looking quite similar to Mercutio and his friends in the town square right before they begin harassing the nurse in Zeffirelli's production of *Romeo and Juliet*.

"Ah, the rose-haired vixen hath slain my heart; to feast upon her would cause my own death," the smallest of the squirrels declared, one paw over his heart.

"Hey!" I snapped, which caused all three squirrels to jump, one nearly losing his balance on the branch. "You watch your mouths and get your minds out of the gutter." I'm not even sure these guys had a clue about sexual innuendo, but depending how much Shakespeare they'd been exposed to, it was more than the average person, or squirrel in this case.

My sisters were looking at me like I'd lost my mind, so without taking my eyes from the squirrel rogues above us, I explained to them what had been said.

"Are you serious?" Meg asked, eyes narrowing as she watched the squirrels shifting around a bit.

Alec started to laugh. "So this is what happens when squirrels live too close to the theatre versus watching too many gangster movies."

"Alas, fair lasses, forgive our trespass; though verily, we hunger most fearsome."

I translated this for my sisters, absently digging in my bag to see if I had any crackers or something to give them.

"Are they hitting on us or really just hungry?" Meg wondered aloud, then directed her voice upwards. "Saucy knaves! Thy guts belie thy hunger."

The squirrels started laughing at her comment. One hopped down to a lower branch, looking us up and down. "Truce, maidens," he began, doffing an imaginary cap. "Forgive my brothers, I beg. Ne'er before have we encountered such wit!"

Before any of us could respond, another voice on the other side of the sidewalk called out dramatically: "Look on my nuts, ye mighty, and despair!"

Turning to this new voice, I found the squirrel version of Ozymandias standing on the back of a bench, an acorn in each paw, which were raised above his head in a triumphant, taunting manner.

"Shut thy mouth, Percy, else I'll stople it!" First Squirrel shouted, or at least, his chattering got louder for those who couldn't understand him.

I was trying to keep my sisters up to date on this little scene unfolding before us when another squirrel joined Percy on the bench. He held a paw out, and Percy put one of the acorns into it.

"Yet he was jealous, though he did not show it, for jealousy dislikes the world to know it!" As he finished this statement, both the Romantic squirrels stuffed the acorns in their mouths, still glaring at their enemies across the sidewalk.

An unsettling silence followed this statement as the squirrels glared at each other across the divide of the walkway, not speaking, but tails twitching menacingly. I nudged Alec and started backing away. "I think an all squirrel version of *West Side Story* is about to break out, minus the dancing." The three of us turned to go and as we did so, First Squirrel scrambled down the tree cursing as he went.

"You whoreson cullionly barbermonger! Have at thee!"

In a flurry of tails, the five rodents started chasing around like crazy. We took the opportunity to flee toward our intended target, the Vista, and the refuge it would offer.

We only slowed our brisk walk as we crossed the parking lot, hoping Richard would be hanging out inside the motor home. As a ghost, he could go wherever he pleased, so he might be out roaming the campus, meeting some of the other spirits I had noticed earlier. Before we could open the door, it flew open, nearly catching Alec in the face, and Richard, being over-dramatic as usual, greeted us.

"It's been ages since I've had company. Put on the kettle and let's catch up!" He shooed us into the Vista, making a big production about plumping pillows and checking for dust, as if we had been away for months.

We took turns filling him in on what had occurred, where Laurel currently was, and that her friend Madi would be there as well, though maybe not in the room. Alec made the tea while Meg approached him with her idea once the background story had been established.

"What we need, Richard," she began, trying to not use the word 'favor', "is to have some eyes on the inside, right inside the room where Laurel is, in fact; eyes that can also ward off any potential threat to this young woman, if you know what I mean." This last comment was meant to flatter, and it worked.

Richard flexed a little. He'd been a ghost long enough that he could interact with solid objects; a feat, he assured us repeatedly, that took time to master. As Alec set all the fixings for tea on the table, he casually filled my mug to prove his point without saying it for the umpteenth time.

"Any idea who is after her?" he asked.

I shook my head. "No, not yet. But the rumor of her waking could set them into motion again. You might also encounter her parents there. I would like to talk to them if they are, so please be nice to them."

"I got you, fam," he said, smiling at his use of slang, and with that, he was gone.

We sat sipping our tea in the wonderful silence he left behind.

"Well that wasn't so bad," Meg finally stated, pouring out the last of the tea into our mugs.

Alec looked over to me, chewing the inside of her lip. "Since you can still understand squirrels, maybe you want to go back to the Monroes and see if any of them saw anything that night. You wouldn't have to hide if you went with Madi on one of her upkeep visits."

"I could ask her if the Monroe's employed a cleaning service as well or if anyone else has a key that she knows about," I mused aloud, my brain thinking over the possibilities this action might uncover.

With the tea gone, Alec started putting things away, looking over to me while she bustled about. "What did you think about the end of the scene, with the kick at Kit and all?"

I handed her my now empty mug. "I liked it. Kit has mentioned she would like a death scene, and I think that kick could be our way into it."

Meg laughed, "Of course she does." She stood then, and began gathering her painting materials. "I might be able to get some of those Kit tiles done before we start performing."

While she put together a backpack with her supplies, I rummaged in the cabinets for some nuts to bring back to the squirrels even though they looked well fed. I realized as I pocketed what was left of a bag of pecans, that I missed Rocko and Mugsy and their no-nonsense gangster banter. Surely if I found squirrels around the Monroe house, they wouldn't be speaking in such flowery phrases as the ones we had encountered on the way to the Vista nor like a gangster Joe Pesci.

By the time we reached the area where we had left the squirrels to their scuffle, the fight had ended, and all five of them were sitting on the bench, singing.

"He turned his face unto the wall
And death was in him wellin'
'Goodbye, goodbye to my friends all
Be good to Barbara Allen'."

At our approach, they stopped their song and turned to look at us, First Squirrel calling out, "Oh beauteous light! Our fair maids have returned!"

I pulled the pecans out of my bag and approached their bench, already tipping the container to spill out the contents. "Share, please," I warned, stepping back with the empty bag crumpled in my hand.

"Oh summer's day! 'Tis a delightful feast!" Second Squirrel chirped; the others were too busy stuffing the pecans in their cheeks to respond.

My sisters and I made our exit, leaving the squirrels singing incomprehensibly as their mouths were full. I chucked the bag into the first trash can I found along our path and took a moment to rub my eyes. The squirrels had been a distraction from the business at hand. Now I needed to figure out how to find the would-be killer before they took another shot at Laurel. And I had absolutely no idea how to do that.

Alec noticed my action. "Look at me," she ordered once I took my hands away from my face. She stared into my eyes for a moment before coming to a decision: "Clock's ticking."

Chapter 9

When we finally made it back to the outdoor theatre, most of the extra cast had left; a few remained, talking with Carlos on stage. Guppy had gathered the rest of the troupe in the back of the seating area, filling everyone in on the events that had been transpiring around us. When she looked up at our arrival, Alec tapped the back of her wrist a few times, the gesture letting Guppy know that the Fury changes that affected me were in motion and we were on the clock.

Guppy acknowledged her with a nod, then turned her attention back to her audience.

"So here is what we know: Laurel's parents were killed by an angry spirit and that spirit has been dealt with and is no danger to her or anyone else. However, someone wants that girl out of the way and has waited eight months to remove her, or try to anyway."

Bri spoke up, which is always a little surprising considering how soft-spoken she is. "So, the whole plan to get rid of Laurel probably wasn't even on the menu until the parents were killed, do you think?"

Many heads were nodding along with this idea. Had Laurel's parents not been killed by Paisleigh, the whole horrendous scenario the poor girl found herself in now probably would not even exist.

Meg threw in our latest move concerning Richard. "Madi says Laurel is waking up; she comes and goes, which is apparently normal for coma patients. Richard is going to be in her room to both keep an eye out for trouble–like a second attempt–and put an end to it if necessary. I'm not sure anyone would try something in a hospital, but desperate times and all that."

"Who benefits from Laurel's death?" Asher, our head tech, spoke up, asking aloud the question most of us were thinking.

Kit had come over to sit with me, bumping me with her head until I looked at her. She, like Alec, studied my eyes for a minute, then sent me an image of snakes writhing around on my head.

"I have some time yet, Kit; no worries," I smiled at her, and the image changed to Dr. K at lunch. It took me a second to grasp where she was heading. When I figured it out, I spoke.

"Dr. K said something about the family lawyer finding her before some big meeting with the general managers of all the establishments the Monroe's own. Kit just reminded me of that," I added that last part to give credit where credit is due. Kit raised her paw, and I fist bumped it before turning my attention back to my mom.

Though Guppy hadn't been taking notes, she had followed the thread of the conversation as it went around and had filed it all away; for as long as I can remember, she never wrote anything down—it just seemed to stick in her head. I wish she had passed that trait on to me; I might have gotten better grades.

Carlos had finished up his conversation with our extras and had sent them on their way. He seated himself near Guppy, and the two of them whispered back and forth for a few minutes before Guppy turned to face all of us.

"Good news is," she started, "that our extra cast have their lines memorized and some great ideas for blocking out the action. The bad news is we might lose our Fool in both productions, what with Miss Drake being concerned for her friend and Tisi, well, Tisi being Tisi. With Richard at the hospital, I think Laurel should be safe, but Asher, if you and the tech crew could also take shifts, that might put Madi's mind at ease. She can introduce you all as 'theatre friends', and that should satisfy people's curiosity. With her mind at ease, maybe the student production won't suffer as much. For the next few days, we are going to start extra early and work extra late, but it will still take a little magic to get this production off the ground. In fact, it might take a little magic to help the students as well, but we'll see. For now, let's go get a good night's sleep so we can hit the rehearsal hard tomorrow."

Everyone took their cue from Guppy's dismissal and headed back to the dorm, walking in small groups and chatting about various concerns about our production. Carlos walked with Kit and I, and I took the opportunity to explain how Kit wanted a death scene, and how I thought we could make that happen.

As we walked, he scooped up the cait sith and set her on his shoulder. "A death scene. Exquisite! What's your plan?"

In *King Lear*, there is a moment when the two older daughters gang up on Lear, take away the remainder of his knights, and piss him off so badly that he storms out of the shelter of Gloucester's castle and heads into the teeth of an oncoming tempest. Of course the fool goes with him, as does Kent in disguise as Caius. The storm scene is the moment in the play when all of the mistakes Lear has made come to fruition, and he quite certainly loses his mind to grief and disbelief of how things have turned sour for him, and he has no one to blame but himself, which, of course, is hard to accept for any tragic character. It is in this storm scene that the audience sees the Fool for the last time.

"So, I made it back in time to see Alec kick Kit, and that Kit dodged it. What if, during the argument in the castle yard with both sisters, either of the sisters kick her, but she doesn't manage to avoid it this time."

Kit was looking at me intently, the expression mirrored on Carlos's face; Carlos spoke. "That will have to be seriously blocked out and practiced to make it appear real."

I nodded in agreement and continued with my idea. "Then, she can limp out after us in all the chaos, and maybe the other sister takes another shot at her, whatever. Anyway, after the mock trial goes down and Gloucester returns to move the king to a safer locale, we all leave except Kit, who at this point will be 'dead,' and Poor Tom will give his last speech. Then I'll come back and look for Kit, find her, scoop her up, and exit the other side, which will explain why we are gone for the rest of the production.

Carlos and Kit looked at each other, then back at me. "I think we need to put the kitten through fight school so this looks real."

Kit's purr was loud enough for me to hear at that point.

"Alec, Meg, and I can work with her tomorrow, among other things that we have to do. Like Eliava told us earlier, 'the show must go on' and if we don't rehearse, it won't."

We continued on in companionable silence, Kit still purring and sharing with me different death poses. When my phone chimed, I slowed to answer it and motioned for Carlos and Kit to continue without me. It was Madi.

"Hey Madi; everything okay?" I asked, crossing the fingers of my other hand.

When she spoke, her voice was calm, a good sign considering the panic she was in when last I saw her. "Yeah, things are fine here. Laurel hasn't come around again, but her room is right across from the nurses station, and they are taking the pushing comment seriously. Someone will be watching her room 24/7."

That was good news; I used it to segue into Asher and the other tech guys that would be coming in and out as well, posing as concerned theatre friends.

"I remember him; I'll make a big deal like I know him when I see him. I'll also tell the nurses some of her other friends will be coming by for added support," she said, the relief in her voice audible.

I really wanted to tell her about Richard being in the room and that he could protect Laurel from certain things if he had to, but how do you tell someone you've arranged for a ghost to guard the room? This has been one of my issues with communication since I could talk. The number of people I could trust with my paranormal skill set was minimal, and for the longest time, the only ones I could share it with were the troupe members. When Officer Larkes saw me in all my Fury glory, I really thought he was going to shoot me. Luckily, he has a touch of the supernatural about him as well, so instead of things falling apart, I had a new friend. That isn't always the case.

"Tisi?" There was hesitation in her voice, but she hurried on before it could stop her from speaking. "I think I should drop out of the production; my head isn't in it, and I don't want to be the weak link."

I held in a sigh. If Guppy were on the phone, she would be able to reassure Madi that everything would be fine. I, on the other hand, wasn't sure what to say, so I just started rambling.

"I get that. I'm not sure what I would do in your shoes, but I promise you, between the nurses and the tech crew, Laurel will be safe. Come to practice tomorrow and talk to Dr. K." In the middle of this spiel, I had a sudden idea. "You could video what you are doing and share it with Laurel; I bet she would love to know you are working with a real, live Ember."

Manipulative? Yes. Necessary? Maybe not. Feeling both guilty and pleased with my idea? Absolutely.

"Kit's going to be in the student production?" Madi asked, sounding a little surprised.

I nodded before remembering to speak, and hoped I wasn't speaking out of turn concerning Kit. "Oh yeah! We have some of the blocking done, and my sisters and I are going to put her through fight training tomorrow.

If she passes, she most definitely will be in the student production if you want her to be."

I could almost hear the gears grinding in Madi's head as she thought this over. I squeezed my crossed fingers tighter, willing her to stay with us, not just for the sake of the production, but because I needed to get back into the Monroe house so I could talk with the squirrels, if there were any, and maybe find some more clues to help lead me to the truth of this situation.

"Okay," she finally answered, "I'll talk with Dr. K to see what she thinks. Hey, I gotta go; the Monroe's lawyer just got here."

And before I could ask any questions, the connection was cut, and I was left alone with my thoughts. I guess the lawyer arriving wasn't too concerning; after all, she was the one currently in charge of the estate, and if the hospital had informed her of Laurel's in and out status, I'm sure she would want to be present to see for herself. I have no training in the art of law, but I would also assume that if the nurses had informed her of the statement about being pushed, the lawyer showing up could be a good thing. Maybe she was there to ensure there was extra security around her client.

I started after Carlos, jogging a little to catch up, my brain shifting gears as it tends to do during the information gathering stage of a fury conundrum.

But, what if the lawyer showed up because she was concerned about Laurel being pushed for another reason, namely that she had been the one to have done the shoving, and thus was about to be revealed? I rubbed my eyes, slowing down so I wouldn't accidentally jab one of them out. I came to a complete stop and shot Madi a quick text, asking about the attorney and why she was there. I didn't expect her to answer right away, and there was no point stressing about it at this moment. Hopefully, the nurses were going to go full rabid dog on anyone who wanted to see Laurel, especially alone, and that would include her lawyer. I picked up my pace again, wishing that Richard could carry a phone; technically he could, I suppose. He just couldn't conceal it. I'm not sure how a floating cell phone would go over in the hospital, but it sure would make my life easier right now.

I stopped again, checking the time on my phone. I wanted to update Officer Larkes on both the issues I was dealing with, mostly because as a law enforcement officer, he might have some insights, at least about the part concerning Laurel and her lawyer. I could see that Carlos had stopped when he heard me approaching, and now he was turned around watching me, waiting for me to close the last ten yards between us. I raised my index finger to him, and quickly typed out a text to Ethan: *Monroes not at the site; took care of the spirit that was causing the accidents. Laurel is in and out, but said she was pushed. What do I do?*

Before I hit send, I deleted the last part. It wasn't his job to figure out my next move–that was my responsibility. I replaced it with *Richard is in Laurel's room keeping an eye out.* Once sent, I rushed to catch up to Carlos and Kit and filled them in as we made our way into our temporary home.

While most of the cast and crew had headed immediately up to their rooms, my family, including Kit, huddled up in a corner around a small table, mahjong game out as a cover for our conversation.

As we played a round, I described the call I had with Madi, and that I think I had gotten her to not leave the production yet, but Kit was mostly to thank for that.

"Well, if Kit is alright with it, that means we need to spend time in fight school with her, Madi, and the two girls playing Regan and Goneril; I don't want someone missing their timing and giving Kit a real boot to her butt," Guppy stated while discarding.

Kit meowed in agreement, studying my tiles. My hand was a disaster, and the last two times I discarded, Alec claimed the tile, as random as they were. I couldn't tell if she was trying to psyche me out or was just building her hand based completely on what I had decided was useless. Carrying on a conversation while playing had never worked out for me, so I just listened, then threw out another random tile that Alec snapped right up, showing off the third collection I had helped her build.

"So tomorrow," Meg chimed in waiting for Alec to finish up her turn, "we'll block out the first fight with Goneril, and the second with both sisters. Once we get that down, training the other crew will be easy." She passed on Alec's rejected tile, and drew, remaining quiet while she ran possibilities through her head.

By the time the game ended—I didn't win, by the way—we had verbally blocked the first fight and had two scenarios we wanted to run through for the second. Tomorrow morning, we would work on both with action and cue lines, and then decide which of the second fights looked best and was easiest for our student crew. I had heard back from Madi and was relieved to hear that the lawyer was there to ensure security for Laurel until she left the twilight zone she was currently in and rejoined the world of the fully awake. This information put my panic on simmer instead of full boil, and I responded that she should meet up with us at Willow's the following morning before the workshop started.

"That sounds like a good plan; maybe you can get back to the Monroe house at lunch," Guppy stated, packing up the rest of the game pieces and snapping the case shut. "But don't stay too long because we have some serious rehearsing to do tomorrow."

"We're going to meet early tomorrow, like when the shop opens, so I'll need to drop Kit off to you before I go," I responded as we all walked to the stairs and headed up to our floor.

By the time we reached our rooms, Guppy had decided she was taking Kit for the night so they could work on her costume a bit before they went to sleep. The cait sith was excited about this prospect, and before I could hand her off, she head bonked me in the chin which I suppose was her way of saying good night. I headed off to my room, working out conversations in my head about how to get into the Monroe place again without sounding like a creeper, but nothing was inspiring me. With my nightly routine finished, I clicked off my light and hoped that something would come to me as I slept.

Chapter 10

When my alarm went off, I hit the showers running, getting ready in record time. I was at Willow's a good fifteen minutes ahead of schedule, and I even had an idea about how to convince Madi to take me to the Monroe's place. Now that I had a plan and was safely at my first destination, I could feel my body wondering why I had gotten up so early if I was just going to sit outside a coffee shop. Just as I was about to go on in and grab something, I heard Madi call my name.

"Any news about Laurel?" I asked straightaway. Depending on her answer, I had two cover stories I could use. And, yes, I had been rehearsing them in my head. Don't judge.

Madi entered the shop as I held the door and followed her in. "She was out all evening, but her lawyer was all over the staff about keeping watch on the room just in case. She even thanked me for filling her in on all the details."

"So you know her, the lawyer?" I asked, ordering and paying for my drink–another affogato; I think I'm becoming addicted.

Madi got her own Americano, filling me in on a little Monroe family history while we waited. "Penelope Faulkner has been the Monroe's lawyer for over thirty years; I've known her my whole life. She's even Laurel's godmother."

Before we could sit down, I blurted out what I hoped would segue into a walk to the Monroe's. "I want to hear more about this, but do you think we could go to Laurel's house? I have an idea. I'll run it by you on the way."

For what seemed like an eternity, Madi looked at me strangely, and I thought for sure I had blown every chance I had at getting to the house and convincing Madi to stay in the production.

"Sure, but get ready for a walk," she finally said, and instead of sitting, we headed down toward Pearl street.

"Okay, so yesterday I mentioned talking to Laurel about working with Ember," I started, hoping this was going to sound as good out loud as it had in the confines of my head. "If you know where Ember is in the house, we could take her back and take pictures of her on the set, or film you practicing with her while my sisters and I are working with Kit."

Madi appeared to think this over. "I'm not sure I'm staying in the production yet."

I nodded, taking a sip of my drink. "I know, and I think I have some strategies that might help you learn your lines despite you being worried." I didn't mention that there was a little bit of magic involved in this process, but what she didn't know wouldn't hurt her. "It works; trust me."

Before she could answer, I recited the Fool's first line: "'Let me hire him too. Here's my coxcomb.' Now repeat that back to me; repeat back whatever I say."

She did, and I continued forward with more lines, changing my inflection and intonation at times, which she also mimicked. We carried on like this for the entire walk to Mapleton Avenue.

Truthfully, this is a strategy that we use before performances. We could put on one play all summer, but it is more interesting to have a wider repertoire ready to go if needed. I have played Lear's Fool since I was in middle school; I know the lines. Madi's brain did not have the years of performance experience in it, but by feeding her the lines with just the slightest charm on them, I was hoping to build her confidence so she would remain with us through the camp, the performances, and the resolution to the mystery surrounding Laurel.

I knew we were nearing the house, but I couldn't slow down like I knew where it was. I was just starting another line when she stopped me and pointed to the house.

"It's gorgeous!" I said truthfully, but like I had never seen it before this moment. "On the way back, you're going to give me the lines to repeat." I didn't want to look too eager to get inside.

She let us in the front door and stood still for a moment, glancing around the spacious living area off the main entryway.

"I love this house, but it's just not the same," she said quietly.

I didn't know what to say to that. "I can't even imagine how you must feel. Will you show me the Elixir Classroom, if it's still around?"

Madi smiled at that and led me to the butler's pantry, throwing open the door with a flourish. She opened a few of the little drawers. "Looks like most of the non-food stuff is still in there. I wish things could just go back to how they were before the accident." She paused for a moment before continuing, forcing a note of happiness into her voice. "Guess I should check the plants while I'm here."

For the next fifteen minutes, I followed her as she watered both inside and finally outside in the back, still feeding her lines which she called back to me.

"Do they put out food for the birds or squirrels or anything? I could take care of that while you water; I'm pretty good with manual labor," I offered.

She looked back at the mudroom. "Should be some seed and maybe some peanuts in there in one of the under cabinets."

Reentering the house, I looked in all the cabinets until I found food for the various critters that the Monroes kept fed, including some hummingbird food powder. While Madi worked her way around the backyard flowers, occasionally stooping over to pull out a weed, I gathered up some peanuts and seed and headed out to the feeders. When Madi looked over to me, I mentioned that the hummingbird feeders were empty and would she like me to make some sugar water for them.

"I got it," she replied, "I'll do that once I'm done with the flowers."

I filled up the seed feeders and placed a couple large handfuls of peanuts on a tray feeder that had a little table and chair on it, just perfect for the dining-out squirrel crowd. Then I sat back in a chair a little ways off and waited to see if the nuts brought in the breakfast club.

Once Madi had finished up and returned to the house, I called out in a normal speaking tone, "I'm looking for someone who might have seen a person in the yard that shouldn't have been here."

No response to my call, but I could hear rustling in the trees above me. When I glanced at the feeder, the fattest squirrel I had ever encountered was sitting on the edge, watching me.

"Like you and those others that were here last night? This is an upscale establishment, you know." The voice was haughty, and the owner of the voice was looking at me very judgmentally. "You might feel more comfortable a few blocks south."

I arched an eyebrow. "You're welcome for the peanuts."

The squirrel actually rolled her eyes at me. "Oh, yes, let me give you my undying gratitude for finally bringing out my order; the kitchen staff must be completely in the weeds to send out the busser with dinner. Where is Laurel? She's the usual server."

"About that," I continued, casting a glance back at the house to make sure Madi wasn't coming out the door. "Aside from my group that was here last night, have you seen anyone come in or out that doesn't normally come over?"

The squirrel brought her front paws together under her chin and started tapping the tips of her fingers. "Let me see," she voiced, eyes staring into the canopy of the tree above her. Aside from you, Madi, and Penelope, the house has been quiet since Lucia and Paul got eighty-sixed on the way home."

The squirrel's familiarity with the family and friends was impressive, but before I could interject, she stopped her fingers from tapping and looked squarely at me.

"Wait. That last storm that came through, the night before all the cops showed up, someone may have been here. I thought it was just Laurel out for another late night walk, but the storm was pretty fierce and I had just woken up, so maybe it wasn't my favorite server? She always brings a few extra peanuts for me, you know—eating for six." She patted her belly with both paws.

Before I could offer congratulations or ask her for more details about the figure she saw, the slamming of the backdoor made me snap my mouth shut with an audible click of my teeth.

"I see you've met Mama Matilda," Madi's voice grew louder as she approached, but she wasn't talking to me anymore. "Good morning, Mama Matilda; I see your order has arrived. How is everything?"

"It's just great, hun. Are you training this new server? She's kind of nosy. You aren't going away, are you?" Matilda responded, turning her attention to Madi.

"I'm not nosy," I protested before I remembered that Madi didn't understand what Matilda had said, so technically, I hadn't just been ratted out for my snooping.

Madi threw me a strange look before commenting, "Sounds like Matilda is upset about something. Why do you think you're being nosy?"

I fumbled for a few, what seemed like a million, seconds. "Lots of reasons, like suggesting we come here to get Ember, and trying to force you to stay in the production. I hope I'm not imposing myself; you just looked like you needed someone to talk to."

Madi laughed reassuringly. "You aren't. And I think I really did need an ear; I was worried you'd think I was annoying."

I joined in her laughter, standing up from my chair. "We should grab Ember and go before we're late."

Still laughing a little bit, we wandered back through the house to the front door. Madi zipped upstairs and returned with the well-loved stuffed black cat with a white heart on her chest, just like Kit. We continued out the front door, pausing so Madi could lock it back up tight.

"Who else has a key?" I asked, hoping she knew and also hoping that the list wasn't super long.

She stuck the key in her purse as we headed back toward the campus. "Well, I do obviously. And Ms. Faulkner has had one for years; as I said, a family friend now and not just their attorney."

"Do they have a cleaning service for the house? Their businesses sound like they would have been too busy to worry about cleaning, yet the house is spotless," I questioned, thinking to myself that Mama Matilda was right—I am nosy.

Madi was nodding, the expression on her face was one of concentration as we continued to walk. "They do, actually; I'd forgotten about that. The same service and people have been cleaning the Monroe house for at least twenty years—it's a family business. They also deep clean the restaurants every month or so." She paused, glancing over to me. "Are you thinking someone with a key to the house pushed Laurel?"

I hesitated. "Well, there wasn't a forced entry, right? I think I read that in the paper shortly after it happened." I don't remember if that detail was in the paper, but it sounded plausible. And it certainly sounded better than saying I heard a squirrel saw someone leave the house on the night in question. Mama Matilda wasn't even sure it was Laurel because of the storm. Officer Larkes said the report noted no sign of forced entry. So someone with a key had let themselves in and out without leaving a trace.

Madi chewed on her lower lip, thinking. "I hadn't thought of that. And now that you bring it up, I think they must have had a key because nothing was broken or showed signs of being forced. Maybe that's why the police were so quick to chalk it up to an accident or . . ." she paused, not wanting to continue that thought. When she broke the silence I knew the conversation was finished concerning Laurel; she didn't want to contemplate that her friend had been depressed enough to take her own life. "If a man's brains were in's heels, were't not in danger of kibes?"

I stated it back to her, and we continued working with scene v for the rest of the walk back to campus.

By the time we reached the amphitheatre, Madi was feeling confident about her lines, the little charm was working like, well, a charm. Before she continued on to the University Theatre Building, she thanked me for the idea concerning Ember and the practice, saying she was already feeling more like she could be successful in the production and didn't want to let everyone down.

Guppy had seen us approaching and came to greet us. "So this is Kit's double. Put her on the stage with our resident diva and let's take a picture for Laurel."

As we approached the stage, Alec was just aiming a kick at Kit, who waited until the last moment to jump awkwardly away, twisting a bit, and landing only briefly on her paws before collapsing.

"That was so close to perfect, Kit!" Meg cheered, then seeing us approaching, started petting the cait sith and calling her a good girl, pretending to slip her a treat. Kit, for her part, pretended to eat the invisible reward, but she was sending me some rather violent images concerning being treated like a child.

Before I could respond, Guppy sat Ember on the stage, and said, mostly for Kit's benefit, "I'm sure she'll come over to check out the stuffie, and then you can take a few 'publicity shots' of our little diva."

I watched as the cait sith slowly closed her eyes and took a deep breath. Her actions mimicked what I did to calm myself down before going on stage. When she had collected herself, she put on her 'curious cat' routine. Eyes growing wide, she cautiously took a few steps forward, sniffing the air; she even let her tail puff up a bit. A few more calculated steps brought her directly to Ember, and she tentatively stretched out her neck to sniff. Satisfied that she was under no threat, she sat down next to the stuffie, slow blinked a couple times, tilted her head a little, and stared directly at Madi, who quickly took several shots with her phone as though she thought Kit would move away and she would miss her chance.

"This is so cute!" she said, the smile coming though in her voice. "I can't wait for Laurel to wake up again so I can show her these."

Kit chirped in response and head butted Ember. After a few more shots, Madi noticed the time, grabbed Ember, and made quick goodbyes to all of us, eager to go speak with Dr. K and begin practicing with the student crew.

Once she was gone, Guppy clapped her hands together and turned to all of us. "Let's get this show on the road."

Chapter 11

Maybe it's cheating, but with a little bit of practical magic and a great deal of dedication, *King Lear* started to come together nicely. We had utilized the entire space for practice, multiple scenes taking place all over the theatre–stage and seating. Kit spent most of the morning with Alec and Meg, perfecting her reaction to being kicked and adding a me-ouch for extra emphasis and empathy.

When I was not involved in the scenes, I took the opportunity to call Officer Larkes. What I wanted to discuss I didn't want in written form that someone else might catch a glimpse of accidentally and then hold over my head as proof I was crazy or something. I was hoping that when I told him about my conversation with the squirrel, he might have some insight for me or a direction to follow next. Having a visible text-thread with the phrase 'conversation with a squirrel' just didn't seem like something I wanted a record of at this point.

He picked up on the second ring. "Tisi, what's the latest?" He sounded happy; I hoped I wasn't about to ruin that mood.

My relationships with people outside my family and troupe have always been a little weird. Being able to see ghosts and interact with them is not something you share with everyone, and you have to be careful with whom you do share that knowledge. In my experiences growing up, people seemed to react one of two ways. The first was the obvious 'she's crazy' response, which hurt, but the second was worse. The second reaction involved people thinking I was just doing it, claiming to see ghosts, to get attention, that I wanted to be special and different. And nothing was further from the truth.

Taking a deep breath, I started what I'm pretty sure was the most surreal conversation the officer had ever held with a sober person.

"So, you know about the snakes and that I can understand Kit's thoughts."

I could hear the question in his vocable response, "Uh huh?"

"Well, there's more." I proceeded to give him an abridged version of the potions Guppy had concocted to help my communication with Kit, and how while neither of those potions really worked, they did give me the ability to understand squirrels and dogs.

The silence that followed was deafening; in fact, I thought he might have disconnected the call, which would have been completely understandable on his end.

"I know I sound crazy, but hear me out," I rushed on, hoping he was still connected and that I wasn't just talking to dead air.

I explained to him about Mama Matilda, and how she thought she may have seen someone leaving the house the night of the 'accident', but that she thought it was just Laurel going for a late night walk. "I realize you can't really rely on a squirrel for information, but I do think she saw the would-be murderer leaving the house."

The silence continued from the other end for an uncomfortably long time; finally Ethan began speaking. "And she thought it might be Laurel, which means this person must have been close in stature to our victim as opposed to some six-five linebacker."

I hadn't thought of that, and I told him so.

He chuckled a little before answering. "You're an actor, Tisi, who happens to also be tasked with seeking justice for those who can't obtain it for whatever reasons. I'm a cop; I have a degree in criminal justice and training from the police academy. It's my job to see things and make connections from them. What else do you have?"

I explained the family attorney and the relationship she had with the Monroes, and the cleaning service that had been on contract for years to do the house and all the restaurants, and that maybe these people all had keys to the residence.

I could hear the clicking of computer keys through the phone. When he spoke, his voice was serious and clinical, like the officer he was. "Okay, so in the report, Laurel is listed as being five foot seven and odd change, so about Meg's height. Because it was stormy and we have no idea how good Mama Matilda's eyesight is, let's give or take a couple of inches. It lists her weight at 133, so again, you're not looking for a linebacker sized person."

My thoughts immediately went to Cal Garrett, who had to be over six feet and probably close to 200 pounds; he was a linebacker sized guy, and apparently, I needed to rule him out as a suspect if I chose to believe Matilda's testimony.

"So," he continued as the tapping of the keys stopped, "you're probably looking for someone either close to the family, like the attorney, the cleaners, or the restaurant people, who have access to the key—and keys are pretty easy to duplicate or go missing only to turn up again—and who closely resembles you and your sisters in build."

He had given me quite a bit to mull over in a short time. It took me a minute to gather my thoughts as my brain started spinning around the new information I needed to apply to the situation.

"I think you have some good information to work with right now. Anything else I can help you with?" he asked, his voice regaining some of its cheerfulness.

I pulled myself out of my thoughts. "I think I need to sit down and do some serious thinking; maybe I'll make a big crime board and connect things with yarn like they do in the movies."

Ethan started laughing at that. "Hey, don't knock it; that works as it frees up more of your brain to make connections when you can physically see them."

I smiled, agreeing with him. Before I ended the call, I remembered to ask about Sherlock, his cadaver training, and his upcoming test.

"It's happening on Monday, and he is doing really well. It's a live find test, and I think he'll pass with flying colors. But if he struggles, we may have to focus on either live find or cadaver; he's young and seems bright enough to be able to work as both. This test will help us determine if he can do both or should specialize in one or the other. As a reward, I might bring him up to Boulder to see *King Lear* if you think Kit wouldn't mind. I think he misses her, and maybe you could talk to him about not chewing on my work shoes?"

I threw a glance at the stage where Kit was waiting, staring at me with her wide greenish eyes. "I'm sure our little rising star would love to greet her adoring fan, and I can try, but puppies will be puppies. Thanks for your help; I hope I didn't freak you out too much. I should get back to practice. Let me know when you want to come up, and I can reserve some seats."

"Keep me updated on any other information you gather and call anytime, Tisi; good talking to you," he said, and the connection went dead.

"Well that sounded less awkward than yesterday," Meg's voice made me jump as I had not heard her sneaking up behind me; I could feel my cheeks flush like I'd been caught doing something I shouldn't. "Guppy's ready to see how the Fool with the cat scenes look, so shuffle it on up there

---

The rest of the practice zoomed by. Carlos, Kit, and I slipped into a nice rhythm, with Kit's involvement in the dialog slowly diminishing as Lear sinks further and further into anguish and madness. We tweaked the ending of the Fool's final appearance by having Kit still on the stage while I help Kent carry Lear out. During Poor Tom's final speech of the scene, Kit tries to jump back on the bench where we had been sitting in judgment of Lear's daughters, but fails to make it and collapses back to the ground. Once Poor Tom exits, I return to find her, wrap her in my tunic, and leave the opposite side I came in. The whole moment is a dumb show, but the death of the Fool, or in this case, the Fool's Cat, is obvious.

By the time we decided to shut down for the evening, the whole cast was starving because we had worked through, and well-past, dinner time. We knew Dr. K had ordered something to be delivered again for both casts and that it would be waiting for us at the residence hall, so we packed up quickly and headed for our temporary home. We had barely opened the door before the smell of barbecue smacked us, and various versions of "I'm starved" and "That smells great" replaced everything that we had been speaking about before entering.

After fixing a couple of plates, I searched for Madi in the crowd of the student cast. She was sitting with Jaime and waved me over when she saw me looking.

"Dr. K says we are going to the opening show tomorrow since the crowd will be smaller; at least she thinks it will be as that's how Thursdays usually are. Are you guys ready?"

I set down my plate and the smaller plate for Kit next to me, deciding I should answer before I started stuffing my face.

"Ready as we'll ever be; mostly we were just getting used to new cast people and finalizing some blocking. Guppy sent them a video of an earlier performance of Lear we did so they could work separately from us until we got here. How're things going for y'all?"

They both started giggling a little. Jaime finally spoke, still smiling. "I forget you guys are from Texas as none of you really have a drawl, but then you throw out 'y'all'."

I returned their grins, but refrained from explaining why y'all is one of the greatest contractions ever invented, because it is, for various reasons. "Well you missed Guppy saying 'fixin' to' earlier when Meg and I caught a case of the giggles over something stupid. That's way more Texan than 'y'all'."

We continued to chat and eat. Dr. K circled around the area stopping to talk to tables as she made her rounds. When she reached us, she put her hand on Madi's shoulder but looked at me as she spoke. "Did Madi tell you she is staying in the production? We recorded several of her scenes today for her to show to Laurel next time she's conscious."

I smiled at this news. "I'm sure she'll love them, especially since Ember is in them."

Dr. K returned my grin, looked over my head at someone, then back to me. "I think your mother is summoning you."

I excused myself, gathered my empty dishes and chunked them in the trash on the way over to where Guppy was sitting, Kit on my heels. When we arrived, she motioned us to lean in. "Richard blipped in earlier. Laurel is conscious and seems to be remaining so, but the police have told the few nurses who check on her to keep that quiet for her safety. She hasn't been able to identify who pushed her, but she is adamant that she was pushed."

We sat silently contemplating Guppy's information; she waited for a few beats, then continued.

"I think tomorrow we'll have a cast meal at the Vista. We need to get a bit of our routine back in place, including our meals." She motioned at Alec and me, "If you two will do the shopping, Meg and I will cook; don't forget to figure in our guest cast."

Alec had already started a grocery list on her phone. We were good on the pantry ingredients; it was the fresh stuff we would mainly need to gather. "We could stop by the hospital before we go, just to check out the situation there, see if Tisi gets any vibes from the place."

"Good idea," Guppy agreed. "Be sure to thank Richard when you see him; we don't want him getting into a snit." She then turned her attention to the cait sith. "And you, Ms. Kit, let's put the finishing touches on your costume tonight so that is taken care of as well."

As Guppy and Kit made their exit, I turned to my sisters to fill them in on the phone conversation with Officer Larkes.

"So, if we think Mama Matilda has pretty decent eyesight and doesn't need glasses, we're looking for someone around our height, so either a woman or a smaller man; and this someone also has to have possession of or access to a key to the house."

I watched their expressions as they thought this over, coming to the same conclusion I had earlier.

"So Mr. Garrett is off the hook, then," Meg stated, rubbing her eyes. "I suppose it was too convenient to think that the biggest jerk we've encountered yet who has a connection to Laurel would be our attempted murderer. So what now?"

I shrugged one shoulder, "I guess we just keep our eyes open."

Chapter 12

The next morning, Alec and I set out extra early, both needing our new addiction from Willow's. My blood may actually be turning into affogato at this point, and I don't care. After ordering from the young woman at the counter, we went to find a table while the barista whipped up our drinks. There were very few people sitting and enjoying coffee this morning; most were coming in and taking it to go.

When Alec's name was called, we both looked over to the counter, and Alec rose to go retrieve them for us. Beyond her, I could see Moira stick her head around the corner of the backroom, and for the briefest moment, there was just the faintest hint of fear or concern in her eyes when she caught sight of us, but it vanished nearly as quickly as it appeared.

Alec returned, and as we lit into our drinks, Moira came to our table, now smiling widely instead of looking scared.

"You have heard about Laurel, yes? I can't wait to go visit her once she is fully awake. Coffees are good this morning?"

Her happiness was contagious, and we engaged in conversation about Laurel, our upcoming opening, and how the students actors were doing. By the time we were finished with our drinks, she had brought a to-go cup over, asking if we would please deliver it to the officer guarding Laurel's door. "Hospital coffee is no good; they deserve something better."

After assuring her we would deliver her gift, we continued on our way, planning to hit the hospital first and pick up the groceries on the way home as there would be perishables we didn't want sitting in the car.

"She seemed genuinely happy," Alec stated, glancing at the map her phone had running. "She might have the right build to be our pusher, but that joy seems real to me."

I nodded, "I tend to agree, but you know me—always bringing up the darkness. She might be happy because she's really regretful for pushing her in the first place." I mentioned then about the brief flash of fear I had seen in her eyes before she came to our table to talk.

Alec chuckled, "Well, she didn't look or act frightened, and she wasn't angry at all this morning, about anything. I had been thinking we needed to pick up flowers for Laurel rather than show up empty handed, but I think the coffee delivery takes care of why we are there."

Neither of us expected to get to see or speak with Laurel if she were awake as we weren't family or even friends, so maybe the coffee delivery to the officer outside the door as a thank you from Moira was actually a better reason for our presence anyway. All we really wanted to do was talk with Richard about what he's noticed, and I wanted to snoop around a bit and find out if the Monroes were in the hospital, watching out for their daughter, or if they had moved on before even knowing she was hurt.

As we approached the building after parking, Alec turned to me at the door. "Let me know if this gets overwhelming for you; there could be a lot of ghosts in here."

I took a deep breath, smiled at her, and walked through the door. Many people don't like hospitals for various reasons. I don't like hospitals for the reason Alec brought up: they can be filled with spirits who weren't ready to die, their grief almost a haze in the air; or they can be spirits that died here alone, with no one but hospital staff to help ease their passing; or they can be the souls of the murdered, screaming for justice, which is why I wore a hoodie and had it pulled up, just in case my hair triggered on a need for vengeance. I also had my sunglasses in the pouch pocket. But, so far so good.

Madi had told us the floor Laurel was on, so after stepping off the elevator, we looked around for a door with a police officer outside of it. Alec spotted him first and headed over confidently; she did everything confidently. I followed behind, looking at the doors and the greenish walls and the old man who was sitting on a bench outside a room several doors away from Laurel's. Alec had continued walking, but I stopped.

The man noticed I had stopped and looked me in the eyes, surprise registering when he realized I was focused on him, that I could see him. He smiled, and I sat down. We both watched as Alec reached the officer and handed him the coffee, explaining it was from Moira. He looked hesitant to accept it, but did finally, removing the lid and inhaling the steam deeply. He and Alec continued to chat, so I turned my attention back to the gentleman at my side.

"Paul Monroe?" I asked hopefully, knowing he was quite a bit older than Laurel's father but not wanting to dig because it's rude.

He shook his head. "Nope; Lionel Stephens. How is it you can see me but no one else here can?"

I hesitated. He hadn't been murdered and wasn't looking for justice. "I'm a witch," I stated. "Tisi Kindley. Nice to meet you."

He smiled at me, "I'm waiting for my wife." He motioned toward the door across from us. "The old battle-axe outlived me by five years; toughest Gunnery

Sergeant the Marines ever had. She's probably in there arguing with the devil himself, keeping me waiting again." His voice was warm, the love he felt for his wife obvious.

I returned his smile, the tension leaving me slowly. I liked encountering spirits like this one because I could relax; there would be no snakes or hunger pangs, just pleasant conversation which I often find to be easier with the dead.

"Are you one of the witches Richard was telling me about?" he asked.

I nodded. I should've had more faith that Richard would seek out any spirits in the hospital; I had asked him to keep an eye out for the Monroes, after all. As a companionable silence fell over us, I didn't notice another man, much younger than my ghost pal, approach our bench, and, because he couldn't see Lionel, half sit on the spirit. The man shivered, more than likely thinking he just hit a cold spot, not that he just sat on a ghost. Lionel sighed, and I glanced over at the newcomer, wondering why he chose to sit so close to me when the whole rest of the bench was free and several empty ones lined the hall on both sides.

I have had what people refer to as a resting bitch face since I was a child, so I don't think I was purposely scowling at this guy, but apparently he thought I was.

"You'd be prettier if you'd smile more," he said, smiling and leaning closer to me. Before I could roll my eyes or open my mouth to speak, Lionel jostled the man's hand that held his coffee, making it slosh out onto his pants. It must have been hot, because he jumped up reflexively and snapped out, "Now look what you made me do!"

My eyes skipped down the hall to where both Alec and the officer were looking at the sudden commotion. The officer was staring at the man's back; Alec was also staring at the man, which was strange as usually she would be looking to me for a visual sign that everything was hunky-dory. But she was laser focused on Prince Uncharming. With a quick word to the officer, she slowly started toward us.

Lionel noticed her coming and asked, "Is that your sister? She looks mad."

"Yes, and she is," I half whispered, which made the abruptly angry man near me even angrier for some reason. If Alec were as mad as she looked, this was going to get ugly.

As he opened his mouth to speak, two women rounded the corner and in a few strides, passed the drama happening at my bench and reached the nurses station Alec had just left. I could see Richard half out the door of Laurel's room, a look of confusion on his face as he registered the scene in the hall. He pointed at the two women, then back at Laurel's room, finishing the mime show with a two thumbs up. I had no idea what he was trying to tell me, so I shrugged my shoulders and smiled.

"Do you think this is funny?" The man finally managed to spit out, stepping closer to me, and bending down a bit to further crowd me.

Before I could speak, both Alec and Lionel responded simultaneously: "Is she laughing?"

The man turned to Alec since he could actually hear her, ready to snap and stopped before he could. Lionel was gearing up to spill the rest of the dude's coffee, but hesitated when I gestured at my sister.

"Just wait," I whispered, feeling an increase of tension that set my ears ringing, and faintly tasting the first bitter hints of guilt.

She had locked eyes with the man, who was frozen in place as she read him, her irises slowly becoming darker, and that small dangerous smile of hers widening as she spoke. "You're why she's here, Kyle."

My heart skipped. Was she accusing this guy of being Laurel's attacker? He didn't fit Mama Matilda's description, but then again, should I really be trusting the eyewitness testimony of a squirrel?

Alec continued, her gaze locked with Kyle's. "All those slips, and trips, and falls. Those weren't accidents; it was you."

Lionel jumped, hands raised up in innocence when Kyle dropped his coffee. Neither Kyle nor Alec noticed, though the officer down the hall looked up, his focus going between us and the two women at the nurses station.

"Sucks, doesn't it; not being able to protect yourself," Alec soothed, her voice trapping him where he stood. For all intents and purposes, it just looked like they were commiserating about a shared loved one.

If only.

She continued, her voice soothing but sharp. "But the doctors are getting suspicious, aren't they? Her file must be as thick as a dictionary. What's she telling them this time? 'Silly me, I tripped again.' You really think that's going to hold up?"

She paused for a moment, digging around in his mind for more; Kyle was caught in her web, unable to hide anything from her, and she was spinning it all back to him, wrapping him in a guilt he seemed incapable of feeling on his own. "Oh, now that is interesting," she purred, finding something to use against him.

I sat perfectly still, wanting nothing more than to pick up the fallen cup and escape from what my sister was about to pull from his thoughts, before the taste of guilt overwhelmed me.

Kyle was starting to tremble, his fear palpable, a new experience for him I was guessing. The darkness in Alec's eyes began spreading to the whites. "Oh Kyle," she said softly, sadly, her hand resting gently on his arm as though she were offering comfort rather than a threat. "You better hope she pulls through. In fact, it might be best for you to go tell that officer down the hall what you did and why you did it, because if she doesn't make it, nothing can save you from my sister. Not even me."

The tremble became a full body shake now as Kyle turned a more sickly shade of pale green than the walls, trapped in the black of Alec's eyes. I could only guess what she was revealing to him, but I assumed it was me and my snakes ripping his soul out. He glanced at me briefly, and I smiled, wondering if he thought it made me prettier than the image Alec showed him. He then turned to the uniform, who had stood and was heading our way, his concern growing.

Taking this opportunity to escape, I stooped and picked up the now empty cup, heading into the ladies' room to dispose of it. When Richard popped in abruptly, I jumped, nearly shrieking.

"What was that all about?" he asked, before quickly rushing on without waiting for a response. "I was trying to tell you that those two women are the lawyers. The older one with the gorgeous white hair is Ms. Faulkner; the younger one is her associate, Ms. Norris."

I took the opportunity to take a few deep breaths to calm myself both from the jump scare Richard provided and from the aura Alec's probing had created.

I could feel my eyes returning to normal as my breathing slowed.

Richard waited a couple of beats before continuing. "I've also looked high and low for the Monroes, but they aren't here. I see you met Lionel, though. He actually sat with Laurel for a while when I went to scope out the rest of the hospital."

As I washed the coffee off my hands, I asked Richard if he had heard any news from the attorneys about developments with the new investigation.

He shook his head. "Not really, but I can report that no one, and I mean no one, including the attending doctor, is allowed in that room without either the officer on duty or two nurses going in as well. When the doctor got huffy about it, Ms. Faulkner shut him down fast; I almost thought she was half fury at that point. The nurses at the station enjoyed that little show as well."

When the door opened, Richard faded into the tiled walls, and I finished drying my hands. The younger of the two attorneys entered, looking flustered and worried. She was texting vigorously, and her eyes caught mine in the mirror for just a second before she turned back to her phone.

The bitter and cold taste of guilt still lingered in my mouth, and I wished I had my toothbrush with me or that I had another affogato to overpower it. As I headed back into the hallway, I was debating asking

Alec if we could stop at Willow's again, but knew it would be best if I didn't load up on more caffeine as we had a show to perform and the last thing I needed was a caffeine crash.

In the hallway, Alec, Kyle, and the police officer were all standing at the nurses' station; the officer was on the phone, his eyes never leaving the door to Laurel's room except for the quick glances to Ms. Faulkner. Lionel had returned to his bench and was engaged in conversation with Richard. I opted to join the ghosts; I was more comfortable with them and didn't want to get another dose of guilt flavor.

As I approached, Richard stood up and saluted, "Back to duty, Cap'n." He drifted up the hall and through the wall of Laurel's room.

Lionel smiled at me; "I think you might be a bit more than a witch."

Alec had left the nurses' station and was motioning to me that we needed to go. "It's complicated," I said to Lionel, then promptly changed the subject. "Do you know how much longer your wait will be?"

He gazed back at his wife's room. "Doesn't matter; she'll come when she's ready. Always was stubborn." He refocused on me, "Did someone really try to kill that young lady?"

I nodded, but before I could speak, he continued on. "Well not on my watch. And when Maxine passes and I tell her about this, I'm sure we'll be sticking around to help Richard."

I smiled and thanked him just as Alec linked her arm through mine and steered me to the elevators. "That was fun," she grinned a bit maniacally, still blinking more than normal, the rush from her encounter with Kyle still dissipating.

I snorted. "You've got a weird definition of fun."

Chapter 13

"And my poor fool is hanged. No, no, no life?
Why should a dog, a horse, a rat have life,
And thou no breath at all? Thou'lt come no more,
Never, never, never, never, never.—
Pray you undo this button. Thank you, sir.
Do you see this? Look on her, look, her lips,
Look there, look there!"

Off stage, Kit and I watched as Carlos finished up the last lines for Lear and collapsed next to a prone Saumia; Cole and Dr. Galloway rushed to his side, both weeping as they finished the scene and the play as a whole. Most of the audience was weeping as well. The ones who weren't had their faces clenched tight, sniffling like crazy, forcing themselves to be stoic.

It never fails. The end of *King Lear* is maybe the most brutal of the tragedies in its understatement. The duel at the end of *Hamlet* is so over the top, with

Hamlet forcing Claudius to drink from the poisoned chalice and stabbing him with the poisoned sword, it borders on overkill. The audience is angry because the duel was rigged, and Hamlet, who probably suspects something is hinky, plays along until it's too late.

There is no anger at the end of King Lear; it's just a morass of pain and despair. The build up to Lear's death is one long heartrending journey, which ends only when he thinks Cordelia is breathing again before promptly keeling over dead. And spoiler alert: she's not breathing. The final act and scene of *Lear* has always choked me up; tonight was no different.

I felt the small tap of a paw on my arm. Kit looked at me, sending me an image of her sharing a plate of bacon and eggs with me, offering me comfort the only way she could express it.

I smiled at her. "I'm not really sad, Kit; this part just makes me cry." Fun fact about *King Lear:* it was so sad that a guy rewrote the ending in the late 1600's, letting Lear regain his throne and Cordelia marry Edgar. I always found that strange. It's a tragedy. The point of a tragedy is to be, simply put, tragic. I suppose it made sense to the guy at the time, but still.

The next image she sent was me carrying her off stage at the end of Act III, and while no one was bawling their eyes out, there was quite a bit of sniffling, a few "oh no's", and one stage whispered "Mommy is the kitty dead?" as I stumbled out clutching her to my chest.

When the applause started, I grabbed Kit and waited for our curtain calls. I straightened Kit's jester cap a little, glanced over at Dr. Galloway, who nodded and took my hand as we strolled out to take our bows. I set Kit down for a brief moment to show the audience she was still alive, and she hopped about a bit on her hind legs before jumping back to my arms. The entire family of Gloucester came out next, followed by the daughters of Lear, and finally Lear himself, whose arrival brought the audience to their feet.

Out in the crowd, the camp students were cheering loudly; many of them had brought their scripts with them and had been making notes as the play progressed. Now they were celebrating with a type of nervous energy that only comes when you know that your time on stage is coming up. They had eight days to pull their show together, but seeing it performed had probably helped many of them visualize it better, see the final product while they were still just working on the individual parts.

When the lights clicked on, most of the audience headed for home, but quite a crowd stayed behind to take pictures with the cast or offer appreciation for our interpretation. As with *Macbeth* in Salida, more than a few people wanted to check out Kit and take her picture. Something she was way more comfortable with than I was. The difference here was that my eyes hadn't darkened obviously yet, so I had no worries about someone freaking out.

Alec's Goneril had been deliciously evil in this performance as she was still channeling the rush she was riding from encountering Kyle and convincing him to confess; the first time she 'kicked' Kit, the audience gasped audibly. It's pretty easy to despise Goneril, but tonight, I was shocked people didn't actually boo when she waltzed out for her scenes.

Earlier at our traditional dinner at the Vista, Richard had popped in with all sorts of news from the hospital. As we sat eating the butter chicken Guppy had made, he filled us in on what had happened after Alec and I had left. The officer on duty had called for another cop to come take Kyle down to the station as he could not leave his post. Ms. Faulkner had overheard enough of the conversation to offer her legal services to the abused woman pro bono. The last item he had for us was to announce that Lionel's wife Maxine had finally passed, and that she and Lionel both were now sitting in Laurel's room, ready to lend a hand until this was over before they began their journey elsewhere.

"I explained what you were to them," Richard continued in his recounting of the events. "And Maxine really wants to meet you."

His comment made me raise my eyebrows. Not many people are thrilled to meet me when I'm in full fury mode, and I'm a pretty basic run of the mill early 20s gal. Maybe she just really likes the idea that there is justice waiting for people who seem to be able to avoid it while living. Or, she might merely be adjusting to not being seen and heard by people any longer and wants to talk to a living person one more time. Either way, I'm sure I would run into her at some point unless someone fessed up to shoving Laurel down the stairs, and we could call this case closed.

Now, while Kit and I posed for a few pictures, Bre ran interference again for me, although I felt more comfortable than during *Macbeth*, mostly because I wasn't hiding snakes under my coxcomb and had been able to freely take it on and off during the performance. Some of the audience also wanted to take shots of Kit with Carlos, which both readily agreed to do. And as usual, our shifter brothers and Saumia had a line waiting to capture selfies.

It was nearing eleven o'clock before we finished packing up all our costumes and resetting the stage for tomorrow's performance. Even though we had eaten before the show, most of us were starving, which happens when you put on a production. Instead of going out for a late bite, Guppy had promised that there was food waiting for us back at the residence hall, so we slowly strolled back that way, reliving some of the highlights of the show, especially Alec's Cruella DeVille take on Goneril, but also how Carlos's raging King Lear in the first act had shocked the audience into an eerie stillness, like they were afraid he would look out, see them, and include them in his wrath.

Kit rode on my shoulder, worn out from the action. Cait sith she might be, but she was also just a kitten; her bursts of energy were followed by serious naps, and *Lear* is a long play. Her head was drooping as we made our way to our temporary home, and the closer we got, the closer she came to sliding right off. I slowed a bit so I could reach up and carry her, but before I could, Cole plucked her up and wrapped his arms around her. Kit didn't protest, and promptly fell asleep, warm and supported, her nose stuffed into Cole's elbow.

"You doing alright?" he asked as a little snore escaped Kit.

I shrugged. "I think so; I've never had the fury part trigger because someone's belief that a murder has occurred, or in this case failed to occur. I wasn't even aware that was possible."

Cole chuckled a little. "Madi fits the description that squirrel gave you; you don't think her belief is so strong because she's the one that did it, maybe?"

He had an interesting point. This situation was new to me, and the guilt I had sensed in Madi that first day floated to the top of my thoughts. Was that guilt more than what I had initially believed? Many people feel guilt when horrible things happen to those they love, mostly because they are happy it didn't happen to them, and that relief can easily become guilt. It's a bit like being told to eat your vegetables because someone, somewhere, is starving; you should be happy you have the food but miserable at the same time that someone else doesn't.

I shrugged again. "I hadn't really thought about that, but I suppose it's possible." I mean, really, what did I know about Laurel and Madi's friendship? I only had one side of it, and for all I knew, it could be totally fabricated.

When I sighed, Cole put his free arm around me and gave me a shake before wrapping it back around the zonked out cait sith. "Didn't mean to put a damper on the night; it's been in my head for awhile and wondered if you'd thought about it."

We continued in silence to Baker Hall, and as we entered the common area, were shocked by the camp cast yelling "Surprise!" at us.

Laid out on various tables were charcuterie boards full of sandwich makings, fruits, and small bite sized desserts. I'm not sure if it was the noise, Cole startling, or the smell of food, but Kit woke up immediately, her ears back but her nose twitching as she took in all the smells.

Dr. K quieted down the crowd and began speaking. "We wanted to show our appreciation and figured you would be ready for some food. Tomorrow my cast is going to grill you about your choices for tonight's performance, so eat well, rest up, and thank you for a brilliant evening."

When she finished, the troupe fell on the buffet like a pack of starving wolves. Many of the camp participants were busily refilling stations as they emptied; others were pouring glasses of iced tea or water or making hot tea on request.

Cole had put Kit back on my shoulder, and as I went along the line, she sent me images of what she wanted. Most of it made sense; she wanted some cheese and some thinly sliced roast beef and turkey, but then she flashed a picture of the celery sticks.

"You can't be serious," I whispered, but loaded several on my plate anyway. I made my way to an empty table. My eyes were itching a little and between the performance and the issue at the hospital earlier, I was really very tired. As I was tearing up the meat and cheese for Kit, Madi sat across from me and set down a cup of hot chamomile tea next to my plate.

"You guys were amazing!" she gushed, distinctly enunciating all three syllables of amazing. "I have so much I want to ask, but Dr. K told us to leave you all alone until tomorrow. But I have something I want to run by you."

I blinked, hoping my eyes were just tired looking and not possessed looking, "Fire away."

Madi glanced around conspiratorially before dropping her voice and leaning in to speak. "Laurel is awake all the time now. I mean she sleeps and stuff, but no more coma. The police want to keep that under wraps for her own safety, but I figured you would be safe to tell."

Her smile was wide, her happiness obvious, but Cole had planted a seed that I couldn't ignore. Was she happy because Laurel was on the road to recovery or was she happy she wasn't going to get charged with murder? Laurel could still remember who pushed her if she indeed saw who did it. I had my doubts about that after the experience I had on the stairs with Meg, but the lighting could have been different the night of the fall. I had no idea how many lights she left on at night, and our little excursion allowed us to turn on exactly no lights.

I swallowed some tea, gathering my thoughts. "That's great news, and the police are smart about keeping it quiet."

She murmured her agreement. "I really want Laurel to see the play, but for obvious reasons, she can't attend." She paused here, chewing the inside of her lip. "I know this is a lot to ask, and I'm probably asking too much, but could I video tomorrow's performance for her? I promise I'll delete it right after."

Before I could speak, Kit snagged one of the celery sticks off our shared plate and started rubbing her head all over it, eventually flipping it onto the floor. She immediately pounced on it, and then began rolling around, trying to rabbit kick it.

Have you lost your kitten mind? I asked her silently, and received nothing in response.

Madi, on the other hand, started laughing. "My aunt had a cat that treated celery like catnip. I thought he was just weird." She looked back at me smiling.

"I think I can do you one better," I started, stifling a yawn while searching the tables for either Asher or my mom. I caught Asher's eyes first and waved him over.

"Asher records the first night of our performances for what we call quality purposes. We check the blocking, the timing, all that stuff so we can see how it looked and fix anything that might need fixing for the following shows. He probably has it on him or can get it to you tomorrow, but you'll have to ask Guppy for permission; she's the boss."

Madi's eyes lit up, and she scanned the room hastily. When she found Guppy, she excused herself and rushed off before Asher even made it to where we were sitting.

"What's up, Tiss?" he asked, his eyes following Madi to where she now stood talking animatedly with my mom.

I explained to him the request, and that Madi had gone to ask for Guppy's blessing.

Asher grinned widely. "I have it alright. Best damn Goneril Alec has ever done. You should have heard the comments from the crowd sitting near me when she kicked Kit the first time. This show will definitely be part of the permanent library."

"Carlos was on fire, too," I added, thinking about both the rage from Act I and the emotional shattering in Act III.

Asher opened his mouth to speak just as Guppy and Madi arrived at the table.

"Asher, would you make a copy of tonight's performance for Madi? And put the original in the library, if you would." She turned to Madi, "I will give it to you personally tomorrow at camp. Please pass it on to Laurel with our wishes for her speedy recovery."

Abruptly, Madi threw her arms around Guppy and hugged her, breathing out her thanks and rushing off as though she were suddenly embarrassed by her show of emotion.

The three of us watched her go, but I was the only one not smiling."

Chapter 14

"You've got five more minutes in your groups, then we will start blocking Act I for movement," Dr. K's voice carried easily through the indoor theatre, simply called the University Theatre; she was a professional, after all.

I looked at Madi and smiled. "Anything else? I know you're nervous about working with Kit, and if the blocking doesn't go well with the evil sisters, we can scrap her from the camp production altogether. She's pretty young to be doing two shows a day."

We both glanced over to Kit; she was paying attention, but her eyes were half closed. Mostly this had to do with our stop at Willow's early in the morning. Alec and Meg had woken us up by pounding sharply on the door. When I rolled to my feet, I noticed that Kit must have been sound asleep as well as she was now standing askew, her fur puffed out and her ears laid back and a small growl escaping her mouth.

As I hurriedly pulled on some clothes, Meg's voice came through the door.

"Get a move on, chickie, or we're going to Willow's without you."

I double-timed getting ready, calling out that I would be down in the common room in less than ten minutes, which would give me plenty of time to make myself a little more presentable. Kit licked her fur back into place, still grouching a little at the rude awakening she experienced, but I noticed that she, too, was rushing her grooming, worried about missing her side of ice cream.

I was happy to see that my sisters had waited for us, even as the rest of the crowd headed out for the theatre or their own coffee fix. Alec's eyes had returned to normal since her confrontation with Kyle; apparently, Madi's belief was not strong enough to trigger my sisters. I sighed deeply at this thought. With all the 'what ifs' spinning around in my head as we walked, I barely heard the conversation my sisters were having.

Kit, still a little grumpy, rode quietly in my bag, her eyes taking in the campus and groups of people strolling around, images of a cup of ice cream, slightly larger than her usual serving, flashing into my head periodically.

I sent back a large affogato; I was going to need some extra caffeine today. Kit sat up a little straighter and reached out to tap Meg with her paw.

"She wants a larger bit of ice cream today," I said, registering Meg's confusion.

"Do we know if ice cream is good for kittens; I never looked that up," Alec stated, already reaching for her phone. After a few moments she gave us the bad news.

"Kit," she said, "I hate to tell you this, but ice cream is, in fact, not good for kittens."

Kit started growling, and slowly dropped from view back into the depths of my bag.

Madi laughed when I recounted this tale before the day officially started. "Did she get her ice cream anyway?"

"Amazingly enough, yes. Willow's has pet friendly ice cream just for all the dogs people bring in. When Meg ordered it the first time, that's what she served us. Well, not in my affogato I hope."

"Yuck," Madi quipped, making a face like she was tasting something awful. "But she does seem really zonked; maybe this is all too much for her."

We spent the early part of the morning going over what she liked about the Fool's blocking and mannerisms and what she thought she might change, especially if we decided that Kit would not perform with the student players. That was where we were when Dr. K brought our attention back to the matter at hand: getting the blocking going for the matinee productions.

One thing I remember about being in theatre, both in high school and in college, was that things were pretty much a disaster until they weren't. There was always this magic moment where things suddenly clicked, but the road to get to that point was long, twisty, and many times slick with tears.

This production was no different, but considering the actors ranged in age from 17 to 22, there was a more urgent panic in the air. Older actors, like Carlos, lend an air of calm to most situations as they are better able to control their anxiety. But it was that buzzing nervousness that could produce the most amazing scenes once the actors learned to channel the nerves into their performances.

Since the Fool doesn't appear until the fourth scene, Madi and I sat out in the house seats watching the tragedy begin to unfold. Dr. K was everywhere at once, offering suggestions, stopping the movement to make alterations, and praising the students as they finished. As each section in the first scene was completed, the students would make notes on their scripts, marking the changes that had occurred. This stage of creation was time consuming and could become very frustrating for everyone involved. Once the scene was roughly blocked out, the students met with their counterparts in our production, and Guppy strategized with Dr. K over the next scene coming up for blocking.

The rest of the morning passed quickly, and by the time lunch arrived, quite literally as Dr. K had ordered sandwich boxes from a local deli, the students had blocked out all of Act I. The theatre buzzed with the noise of lunches being eaten and discussion over what had been accomplished.

Madi was texting someone when I dropped down next to her on stage to eat. When she finished, she looked up and smiled. "I'm going to the hospital after practice today to show Laurel the play. She's really excited about seeing it."

"Maybe she'll be able to see it live by the end of next week," I said, having no idea about recovering from a fall such as she took or how long a brain needs to recover from that type of injury. And then of course, if someone was trying to kill her how that might mess up those plans.

Madi shrugged one shoulder and finished swallowing before she spoke. "Maybe. Right now, Ms. Faulkner is holding fast to the twenty-four hour guard outside the door. There's still a police presence around the hospital, but she's arranged for private security as well."

Once lunch was finished, the blocking continued and was still going on when our crew left to go prepare for our own performance that evening. The stage dressing was checked and a few pieces shifted around per Guppy's orders. Dr. K had packed up the previous night's after party food, and it was waiting for us in case we started getting peckish.

Kit stretched luxuriously from her nose to her tail tip after I set her on the stage, then flopped over onto her side, her eyes half closed.

"Maybe you should take a nap before the performance starts," I suggested, looking around to see what Guppy was up to at the moment. I was beginning to think that being in the student show was going to be too much for the cait sith.

"Kit looks worn out." Guppy's voice immediately behind me caused me to jump, which startled the kitten as well.

I nodded in agreement. "I don't think she can handle the pressure of nightly shows and all day practices; she's pretty young."

Kit chose that moment to sit up, trying to look more awake, but instead yawned so wide I could see the back of her throat. She sent me an image of her being wide awake, performing with me and with Madi. I translated for Guppy.

My mom looked at me and then back to the cait sith. "Tisi, could you excuse us for a moment?"

I knew that tone of voice. That voice belonged to Producer / Director / Head of Mustardseed Productions Guppy Kindley, not everybody's mom or stand in mom, shoulder to cry on, ears always ready to listen Guppy Kindley. I also knew better than to try to stay at this point because one never argues with the director about another actor, especially in front of said actor; Kit was on her own.

"I'm going to grab a snack plate," I informed them both. "I'll get you some snacks, Kit."

I hurried away, hoping that Guppy could make Kit see reason. Exhaustion has sidelined many actors, and it can be brutal. It would be a one-sided conversation without me there to translate, so I knew Guppy would explain her position, offer reassurances, and ask her to think it over; but I also knew that Guppy's word would be final. The funny thing is, most of the conversations of this type with any of her actors is usually a one-sided affair; she never makes us defend or argue on the spot, but allows time to think over what she has said before responding. I'm not sure where she learned this technique, but she's been using it on me since I was a little kid.

Meg had watched me approach the snack table, casting occasional glances past me to Guppy and Kit, still on the stage. "That looks serious; Guppy wants her out of the student production, I'm guessing. Hope that goes over well."

I hoped that, too. "I should have had a discussion with Kit earlier about not just how hard being in a production can be but also how tiring working a camp is as well. We just never had the time, and I really wasn't sure she was going to keep wanting to be in the shows."

Meg laughed. "That cait sith is the biggest diva I've ever encountered. Guppy will be kind, she always is. Are you worried Kit will leave us?"

I shrugged. "Well it's not like she's our house cat; she's an entity all her own, and she may decide to move on if she feels hurt. I would worry about her, and I've gotten used to her being around, and, surprisingly enough, being inside my head."

Meg thought for a few seconds, then gestured around to the rest of the crew. "Everyone here has had 'a talk' with Madame Producer, and we're all still talking to her and to one another. I think Kit knows she's got a sweet gig here. Maybe she thinks she's letting us down if she doesn't do both shows."

I half-smiled. Meg was probably right. I had never even thought that maybe we had pressured Kit into doing something she wasn't ready to do. "If Guppy takes her out of the student show, she can get more sleep because she won't have to be at their practices. I'm guessing she'll still want to come along for coffee in the morning."

"Never stand between a cait sith and her morning ice cream," Meg intoned ominously, then nudged me. "Guppy's waving you over; I'll be right behind you."

When we reached the stage, Kit was still sitting, eyes half closed, but she reacted when I set the plate of meat and cheese in front of her, beginning to eat it immediately.

Guppy accepted a plate of nibbles from Meg, then spoke to us all. "Kit is going to remain in our show, but we feel it is best if she drops out of the student production. I have reassured her that no one expects her to work until she drops, and that we will help Madi find another way to present the Fool. For now, we have four hours before curtain, so Tisi, if you would take her back to your room so she can get some serious rest, we can finish what we need to do pre-show and pick her up before showtime."

With that said, Guppy slapped her hands on her knees and started to rise. "So let's hop to it!"

"Your carriage awaits, Kit," I said softly, holding my bag open. "Unless you want to ride on my shoulder."

Licking the last of her snack up, Kit slowly walked over to my bag and climbed in, the image she sent me was her being very small in my bag, but me struggling to pick it up.

"You're not a burden, Kit," I said, hoping I was translating that right. "Guppy is worried about you. We've had players get sick before because they were trying to do too much; then the whole show suffers." I paused for a second before hurrying on. "And you aren't letting anyone down; Madi was beginning to worry about you as well."

When the bacon and eggs image hit, I smiled to myself. Meg had been right; we had put too much pressure on our youngest cast member. "No worries, Kit; I'll fluff up your fleece and you can have a serious power nap. And I promise I won't forget to come and get you before call time."

Once in our room, I repositioned Kit's nest and waited for her to climb into it. Before she curled up into a very small cinnamon roll shape, she head-butted my arm, which I think meant she was okay with all decisions and agreed with them.

"Sleep well, Kit; I'll be back to get you in a few hours." I then covered part of her body with a free corner and tucked her in. She was snoring before I made it to the door.

Chapter 15

Friday night's performance went exceedingly well. Alec was still riding the high from the encounter the previous day, and Meg had siphoned some of that energy into her interpretation of Regan, so both of the elder daughters exuded a level of evil which had the audience enrapt at times. The preproduction nap had done wonders for Kit, and her death scene again elicited murmurs of sympathy when she collapsed on stage.

With no celebration waiting for us when we returned to the residence hall, we were all able to go straight to bed to catch up on our rest the way Kit had earlier. Except for me. I was still worried about Kit. She really didn't like any of the cat food we tried to feed her, and I didn't know if it was because she was holding out and waiting for the people food, or because it was truly terrible, which, as I think I've mentioned before, I know first hand from eating some cat kibble at our neighbor's house once when I was about four.

So I spent about an hour Google-fu-ing kitten nutrition and other needs, thinking that maybe Kit's weariness was a combination of factors, one of which could be diet; no one can live on bacon and eggs alone, no matter how much they might wish they could. By the time I finished my research, my eyes were wanting to slam shut, but I had a mission for the following day, whether Kit liked it or not.

True to Meg's guess, the next morning Kit insisted on coming along for her ice cream fix, which, as we now knew, was perfectly safe for her as it was designed for animals and met her high standards of taste. When it was time to head to the University Theatre for camp, Kit and I hung back; I wanted to talk to Moira about not just the ice cream, but other pet friendly foods she might recommend. I waited for the majority of the crowd to move on to their days before I approached the shop owner. She was a little taller than me, and I couldn't keep my mind from flashing back to Mama Matilda's description of the figure she saw leaving the Monroe's house the night of the fall. Moira fit the bill, but Meg and Alec had only ever perceived anger from her directed at Mr. Garrett.

"This is going to sound like a stupid question," I started after she looked up at me, concern in her eyes, as I neared. "I'm worried about Kit's nutrition, and I wondered if maybe you had some recommendations about brands or types. She's really picky about cat food, and I've never had a cat before."

Moira didn't even pause from her chores to speak. "I know just the thing. I've got a finicky kitty myself." Finishing the table, she walked back to the counter and scribbled something on the back of a business card. "It's a bit more expensive than the average food, but Felicity Whiskers just loves it." She passed the card over to me. "You can buy it at a couple places, and I'm sure you can find it online, too; the brand is sure to have a website if you need to have it shipped somewhere. I wrote the local store names on there for you as well."

Kit was remarkably silent during this conversation. She sent me exactly two images: the first was the ice cream; the second was a beautiful cat with incredibly long whiskers.

"Is this where you get the ice cream for the pet guests?" I asked, understanding the first image immediately.

"Indeed it is. They have all kinds of treats for dogs and cats; all healthy options. I've never had a complaint from either the human or the pet." She smiled at me and Kit, and I thanked her again before heading out of the shop.

On the walk to the theatre, Kit sent the image of the cat with the whiskers again.

"I'm not sure I'm picking up what you're laying down, hep cat," I joked, and the image shifted to Kit with long white whiskers, more whiskers than a cat would usually have.

"You want more whiskers? I think your whiskers are nice," I responded, not sure I fully understood yet. "We'll go shopping after we're released from camp today."

The image vanished, and nothing replaced it. Kit sighed and curled back up in the bag.

By the time we reached our destination, the camp was in full swing doing multiple different tasks at once and utilizing the entire space in the theatre and some of the hallway just outside. Act III was being blocked on the main stage, and the players that weren't involved in the scene at hand were in various spots practicing their lines, working on vocal variation, and attempting to put in natural gesturing as well, which can be difficult when you aren't actually talking to someone. Each one of these groups had either one of the other theatre teachers helping them or a cast member from the professional production. Eliava and Bre were flitting between groups, more than likely sharing a little magical energy with the students to help with their memorization of both word and action.

I settled Kit in the quietest corner of the theatre, removing my zipper hoodie so she would have a nice nest to curl up in whenever she wanted, and headed over to Madi to check in and start working with her on her interpretation of the Fool.

When she saw me approaching, her eyes lit up, and she waved like I might not have seen her.

"I have so much to tell you," she gushed, skipping right over the greeting and heading straight to business. I appreciated this; it meant I might not have to fish around for ways to steer the conversation in a direction that would feed my need for information.

"Laurel and I watched the video last night, and she loved it! In fact, she loved it so much and is so disappointed she's missing the workshop, that she wants to start some sort of foundation or trust or something to help scholarship more students, especially high school students, into the camp. I have no idea what that really means, but she's going to talk to Ms. Faulkner about it over the weekend."

Much like Madi, I, too, was in the dark about what exactly Laurel was trying to set up, but it sounded very much like she was trying to carry on her parents' philanthropy in the community, and especially the theatre community.

Madi rushed on. "I told her all about you guys, and how wonderfully nice you are; I think she wants to meet Guppy at some point, but she's going to be stuck in the hospital for a while. She still has really bad headaches sometimes, and Ms. Faulkner is taking no chances with her brain."

Before I could speak, all the actors needed for Act III, scene ii were summoned to the stage for blocking. While the students arranged themselves to take direction from Dr. K, their counterparts—me, Carlos, Cole, and Dr. Galloway—stood in the apron so we wouldn't get in the way but could still offer suggestions as the process moved along.

I was half listening as Dr. K began explaining to the actors on stage why this act was so pivotal for the play as a whole and that Poor Tom would be taking over the role the Fool serves for Lear as all the secrets and betrayals and lies are going to explode and leave Lear awash in madness and remorse and Gloucester thrown from his own home and literally blinded a few scene later to match his metaphorical blindness concerning his sons from earlier. And it is, perhaps, this literal blinding, done on stage, that is the darkest part of the drama. No pun intended.

We worked on Act III until it was time to break for lunch, and, just like the day before, our crew was free to go relax, eat, and prepare for our own performance. Before I left, Madi hugged me, thanking me again for the video and all the help. "You're a great friend," she said before rushing out to go fill her plate with whatever lunch the camp was providing that day.

I didn't hear Meg sneak up behind me, so I jumped a little when she spoke.

"You look confused. Are you still getting guilt vibes from Madi?"

I shook my head. "Not really, but this is all new to me." I didn't add that I was confused a bit by Madi referring to me as a friend. I never had many of those growing up for various reasons—my anxiety, the fact I'm an introvert, those times people caught me talking to ghosts but thought I was having a full on conversation with myself. For Madi to decide I was a friend after a few days was new to me, and the feeling was . . . nice.

I brought my attention back to my sister. "I'm going to take Kit shopping for some actual kitten food; cait sith or not, I'm not sure she's getting all the nutrients she needs to help her grow." I paused for a second, "She's also having some kind of infatuation with whiskers or something." I explained what had happened at Willow's that morning and that Kit seemed a little down.

"When you get back, talk to Guppy; she might have an idea. But I'm guessing she's still a little worn out from the busy schedule and a little disappointed she can't be in both shows."

Those seemed to be as good reasons as any, and so with Kit tucked safely in my satchel, the two of us headed out to the first shop, the closer of the two, to try some food and see if we could find one she liked. It wasn't a long walk and it was a beautiful day, again, which seemed to be the norm for Boulder. No wonder Guppy always liked to return here, not just because of her lifelong friendship with Dr. K or the ley line that was said to run through town.

Kit had arranged herself so she could see out, her whiskers twitching as she took in all the sights and scents around her and sent me images of what she was smelling that would make for a good meal. I was getting hungry myself, but I wanted to get Kit's lunch—her kitten appropriate lunch—first to see if she liked it. When we entered the store, she squiggled around a bit, so I opened the bag enough to let her scramble onto my shoulder. Before we entered, a woman left with a large dog on a leash, pulling her along and barking excitedly about going to the park, so I knew that Kit would be welcomed if she were seen and wouldn't need to wear her service cat disguise.

Once she was settled, I commandeered a small cart, and off we went. The store wasn't large, but between Kit, my satchel, and the food I was hoping to find, I didn't feel like wrangling a carry-basket.

As we hit the first aisle, Kit hopped into the purse / cup holder section of the cart, her eyes wide and her nose twitching with all the new smells.

"This is the dog food section," I said after a quick look around, speeding up a bit so we could get to the cat section and get serious. However, before we could find it, we stumbled into the toy aisle. I had no idea if Kit wanted a toy or would even deign to play with one if I offered, but before I could ask, she was flashing me images of the things she found interesting, or maybe insulting; at this point, I wasn't sure.

"Looks like we'll do this the old fashioned way," I whispered to her, and began holding out various items for her to inspect. By the end of the toy row, we had a feather thing leashed to a long stick, a catnip (was she old enough for catnip; is there an age limit?) stuffed pouch with the word "laundry" on it, several felt mice with leather tails and ears, which, according to the image she shared, were good for batting around and chasing after, and a tiger-striped skinny stuffed pillow with a faux fur tail, a satin ribbon bow tie, and a tag that said "kick me" clipped to it. I wasn't sure what the attraction was there, but Kit sent me a vision of her violently rabbit-kicking the thing with her back legs while simultaneously hugging and biting it.

"That seems a tad disturbing," I said to her, but her eyes widened and her pupils dilated as I set it in the cart.

The next row was a clothing row with coats and sweaters of all sizes from XXXL all the way down to XXXS. However, none of these were as fancy as her witch's cape and hat or her new jester outfit, but she did want to look them all over. She was very interested in a couple of the pullovers, especially the ones with flashy sequins as decorations, but I reminded her of my mom's skill with a needle and thread.

"Guppy can make you anything you want," I stated, and we moved on to the collar and leash section, which I thought for sure she would eschew as being beneath her status. She did seem rather unimpressed until a sparkling silver rhinestone number caught her eye. To be honest, it did look like something designed by Tiffany's, more like a necklace for a cat than a collar. The price tag let me know that this was a handmade item or maybe actually from Tiffany's, and I was about to attempt to talk her out of it, but her expression and the image she sent me had me tossing the collar in the cart as well.

"You are incredibly spoiled," I whispered, and then startled when a voice behind me spoke.

"Cats are meant to be spoiled. Can I help you find anything?" The voice belonged to a large middle aged man whose name tag proclaimed him as "Gravy".

"As a matter of fact," I started, and then proceeded to tell him about Kit, how she was acting, and that Moira from Willow's had advised me to come here as a first time cat owner.

He laughed when I told him about Kit's ice cream addiction. "Moria is one of my best customers. Let's open a few different types of food to see what your kitten 'purr-fers'." He smiled as he spoke the pun, and I returned it. I liked this guy; there was no guilt in him whatsoever, which is rare.

"So is Gravy your given name?" I asked, genuinely curious. Kit was sending me images of her with the long whiskers again, only this time she was sitting in a saucepan.

"No," he said, grabbing a few different cans and a couple sample bags from the shelf. "My last name is Graves. I played football for the Buffs many years ago, and my teammates called me Gravy. It just stuck, and it sounds happier than Graves. After all, who doesn't like gravy?"

Kit was staring at him as he opened the first can and scooped some out onto a crystal saucer. When he stepped back, she cautiously leapt from the cart to the counter, sniffed her way to the food, gave it a serious once over, and then took a small bite. I hadn't realized I was holding my breath until she went in for a second bite, and then started eating in earnest.

"Never fails," Gravy said. "All the cats I know love this food." He proceeded to explain to me how much Kit should be eating as she was still growing, and other things about wet food versus dry food and proper hydration. "I'd suggest getting a variety of flavors so she doesn't burn out on one, which can happen with finicky eaters."

As Kit finished her wet food sample, Gravy opened a few of the sample pouches of dry food, poured a bit from each into some small china dishes he pulled out from under the counter, and offered them to the cait sith, who approached them warily. She sniffed each one before beginning to try them. The one she went back to was the one she wanted me to get.

"I see the young miss has a discerning palate," Gravy smiled, watching Kit finish the sample she liked best. "A wise choice." He handed me the sample bag and the can of what she favored, pointing out which shelves they were on so I could finish my shopping.

With Kit back in the top rack of the cart, I wheeled it back to the food aisle and chose an assortment of cans, two of the smaller bags of the dry, and held out several dishes until she chose one that resembled the crystal Gravy had used for her sample. I grabbed a small china dish for the dry food and a larger matching one for water before turning my cart to the tiny freezer section near the check out. It wasn't until I went to grab some of the ice cream that I remembered I really had no place to store it. I would have to explain that to Kit, but once we moved back to the Vista, I would definitely be picking some up.

As Gravy rang up my purchases, Kit sent me a picture of him sitting in the audience. I acknowledged her suggestion, and spoke.

"I don't know if you're into Shakespeare, but our company is putting on *King Lear* at the Mary Rippon Theatre. You've been so helpful and Kit is in the show if you'd like to come see it some night. I can swing tickets for you and a guest if you'd like, as a thank you for your help."

"My wife and I love going to the outdoor theatre," he said enthusiastically, handing me the receipt to sign. "You don't have to do that, but, yes, I'd love to take her."

We discussed what night would work for them, and I told him where he could pick up the tickets for that show. He smiled, and then moved into the store to help another customer.

I stood for a minute staring at my purchases. I hadn't thought this out thoroughly before starting out for an adventure. Setting my satchel on the counter, I began to rearrange the interior, placing the bags with the wet food cans first, which nearly filled it, and then the toys. I asked Kit if she wanted to wear her collar out, which she did, so I fastened that around her neck.

With my much heavier bag settled back across my body, and the sack holding the dry food held firmly in one hand, I helped Kit back up to my shoulder. It would be a long walk back to the dorm, and I considered stopping back in at Willow's for another fix, but decided against it, knowing I needed to get some of this food into Kit before the performance this evening and she needed to get a nap in as well.

It was going to be a long walk loaded down, but standing around stewing over it wasn't getting me any closer to my destination. I swung open the door and started my trek, Kit purring all the while.

Chapter 16

By the time we wrapped up both weekend shows, Kit was feeling better, but still seemed a little down in the dumps. She scarfed up her food each time I set out a meal for her and didn't complained about it not being eggs and bacon or ice cream. I hadn't yet spoken to Guppy about her malaise because between the camp obligations and our own performances, there wasn't much time for conversations that revolved around other issues, and with the acceptance of the new menu for her meals, she did seem a little perkier.

We all slept in on Monday morning with Dr. K's blessing. Doing a show four nights in a row, especially a longer one like King Lear gets tiring; throwing in a theatre camp just adds to the exhaustion, which starts to catch up no matter how many affogatos we might have. And believe me, we had plenty.

In fact, I was just finishing the dregs of my morning fix as our troupe entered the theatre, just in time to see the young man playing Lear yelling at Cordelia, who was trying to look hurt but resolute at the same time. I refrained from slurping the last few drops up the straw, opting instead to take off the lid so as to not make as much noise.

We filed in silently, waiting for the scene to end, and when it did, we gave the student performers a round of applause. As both Dr. K and Dr. Galloway began offering feedback, Guppy headed up to the stage to find out exactly what our duties were for the day, which could be anything from running lines to altering costumes.

Madi was waving her arms at me, a wide smile on her face. My sisters and I began to make our way to where she was sitting, Ember on the floor next to her. We joined her on the carpet, and Kit wiggled out of my satchel, images of Ember in a costume similar to her own sliding into my head. *We have some fabric scraps left over,* I thought back to her; *it might make a nice gift for Laurel.*

Madi started speaking once we were all as comfortable as we could get.

"Laurel is getting better every day," she started, then the smile slipped a little. "But she still doesn't know who pushed her. She said if she thinks about it too hard, it makes her head hurt. I told her to focus on something else."

"Sounds like solid advice," Alec stated, throwing a quick glance at me. I knew she was wondering if I was gathering any vibes about Madi being our shadowy figure leaving the Monroe house the night of the incident.

"Meanwhile," Madi continued, "Ms. Faulkner spent most of Saturday evening with her talking about the trust she wants to start. Laurel wanted me to stay for the meeting, saying I would be able to help her remember things, especially if I took notes. I think I might be part of the board now."

Alec threw another glance at me before speaking. "Well I think it sounds great, for both of you, and for Dr. K and the theatre department here."

Madi's smile returned. "Yeah, I think so, too. I wasn't sure what I was going to do after graduation, but I do know I want to be here for Laurel, for as long as she needs me. I might go ahead and pursue a graduate degree in theatre. Who knows, I could be the next Dr. K!"

As we began chatting about theatre in general and Dr. K's bona fides and work with the Royal Shakespeare Company, Guppy sat down to join us, patting Madi on the leg. "You're needed on stage; I'm glad to see you looking happy."

Madi's smile widened as she stood, grabbed Ember, excused herself, and hurried to the stage, ready to start her scene with Lear.

Once she was gone, Guppy turned to us. "So here's the skinny. I've got good news and bad news."

Meg groaned. "Good news first please, so I can dwell on that and ignore the bad news."

Guppy grinned. "Tonight, we're going to Azafrán for dinner."

She paused, the four of us looking at her confused.

"It's the third restaurant in the Monroe's food empire: the 'fancy place'."

"Well that doesn't sound like it will suck," Alec quipped, relaxing a little. We all enjoyed trying out new places to eat, and it would give us a chance to meet or at least see in action the final general managers in the Monroe's stable.

"So, the bad news is we have to wash dishes to afford it?" I asked, only half joking.

Guppy shook her head, laughing. "No; the bad news is we have to dress up a bit more than usual."

None of us spoke. I know that I was personally going over in my head the clothes I had on hand, wondering if anything would be nice enough to not draw disparaging glances. I could tell from the looks on my sister's faces that they were contemplating the same thing.

When we're on the road for shows, we don't bring an entire wardrobe ready for any occasion with us, aside from the costuming we need for the productions we have chosen, and those were probably a little much even for this place. Throwing a semi formal outfit together might be a bit of a stretch.

Guppy glanced around at our silence. "Dr. K has some things we might borrow, so start thinking about what you have and what you'll need."

"Why are we really going?" I asked finally, breaking the silence that followed Guppy's statement; "I mean, I know we need to, just to meet all the players, but why tonight?"

Guppy cast a look over her shoulder at the stage before speaking. "Everyone who is going to be either part of the trust or involved in it in another manner will be there for Ms. Faulkner's unveiling of the plan. Dr. K has been asked to sit on the board that will consider applicants. She thought if we were there, we could get a good look at all the managers, the attorneys, and anyone else who might have an interest in Laurel's future."

Kit meowed. In my head I heard 'me, too?'.

I turned to face her. "I don't think so, Kit. This isn't a place that is likely to welcome animals. I know service animals are allowed everywhere, but I'm not sure we should push that tonight." I knew immediately I had hurt her feelings, and to be honest, I could really use the support, fake service animal or not.

Kit sighed loudly, turned her back on us, and pushed back into my satchel.

Guppy's smile slipped off her face. She looked at me questioningly.

Now would be a great time to explain to her the melancholy I thought Kit seemed to be experiencing, but I didn't want to do it with Kit in hearing range, so I stood up and motioned my mom to follow me to the back of the theatre.

"We've got this," Meg assured us as we walked off, already lifting the edge of the satchel, trying to coax Kit out.

"What's going on," Guppy finally asked when we were well out of hearing range.

I explained to her the past few days, the weird images Kit had been sharing with me—the long whiskers and saucepan, and Meg's idea that Kit might think we were disappointed in her lack of stamina. I also mentioned my own belief that at first I thought it was malnutrition or some form of unbalanced diet that was making the cait sith listless at times, and told her I had already remedied that issue by finding some cat food she actually liked.

Guppy nodded the whole time I was speaking. "I see," she finally said, her expression one of thoughtfulness. "What exactly was happening when she shared these images with you?"

I took a moment to replay the conversations I had been having with Moira and Gravy when Kit had flashed me the pictures.

"Moira was telling me what cat food she bought because she has a finicky cat, and the guy at the store was letting Kit taste some of the food he thought she might like."

Guppy pondered what I had said. "Did either mention whiskers at all?"

I again revisited the conversations in my head. "I think Moira did, but it was part of her finicky cat's name: Felicity Whiskers."

"And were you talking to this Gravy person about his name, by any chance?" she asked, her eyes beginning to sparkle as she hooked all these clues together.

"I think we were; he said it was a riff on his real name, Graves, but his teammates called him Gravy because, and I quote, 'who doesn't like gravy'."

Guppy's smile returned in earnest. "Kit is searching for her name. I'm not completely sure about all of this lore, but between my grandmother and Everything's Bigger, cait sith appropriate several names over their lifetimes. You've already given her one."

I let her words settle in my head. "Is she not happy with it? I wouldn't be either, I suppose. It's not very imaginative. I just called her Kit because she was a kitten; I thought it was more polite than 'Hey, You' or 'Furball'. I didn't mean to christen her with it."

Guppy chuckled, resting her hand on my arm. "No, you've given her a heart name—a first name. Heart names are meant to be used only by those closest. And we've been using it with everyone. I hadn't even thought about this until you brought it up—too many snakes, visits by the police, and whatnot. I thought she wasn't old enough to be concerned about her names, but apparently, she is."

I was starting to feel a tug of worry. "Can we give her another heart name? One that only we use?"

Guppy shook her head. "No, but we need to stop giving the one she has out to everyone. Basically, she needs a stage name, or what is also called a hunter name. That's the one we should be sharing with people outside the troupe. We also need to start putting her in the programs, but not as Kit."

The sigh I let out mirrored Kit's before she hid in my bag. "So I blew it. She could have had a really cool heart name, but I screwed it up." I was thinking back to my first meeting with the little cait sith at the Salida Amphitheatre. She had been shadowing me, but I had snuck up on her and startled her into an arch-backed hiss. Not the greatest of introductions.

"Heart names don't have to be 'cool.' I don't know Everything Bigger's heart name, but I know most of his other monikers. Cait sith collect names to help reflect their experiences. Kit is actually a very sweet heart name as you met her and gave it to her when she was so young."

I sighed again. "So what do we do? And she's mad that she can't come to Azafrán with us tonight."

Guppy tapped her chin with her index finger. "Well, let's go figure out a hunter name for her. If we find one she likes, that may go a long way to assuaging her current miffed state at being unable to go out with us. And we can get an updated program to the printer before our next run of shows."

When we got back to Alec and Meg, Kit was half out of the satchel, grudgingly playing with Alec and the catnip bird toy I had gotten for her earlier. She stopped when we approached, and sat up, looking at me quite disdainfully.

Guppy quickly gave my sisters an explanation of what was going on, and both of them looked quite surprised and excited at the prospect of coming up with a hunter name for Kit.

"Let's start with the Dames," Meg suggested, which we all readily agreed to, especially me because I had no idea how to go about finding a name for our feline cast member.

Kit tilted her head, not quite understanding what Meg was suggesting. Alec jumped in to explain.

"Some of the best actors in England get knighted for their work, and many of those actors have some serious chops as Shakespearean actors. We can start there and branch out if you don't find one that you like." She smiled expectantly at Kit as she finished speaking.

Kit's expression changed. Her eyes widened and she sat up straighter, flexing her front toes in anticipation.

"I'll start," Meg piped up. "Dame Diana Rigg; she has the most evil Regan ever; and she was so cool as Emma Peel in *The Avengers*."

Kit's eyes grew bigger. Alec spoke up next. "I have two: Dames Maggie Smith and Helen Mirren. Dame Helen has won pretty much every acting award that is available, both in the States and in England, and Dame Maggie is also a highly decorated and respected actor with impeccable comedic timing."

"Don't forget Dame Judi Dench," Guppy threw in. "She's amazing as well and quite versatile in the roles she plays."

Kit looked over to me, narrowing her eyes a bit. I wondered if she thought I would blow this as well and not have anything to add to the conversation. "I like Dame Emma Thompson, and I can't really explain why; I just like her voice and the way she portrays her characters," I finally said. "But all of these women are incredible. You could have any of their names as a hunter name and people familiar with acting would know the connection."

Kit sat still, gazing down at her feet. From the images she was sharing, I could tell she was trying on the names for size; was she an Emma or a Diana, a Judi, a Maggie, or a Helen?

While she thought, Alec threw out some more information about some of the names offered. "Diana is also the name of the Roman goddess of the hunt, which is pretty cool. And Helen is the face that launched a thousand ships in Greek mythology."

Guppy sat back, eyes focused on the stage. "I have one more name I would like to add to this list, but she wasn't knighted and didn't win any serious awards for her acting. She was, however, one of the biggest reasons, if not the number one reason, I decided to start Mustardseed Productions: My grandmother, Fiona."

My sisters and I sat back, focused on Guppy who was lost in a memory of her past, her hand absently toying with the ever-present Celtic pendant around her neck.

Kit was watching her closely, slowly blinking as she stretched out a paw and set it on Guppy's leg.

In my head, the scene of an elderly woman tending a fire, her surroundings reflecting a well kept hearth in a cottage lit by candles, drying bunches of herbs hanging on the walls—a warm and cozy setting. The sound of a soft purr started in the image, but soon was enveloping the five of us where we sat.

"I think she likes Fiona," I said quietly, holding my hand out for Kit to sniff, or bite depending on my translation. She bumped it with her head.

"Fiona it is, then," Guppy stated solemnly. "Fiona it is."

Chapter 17

With the hunter name decided, Kit seemed to cheer up a bit, though I let Guppy further explain to her why it would be better if she didn't come to dinner with us. While she did that, my sisters and I worked with various student actors on their performances. The entire theatre was buzzing with small workshops happening everywhere but on stage, where Drs. K and Galloway continued to perfect Act I.

For simplicity's sake, the students were using our lighting set up and various parts of our costumes. This was an actors' camp after all, not a tech theatre or costume designing camp. Dr. K had mentioned to us she was hoping that with the trust being set up by Laurel, a tech camp, including costuming and make-up, could be offered as well, meaning all aspects of the matinee productions would be student created and run. Part of tonight's meeting over dinner was going to involve what all Laurel wanted the camp to achieve and how much that would take, both money- and time-wise. If she wanted it to grow, the best way to achieve that would be to have the camp grow as well in the offerings it provided for students, including those interested in the aspects of theatre that weren't acting.

Things were moving along quite nicely with the student show; I'm not sure how much magic was involved and how much was just a drive, under pressure, to produce a knock-out production. As the date for their debut grew ever closer, the campers had hit that nervous excitement stage–staying late, living off of caffeine and sugar, and bonding with each other over a common goal. While some of them had known each other before the camp, there were no longer any strangers in the room; the older students had adopted the high school participants, and the two professors had become surrogate parents to them all. And Mustardseed Productions? I guess we were the strange know-it-all relatives–aunts, uncles, cousins–that came to visit.

When my family left to go find suitable outfits for our dinner that night, the rest of our actors and our tech crew stayed with the camp, the enthusiasm of the students and the drive for success spreading like wildfire across everyone involved. Kit opted to stay late as well, and Carlos promised he would get her home and make sure she had dinner. I gave him my key–any clothes I had that might work for dinner tonight were in the Vista—and informed him about the food, and told him I was sure we wouldn't be late, so I would stop by for Kit when we got back. I also explained to him about the heart name/hunter name, hoping he had ideas on how to introduce the newly dubbed Fiona to the student cast without making it sound like we were all a little bit off our collective rocker.

He plucked Kit up from the floor and was holding her so he could look her in the eyes. "Don't you worry, Lady Fiona; I know exactly what to do." He helped Kit up to his shoulder as he walked to the cast, who were in the middle of a break. I wasn't sure, but I think she had started purring the second Carlos used the title 'Lady' in front of her new name.

Though I couldn't hear what he said, I could hear the cheers from the students as we walked out of the theatre and headed to the Vista to search for clothes. Whatever Carlos had done, it must have worked to elicit that response. Feeling better about Kit, like I had righted some awful wrong I had committed, I jogged a little to catch up to my mom and sisters, who were in the middle of discussing what we might have that we could dress up with a little work and help from Dr. K's closet.

"It's going to be the shoes," Meg said, looking down at her well-worn sneakers.

We all looked down at our feet as we walked, knowing Meg was right. The nicest pair of shoes I had were Birkenstock sandals, which would probably be okay, especially here, but they weren't in the best condition.

Alec was staring at her phone, typing and swiping and finally looking up. "I think we should hit a thrift shop; there's one in that area around Willow's, practically on our way to Dr. K's."

"Just need to find a couple of cool tunics to go over leggings, and we'll look about as good as we can get on such short notice," Meg's tone was light as she dropped back a little to walk with me.

Before I could agree with her, a familiar voice called out from somewhere above us.

"Brava! Brava! Our fair maidens return, triumphant from treading the stony stage!"

Alec cast a glance over her shoulder and up into the trees. "They're not hitting on us again, are they?"

I shook my head and stopped. "Thank you, kind sirs, for your generous words."

A small shower of leaves began falling on us. I guess they couldn't find flowers on such short notice.

Guppy's voice broke in, a note of concern in it. "I wonder if that potion is ever going to wear off, or if you just have a new permanent talent."

I waved to the squirrels, who were much better versed at ad-libbing iambic pentameter lines than I could ever hope to be, and we continued on to the Vista, making short work of finding a selection of clothes that could be paired with some accent pieces to make us presentable in fine company. Then we packed it all into the hatch of the Fiat, piled in ourselves, and headed to the thrift store in the University Hill retail area.

Originally, I had thought we were going to blow in, shop quickly, and head out, but after entering the store, I, like my mom and sisters, stood, mouths agape, staring at what had to be the largest selection of vintage 50s and 60s clothing any of us had ever seen in one place.

Guppy's eyes were bouncing from display to display. I could practically hear the wheels turning in her brain as she scanned the shop, picturing various Shakespearean titles being set in a post WWII world.

Before I could open my mouth, Alec set her hand on Guppy's shoulder and gave her a little shake. "We can come back; right now, stick to the mission."

Guppy's eyes continued to wander, but she nodded a few times quickly, shaking herself out of her clothing-induced trance. Believe me, I get it; I'm the same way with shoes.

As I followed Guppy further into the store, Meg was suddenly beside me, holding a robin's egg blue swirled with faded pink A-line sheath dress up to me, judging the size, and then handing it to me. "This is you. One down, three to go."

I didn't argue with her. I'm not good with choosing clothes. Costumes, yes, but I was always the one most comfortable in jeans or shorts and t-shirts. I figured that Meg's artistic talents helped her piece together outfits that I could never dream of myself. She hurried off, continuing to search, while I milled around carrying the dress and holding it out to different shoes I found. And there were plenty, but most of them would probably have me breaking my neck trying to walk in them. Yet I wanted them all.

It wasn't long before Meg cruised back by me, holding a pair of ivory Go Go boots and a primary color block capped sleeve tunic. She held out the boots to me. "These are also you; check the size." With her shoe hand free, she slipped back over to Alec and handed her the dress.

I smiled to myself. I had nothing left to do now but follow Alec as she poked through the shoes, which I didn't mind doing at all, before finally settling on a pair of red block-heeled Mary Janes. Together, we continued to browse, watching as Meg kept trying to focus Guppy's attention on the clothing we needed now, not the clothing she was basing a whole new scenario for a play we would be performing much later.

When we heard Meg cry "Huzzah!", we both turned to see her, hands on Guppy's shoulders, conga-lining our mom to the checkout counter. We headed over to meet them, setting our items on the surface in front of the cashier. Meg had chosen a past the knee halter dress in an understated floral pattern. She had no shoes. I cast a glance back at the shoe section. How could she have been in here and not found a million shoes that she needed, even if only just to look upon and dream of being more graceful?

"I know that look," she smiled, noticing I was still staring at Shoe Paradise. "My sandals will go quite nicely with this."

The cashier greeted us and began the checkout process. She and Guppy soon fell into a discussion about the inventory and if there was a chance she could get a bulk rate if she wanted to do something like stage *Romeo and Juliet* at a college campus during the Vietnam Era.

My sisters and I glanced at each other.

"That might actually be kind of cool," Alec said, taking the bags Guppy was handing to her suddenly, the conversation with the clerk over.

"She gave me the owner's business card; I think we might have struck the motherlode here," Guppy smiled, tucking the card in her purse as she took one last wistful look at the contents of the shop before Meg and I dragged her out.

Dr. K's house wasn't too far a drive from the shop, a few blocks west and north off of Marine Street. Alec parked the Fiat in front of the modest sky blue house, and we headed inside once Guppy had unlocked the door.

I've always loved Dr. K's house. She bought it after hanging up her traveling actor shoes to take a permanent position with the University. Her house, decorated in warm colors, had mementos from all of the places she had ever performed, and somehow, she had managed to make them all work together organically. A tea set from Japan sat comfortably next to a small statuette of Anansi on one of the shelves of a built-in floor to ceiling entire wall bookcase. This was my favorite spot in the whole house. The walls that weren't part of the shelves were covered with souvenirs and framed posters from the productions she had been part of, the language on them not always English. When I was little and we would visit, I would spend hours in this nook, reading books, coloring, or just studying the artifacts she had collected.

This was my second home, well, my second home that didn't have wheels. Before my sisters and I were old enough to be in the productions, we would split our time between traveling with the troupe and staying with Dr. K, who had joyfully accepted being made our legal guardian should anything happen to Guppy. One by one, as we grew up, we became part of the production company officially, starting out with stage crew positions and slowly being brought in to the smaller roles. All of our first major roles had been the

Fool in *King Lear*, starting the summers before we entered high school. To be honest, the Fool is still my favorite role, and while there have been shows where I've doubled as Cordelia, I'm quite happy to leave the role of the youngest daughter to someone else. Saumia is a great Cordy, and really, the other two sisters are the fun ones to play because of how evil they are. It's fun to be the bad guy, or gal in this case, on stage.

It wasn't long after we finished gussying ourselves up that Dr. K waltzed in the front door, set her batik backpack on the floor, and called out, "Let's see how you look."

My sisters and I lined up in front of her like soldiers awaiting inspection. Guppy slipped into line, still fussing with a recalcitrant earring back.

"Lovely, my lovelies," her smile wide, a bit of East London in her accent as she looked down the line we made. When she got to Guppy, the smile broadened. "One of these things is not like the other. I've got three sixties mod hippies and a fifties astronaut's wife."

Guppy, finally finished wrestling with her earring, smoothed down the skirt of her deep rose shirtwaist dress, and grinned back at her best friend. "If I hadn't been so rushed" and here she threw a knowing glance at Meg, "we could have re-enacted that pose from the book cover. They had this dress in all colors; I think we would have looked adorable."

Alec and I also looked over to Meg, but with completely different expressions than the one on our mother's face.

"You can thank me later," she said, lacing her fingers together and cracking her knuckles.

"Coffee's on me the rest of the week," Alec said out of the corner of her mouth to Meg.

It took another twenty minutes for Dr. K to disappear into her bedroom and then reappear dressed in a wine-colored pantsuit and decked out with gold accessories.

"We should take two cars as I don't know how long this meeting will last; there is a table reserved in the tapas bar section, which overlooks the dining area. You should be able to see the meeting from where you'll be sitting. They may want to meet Guppy; in fact, they may want to meet all four of you."

Now I was really wishing Kit had been able to come along.

Alec saw my face and nudged me. "Just pretend it's another role you have to play: courteous daughter, smile and nod and politely laugh when someone says something funny, or that they think is funny, anyway." She then turned to address Dr. K. "We'll follow you."

Chapter 18

Guppy had chosen to ride with Dr. K, probably so they could talk about the meeting and sketch out an "in a perfect world, the trust would be able to do . . ." type of plan, or at least construct a list of objectives that the camp would hope to meet in the upcoming years, including a timeline for growth. Before we left, Meg had asked Dr. K why the meeting was at the restaurant and not in some boardroom at the firm.

She had responded with a shrug of her shoulders. "From what Madi has told me, it is easiest for the managers of Azafrán to meet there as they both want to hear the plan but cannot be absent at the same time. And also, the other managers like to go there, especially if it is on someone else's dime."

The arrangements around the meeting were the topic of conversation for those of us in the Fiat.

"Is it favoritism, you think?" Meg asked, gazing out the window as we began the climb up the pass. "Like the managers of Azafrán are the 'golden children' out of all the others?"

Alec tapped her fingers on the steering wheel before answering. "Could be; but I imagine that Azafrán is the big money maker in the triad of businesses, and catering to their needs, especially when it sounds like the restaurants will be expected to support this trust in some way, would be the most beneficial. Plus, even if they were, they would have been the Monroe's favorites, not necessarily Laurel's."

"Maybe that's part of the problem," I voiced the newly forming thought that was taking shape in my brain. "Maybe they're worried about having a new overseer; maybe they're worried about her discovering something about the business that her parents didn't know about."

My sisters were silent for a moment. It was Alec who finally spoke. "Like cooking the books or skimming a little off the top in some way? That's a pretty good motive for murder."

"But wouldn't a discrepancy like that stand out in an audit or something or be discovered after the Monroe's accident by investigators?" Meg questioned, turning sideways in her seat to include me in the conversation.

"Considering everything Ethan has shared with us about the car accident investigation," I started, "it was pretty obvious to all involved that it was nothing but an accident, especially once the car was examined and found to be clear of any tampering."

Alec's fingers started tapping on the steering wheel again. "No murder, no need to do any forensic accounting, as it were."

Her fingers continued their rhythmless tapping as we neared the place Kit and I had taken out Paisleigh; I leaned forward and pointed it out, warning Alec that the road was still tricky even though the supernatural threat was gone.

The spirits had all departed, and the place seemed to be at peace, but the road was still dangerous.

Several switchbacks later, we found the turnoff to the parking lot, and pulled in next to Dr. K's dark gray Forester. Before we left the car, Meg added a final thought to our discussion concerning the managers of Azafrán.

"So we're back at square one with no evidence to suggest that Laurel was pushed except her own memory which could be a side-effect of the head trauma she suffered on the staircase."

We all sighed in unison.

"Let's go eat; maybe something will show itself at the meeting and give us a new trail to follow," Alec stated, unlatching her seatbelt and opening her door.

The most noticeable thing upon exiting the car was the silence. Set back from the road, the parking lot, which only had a few cars present, was cloistered enough by the trees to block any noise that might be happening on the road. The second thing was the deep, rich smell of pine and earth, and the occasional whiff of something grilling. I felt relaxed almost immediately; the silence and the scent of being in what seemed to be an endless forest was very calming.

Alec was breathing the scent of the woods deeply into her lungs. I could tell she wanted to wander out of the lot and into the trees, maybe touch a few, maybe sit down on the forest floor and just exist for a while, recharge a bit. But before she could wander off, Guppy linked arms with her, and we all headed for the door.

Azafrán looked like a cross between an old English hunting lodge and a Frank Lloyd Wright experiment with glass, all heavy timbers, stone, and huge windows overlooking both the surrounding trees and the city laid out below. Once inside, it was easy to see that there were no "bad seats" in the house. The inside was tiered, allowing views from every chair. The main dining area on the lower tier had windows that were currently slid aside, letting the soft, pine-scented breeze drift through the tables.

The upper tier held the tapas bar and was smaller, overlooking the dining area but still getting both the views and the fresh air. Outside there was a lower tier consisting of a multi level deck with patio seating, and on a night like tonight, I was sure that area would fill up fast.

The host greeted us, checking his reservation book with a smile. "Ah yes; the Mustardseed Production party. I have the perfect table waiting for you. Please follow me, and watch your step."

We tailed him like a line of baby ducks around the corner of the host station and up a small staircase which opened onto the upper tier. A full and magnificently stocked bar lined the back wall; a hip high dark metal and glass barrier snaked along the edge of the tier to keep guests from falling onto the diners below should they imbibe too much and stumble. The table he led us to was a half circle, the flat side pressed up to the barrier, so the five chairs that surrounded it all had views of both the outside and the diners below.

"May I start you with an aperitivo?" He asked, glancing around at us, not sure who was in charge.

Dr. K stepped up first; she's the one who was familiar with this place after all and made the reservations. "I know you offer a Chef's Choice four or five course dinner; do you offer that equivalent for the tapas menu?"

The host nodded along as Ike wrapped up her question. "You're in luck. Marisol herself is running the tapas kitchen this evening. She likes to choose the drinks for each course as well. You can have up to seven different tapas, but she gets to choose what they are."

After a little quick math, Dr. K glanced around at us and ordered. "Well then, we'll go with six as I might be missing a couple while I'm at the meeting."

The host smiled widely at us and bowed his head a bit before speaking. "Your server, Jonas, will bring your mystery aperitivo shortly."

With the exit of the host, we were finally able to scope the rest of the restaurant out. It was astoundingly beautiful yet cozy-comfy at the same time. I've been in places that made me nervous to breathe; but instead this whole structure made it feel like you were just sitting down in your favorite chair in front of a nice warm fire on a cold night. Of course, your chair wouldn't care if you were wearing your pajamas; nor would it hand you a three or four figure bill when you got up to go to bed.

Dr. K was motioning toward the corner on the lower tier nearest to where we were sitting. "See how the aisle surrounding that large table in the corner is so wide? That's where the meeting will be. And also, the Marisol the host mentioned is half of the couple that manages this establishment."

"Kinda exposed," Alec stated bluntly, "Of course it is a Monday, so maybe it isn't their biggest sales night. What do I know; I've never waited tables nor had to set up a philanthropic trust fund in a restaurant I inherited."

Meg and I traded glances. We had both waited tables in college, part of Guppy's "know yourself, know your audience" exercise program she had devised so we would learn better financial responsibility, have a little extra spending money, and be exposed to all types of humanity. Alec had worked at a university spirit store, which was the other option instead of food service. We had all gotten the same speech, just at different times, about how some lessons can't be learned in the classroom and involve going into the world to understand it first hand. Hence, we had all worked in the customer service field in some way. However, the restaurant that employed Meg and me was more of a Cesare's than an Azafrán.

"Marisol is also the curator of the wine cellar, apparently," Dr. K added, her voice dropping off as a different young man approached our table with a tray full of glasses and several small bowls of olives.

He set the tray on a caddy he had provided, and presented the bottle to us. "I'm Jonas, and I'll be your server this evening; I'm also training a new hire. Her name is Michelle, and she'll be assisting me. Please don't hesitate to ask either of us questions." Then he turned his attention to the bottle he held and announced the name, described the notes we should detect while drinking, poured a small measure, and offered it to Dr. K who had ordered for us. She went through the steps of sampling the drink, and finished with a nod to Jonas, who then proceeded to pour us all small tasting glasses.

We sipped our drinks and nibbled a few olives and mostly talked about what the trust could do in the upcoming years.

"You know you can always rely on us to help, with any of the areas, whatever you need," Guppy said, responding to a worry Dr. K had about inviting in other acting troupes, like it might offend us. "You'll need more outside voices' input for this than just ours; but you know if you can't find takers right away, we'll always step up."

Ike reached out and squeezed Guppy's hand. "Thank you, Kindley," she smiled at her own play on words, then dropped her voice to a whisper. "There; they are arriving."

We watched, silent and unnoticed in the balcony above, like goddesses looking down from Olympus at the chess pieces that were mortals below us. What kind of game or drama would unfold from this dinner that was only happening because someone, more than likely one of the people arriving at that table, had tried to kill a young woman and failed?

Our quiet study of the corner table was interrupted by our server returning to speak to us about our drinks and to inform us our first official tapas would be arriving in fifteen minutes or would we like more time. Meg and I had both startled at his voice as we were in the least accommodating seats for eavesdropping on the big table. I noticed she had a faint blush across her face that mirrored the heat I felt in mine. Whether or not he knew we were spying, we both had that initial shame of being caught, and it showed in the pink on our faces.

Dr. K assured him the timing was perfect, and we continued chatting instead of staring, especially Meg and I, who would wait for the play-by-play commentary from Alec and Guppy who had the choice seats for snooping.

The first to arrive was Penelope Faulkner, her protege, Beth Norris, trailing behind. The table was set for ten, and Ms. Faulkner sat at the head, motioning for Norris to sit at her right, putting the younger woman's back to the restaurant.

"Read anything?" Dr. K asked quietly.

I immediately shook my head. If I started reading something, believe me, she would know, the whole restaurant would know, and maybe the whole world would know if someone caught it on camera.

Alec had her head tilted to the right as she watched two more people arrive. Moira Amin and a younger version of Moira sat on the left of Penelope, leaving the two chairs directly to her left empty. They had barely seated themselves before a man I'd never seen before approached and sat on Faulkner's left, reaching to shake hands with both versions of Moira, and nodding to the two attorneys.

Alec shook her head, "Not really; nervousness, but that's natural. Everything seems fine. I'm not picking up any malice at all."

Meg agreed, sneaking a quick look before speaking. "Don't tell me when Garrett comes in. I bet I can sense him before you can see him."

"You're on," Alec took the bet, holding out her fist to get a confirmation bump from Meg.

Our first course, dates stuffed with fig paste and wrapped in a paper thin strip of Iberico ham, arrived along with a new drink, a small glass of what Jonas declared to be Albariño. While we all sampled this new fare, and it was delicious, Guppy motioned with her chin to the table.

"There's Madi," she said quietly, and both Meg and I turned to look.

Madi sat at the other end of the table, setting a notebook and a pen on the surface to her right. We could tell when the introductions started just by watching the rise and fall of Madilyn's smile. When that was over, she began chatting to the young copy of Moira on her right, who looked to be the youngest person at the table.

"Well," I started, turning back to the table. "She did say she thinks she's a de facto member because Lauren wants her to be; probably because Madi's the only person she feels safe with right now."

"And yet, Madi also fits the description the squirrel gave you," Alec reminded me, glancing around to see if any of the dates were left. Wishful thinking.

Meg, who had also turned around to face the table again, added, "Well so does Moira." She cast a quick glance over her shoulder. "And Moira Junior."

Alec scanned the table below again. "If you want to be picky about it, so does the associate lawyer. And if you want to get super picky, that guy to the left of Faulkner isn't much bigger."

Our server returned to the table, clearing dishes no longer needed, asking us if we liked the course. We assured him we did, and at this point he told us that Marisol would be joining the meeting for a bit, but we wouldn't be forgotten.

I looked around the tapas bar, realizing we were the only people present.

Dr. K noticed my studying of the bar. "It helps to have connections," she said. "Madi told me Laurel wanted you all here. The tapas bar is usually closed on Monday, though the bar itself remains open; Laurel arranged for us to have this table and be here–me for the meeting, you guys for the support you have given Madi and the theatre department."

"That's a big bill for the restaurant to eat," Guppy said. "Unless Laurel herself is footing the tab for both the meeting and for us."

Ike stood to go over and introduce herself to the growing gathering. "I have no idea who is going to have to pay this bill, but I'm happy it is not me. I'll be back; but please eat my portion if I don't make the course. Leave me my drink though."

As Dr. K made her way down to the table, Meg suddenly spoke.

"He's here."

Chapter 19

W hile I'm sure it was just a coincidence, as Meg spoke, claiming that the manager of Cesare's was here, I felt the breeze, still softly passing through the dining area, turn suddenly chilly. I couldn't tell if it was just an errant wind, Meg throwing a little magical special effect in to accompany her announcement, or if Mother Nature was trying to warn the whole restaurant that a dark presence had entered and to flee the coming storm. I'm pretty certain it was the first, but you never know with Meg.

To our credit, none of us moved for a few beats, instead just surreptitiously looked around, trying to be casual rather than be caught out gawking as before. It was a good five seconds before Cal Garrett appeared, scowling as the meeting table came into his view. Only one seat was available—the one next Moira—as the managers of Azafrán had joined the party just as Dr. K had taken her seat on Madi's left. Slowly, as he approached, the scowl lifted from his face, and for a moment, it looked like he was practicing trying to look nice; he didn't quite get there.

"Now you owe me twice, Alec," Meg grinned when she said it, but the smile immediately fell when she started her next sentence. "Still so much jealousy and resentment in this guy."

Meg and I both turned back to our own table, reaching for the last sips in our wine glasses, when Jonas returned carrying another round of drinks, followed by a young woman who set up the caddy and deposited our next course on top of it.

Our server thanked her, then turned his attention to us. With Dr. K missing in action, he proffered the first glass of red he poured to Guppy for inspection. After she nodded approval, he began setting down the next course.

"Champiñones al ajillo," he said while we all breathed in the deep earthy smell of mushrooms. "Or simply, mushrooms in garlic, paired with a medium bodied Garnacha." He poured and placed one last glass down at Dr. K's empty chair and glanced around at us, silently inviting questions if we had them.

"Oh these are delicious," Alec finally broke the silence, already eyeing the plate in front of the empty chair.

A sudden burst of laughter drew our eyes back to the meeting. By the body language of both Dr. K and

Madi, we could tell they were more than likely regaling the table with stories of the camp and how the preparations for the matinee shows were going. Most of the table was laughing as Dr. K explained something that had her waving her arms over her head like she was panicking. When the story ended, we could see her turn to Madi, giving the young woman a chance to continue or add more to the it.

Marisol had one hand resting on the table, her husband's covering it, and occasionally they turned to each other to smile

"A very handsome young couple," Guppy sighed, and glanced at Jonas. "What is her husband's name?"

Jonas smiled. "Marcos," he answered, then helpfully added more information so we didn't have to pry. "While Marisol stocks the wine cellar, Marcos pours over the menu, constantly changing or altering dishes as the seasons change. Of course, there are some favorites that he will not take off for fear of disappointing some of our guests, but he is a firm believer in sticking with seasonal ingredients."

We all nodded before Alec picked up the conversation. "Does he design the tapas menu as well, because everything we've tasted is just incredible."

"Indeed he does," Jonas confirmed. "Especially since the accident which took the Monroes from us. Before that, the two of them, Marcos and Paul, would sit at the bar designing the tapas while Marisol and

Lucia would discuss wines that would work with their ideas." His voice dropped a little in enthusiasm, which Meg picked up immediately.

"Sounds like they were good friends; from everything we've heard about the Monroes, they were wonderful people and very philanthropic."

Jonas's expression turned wistful, but his smile returned. "They were more; Marcos was like a son to them. He and Marisol are still grieving the loss."

"I'm sorry we've brought down the mood," Guppy slipped in sincerely. "Please let them know that everything is just exquisite and we are so thankful to have been invited."

"I definitely will; and I'll give you a little extra time since I took up so much of it talking. Please enjoy." He nodded to all of us and headed back down the stairs to either tend to other tables, though the restaurant was nowhere near full, or check on the kitchen and the food for the table of bigwigs.

Guppy glanced around at each one of us in turn. "Okay, which one of you is responsible for his glibness?"

I shook my head, "You know I suck at that," and then I turned to stare directly at Alec, as did Meg. Convincing people to talk had always been one of Alec's skills.

"Guilty," she admitted with a grin, "but to be fair, he really did want to share all of that with someone. I think Jonas is really fond of his bosses."

"Unlike the employees at Cesare's," I stated, throwing a glance back at the meeting. "You know," I went on, "Marisol fits Mama Matilda's description as well. And if Marcos was like a son to the Monroe's, he probably has a key to their house."

My comment dampened the mood at our table, but that didn't make it any less true; just because the young couple loved the older Monroes didn't mean they extended the same loyalty and love for the only daughter and true heir of the kingdom.

My family all glanced down to the gathering below as well. Madi was writing furiously in her notebook, glancing up occasionally at whomever happened to be talking at the time. Dr. K sporadically leaned over her to help her add things while still participating in the conversation. Four ears are always better than two when trying to keep track of important matters.

"So," Guppy started up the conversation again. "I've been thinking that we could maybe use our performances to publicize the trust, help get the word out to the community. The people in our audience are the type that would support the theatre. Not in the typical 'pass the basket' type of fundraising, but something more informational and a little more professional."

Meg was the first one to respond. "I'm sure there's a plan for that already, but yeah, I think we could use the performances to drum up some donors or sponsors, if that is part of what Laurel is wanting to happen. It would be a nice gesture, especially after this treat." As she finished she gestured to our table and the restaurant in general.

Her idea of thanking Laurel for a wonderful night out reminded me of the cait sith's costume idea. "Kit wants to have a small jester outfit for Ember. If we have enough scraps and Madi trusts us enough to give us the stuffie for a fitting, that would be nice, too; and a little more personal."

"That's simple enough," Guppy said. "I can whip that out in no time flat."

Alec finished up her wine before speaking. "Maybe you could suggest it when you go down to meet the elite of this trust. If they like it, we can start on Thursday, but it might be more impactful to do something on Saturday, either before the student show or in between their matinee and our performance."

Guppy processed that information, nodding in approval. "Well, I'll go ahead and suggest it when I meet them. If they aren't interested, we could still do something for Laurel on our own, including the jester outfit for Ember."

Jonas and Michelle visited our table three more times with more plates of deliciousness and small glasses of wine before Dr. K excused herself from the meeting and returned to collect Guppy. We hadn't devoured her plate of mushrooms, mostly because Guppy said mushrooms were one of Ike's favorite things, but we had lit into her patatas bravas when given the go ahead. As per her request, we didn't squabble over her wine.

She sat for a moment to fill us in, eyes growing wide at the mushroom plate in front of her, and taking bites between filling us in on the goings-on below.

"The man sitting to Ms. Faulkner's left is Peter Dandridge, the financial representative; he'll be in charge of the funds to make sure they are going to the correct place and not being misused. So far, all the managers are on-board with the concept, but it remains to be seen how much they will actually participate in the process. Faulkner assured them that their respective salaries would not be affected nor would their establishments be expected to drop everything at a moment's notice to cater to the needs of the trust. Dandridge has been in charge of investing the profits for the Monroes for years, and is almost as familiar with the family as Faulkner herself."

"Does he have a key?" I blurted out. I can't help it; I have a one-track mind when it comes to vengeance, and the fact that the people who fit the squirrel's description were all vying for the title of The Monroe's

Biggest Fan had me spinning my wheels and rubbing my eyes constantly.

Dr. K caught my gaze and smiled. "I can try to find that out, but subtly is not my strong point."

At that comment, Alec laughed, "That's okay, it's not Tisi's either."

Before Dr. K could whisk Guppy down to face the trust board, Jonas returned with more tapas and wine.

"Manchego croquetas with Serrano ham," Jonas informed us, setting down the plates while his shadow uncorked the next bottle of wine. "Paired with a light Spanish Malbec." He offered the glass to Dr. K again even though she and Guppy were getting ready to go.

She went through the wine tasting motions again, declared the malbec perfect, and warned us away from her plate, pointing at us in turn. "I'm coming back for this." But this time, she took her wine with her, as did Guppy.

When they left, Alec stretched her back, patting her stomach as she did. "Between the timing and the portion sizes, I feel neither stuffed nor tipsy. Wouldn't you like to see the bill for this, or at the least, the cost of a full glass of one of these wines?"

Meg finished off her croqueta, licking the last of the Mornay off her fingertips. "I am loving this meal, and to be fair, the portions of wine are perfect for the servings." She raised her glass and Alec clinked hers against it gently. "We should add some of these to our own travel menu. I wonder how hard they are to make."

"You're more of a kitchen witch than I am, so I'm sure you could pull it off; make this one first," Alec laughed as Meg rolled her eyes.

I was only half listening. Something seemed off to me with the croqueta; it had a bit of a metallic bitterness to it that I hadn't noticed until I was nearly finished; or maybe it was the malbec.

"How about Garrett's anger level?" Meg asked, noticing that Alec had refocused her attention on the table below. "His resentment is still pretty high, the jealousy has tapered off a bit. Maybe finding out he wouldn't have to personally lose any of his salary had a calming effect on him."

Alec took a few seconds to think before answering. "Not nearly as high as it was, but it's still there, so maybe you're right. She glanced over the barrier to the table. "Seems like everyone is making nice. Madi looks comfortable, considering; even Mini Moira seems to be lightening up a bit. Maybe all the resentment and anger was stemming from thinking they were going to have to take pay cuts or lose bonuses or something."

I shrugged, taking a sip of my water to clear my mouth. The metallic taste hit me even stronger. "Does your water taste funny?" I asked, but both of my sisters shook their heads no. I turned my head to the table below, chewing on my lower lip.

Guppy and Dr. K had finished whatever part of the presentation they had been asked to present and were now listening, as the rest of the table was, to something that Penelope Faulkner was explaining. There was no laughter now, her audience seriously focused on whatever it was she was saying.

Jonas returned to clear away more plates, and he and Alec started a less formal conversation about the food and wine pairings now that the 'adults' were away.

"Is one of the tapas a dessert?" Meg threw in, her sweet tooth starting to call out for attention.

Jonas laughed. "No, but dessert is part of your menu anyway, compliments of Ms. Monroe. And," he added, looking specifically at me, "Wait until you see the coffee service that comes with it."

He cleared more of our dishes and let us know our next course would be coming out shortly; then he vanished down the stairs to continue with his duties.

Before we could start discussing the mystery surrounding the coffee and dessert portion of our experience, Alec, who had the best view of the meeting, stated, "It looks like they might be breaking up, or at least Mom's part is done."

I took the last sip of my wine, grimacing at the sudden bitter notes it had, and following closely on the bitterness, the familiar damp earth flavor of guilt, so light and subtle I almost missed it.

"Tisi?" I heard Alec's voice, a hint of concern lacing the simple one-word question.

"Guilt. I can taste guilt, but it's laced with something else, something burnt but cold." I was relieved to hear that my voice was still my own, and I unconsciously reached up to run my fingers through my hair, which was still, fortunately, just hair. "Just the lightest touch of guilt mixed with a newfound fear."

The three of us openly focused on the table below, our expressions grim. Guppy was rising to leave, going through the obligatory 'thank yous' and 'nice meeting yous,' her smile wide and genuine, before she turned to go.

Moira looked up suddenly and caught the three of us observing them, and though I couldn't be sure, she appeared to shudder as though an icy cold hand had grazed the back of her neck. Her gaze flicked briefly to Guppy, who was already heading back to us, before meeting mine for the briefest of seconds. Then she turned back to the conversation at hand, a fragile smile on her face as she nodded in agreement at whatever Ms. Faulkner was saying.

I rubbed my eyes, feeling the itch growing deeper. I wasn't sure who exactly was feeling the guilt or the fear, or if they were even being experienced by the same person. But the look on Moira Amin's face spoke volumes to me: she was scared.

"You've got that look on your face, Tisi," were the first words out of Guppy's mouth as she scooted her chair back up to the table and reached for her newest serving of wine. "Is everything alright?"

"Moira is scared of something or someone," I stated; internally I was wondering if I should add that she didn't seem to be frightened until she looked up and caught my sisters and me watching them. Annoyance would have been a better expression at our eavesdropping than fear, and to be fair, she may have just been startled to see the three of us staring down at them, but again, there is a difference between being caught off guard and being scared.

Dr. K turned her attention to me. "Ms. Faulkner was going over Laurel's condition there at the end and the measures being taken to keep her safe. Maybe Mrs. Amin is just worried about Laurel."

"Maybe," I conceded, "but the look on her face didn't look like worry; it looked like fear."

We stopped talking as Jonas appeared with the last course of tapas before dessert: a small individual serving of paella for each of us with a sparkling rosa as the wine pairing. He smiled as he set it down. "Coffee and dessert will be out soon. Would you like fully caffeinated, decaf, or a blend of the two?"

After a quick debate and everyone checking the time on their phones, we opted to get a blend, heavy on the decaf. Once he left, we resumed our discussion.

"From what Madi told me," Dr. K began, "when Laurel was in middle school, she would go to Willow's and keep Moira's daughter, Destiny, entertained during the afternoon rush so Moira could finish up orders and start the evening cleaning allowing her to close on time. Madi used to go with her sometimes. It was important to the Monroes that Moira was able to spend time with her daughter and go to her events. That's one reason why Laurel would run the shop some days while she was in college."

Alec set her spoon down. "The first time we were in Willow's, Moira mentioned that the shop belonged to her mother until the Monroes bought it. She didn't give off any negative vibes over the sale, but I suppose she could be harboring some fear about what the trust means for her business. They all could, really. It's new, and it sounds like Laurel wants it to grow, which could bring about some changes in how each business participates. Some people just aren't good with change, especially when they don't have the option of opting out. Unless they quit, that is."

We sat in silence, finishing off our paella and digesting what Alec had said. I had forgotten the Monroes had bought the coffee shop versus starting it up from scratch as they had the other two. But, considering how the shop was still decorated with the older Amin's kitsch and that the Monroes seemed to care about her work / life balance, I wasn't convinced there was something dark hanging over Moira's head concerning what had been her mother's business, unless she was worried about losing it.

By the time the coffee and dessert arrived, we were in the middle of a discussion concerning the student matinee, which, Dr. K assured us, was coming along nicely. We all sat back as Jonas and his shadow returned to our table. While Michelle placed beautifully painted coffee cups in front of us, Jonas placed what looked to be a repurposed deviled egg plate in the center of the table. In each of the divots for an egg was a condiment that could be put in coffee. There were dollops of whipped cream in some, sprinkles and mini chocolate chips–white, milk, and dark–in others. Several cinnamon sticks and nutmegs with a small microplane were in the center. As he explained what each additive was, Michelle put three small pitchers on the table, which Jonas immediately named.

"The white is Rumchata, the red is Baileys, and the gold is Kahlua. And tonight's dessert is tarta de queso." As he finished speaking, his trainee set the last of the plates down in front of us, smiling.

We stared at the dessert course, oohing and ahhing appropriately, no one reaching for anything just yet.

Jonas grinned at our reactions. "Again, let us know if you need anything else. Oh, I almost forgot . . ."

He nodded at Michelle, who set a small dish of ice cream down next to me, and for the first time spoke. "Ms. Drake told us you had an affogato addiction. Enjoy."

Once they left, we fell on the dessert like we hadn't just been stuffing our faces for the past few hours. With the ice cream there, I added a little of that to my coffee first, then dumped in some Kahlua for good measure.

"We should have gone full decaf," Meg stated, grating a little nutmeg into her coffee before adding a dollop of whipped cream and a quick pour of Rumchata to it.

Alec had added an assortment of the chocolate chips to her coffee, then started nibbling the ones left over. "This would be a fun thing to do for the cast some night, like maybe the last night of a run."

Guppy nodded in agreement while sipping her coffee, doctored only with Bailey's, her biggest weakness. "A good idea and very doable, although we won't have dish-ware nearly this gorgeous."

Dr. K was sitting back in her chair looking like a cat who had polished off a saucer of cream, holding her coffee up to her nose to breathe it in. "I wish you would consider moving back here, Guppy. Make this your home base. I miss spending time with you all."

"It is so very tempting every time we visit, but our winter commitments are all in Texas. The weather is a little more amenable to outdoor performances, usually." Guppy pondered her coffee, setting it down when Michelle returned with a carafe to give us refills.

We talked for another thirty minutes, sipping our various coffee concoctions, discussing the plays, the students, pointedly avoiding the ever looming issue that was Laurel and her 'accident' which had dominated our conversation all evening.

After Guppy set a few bills on the table, adding to the tip already taken care of by the last living Monroe, we made our way out to our cars, wishing Dr. K goodnight and trading hugs with her. The sky was clear, the stars shining brightly with the lack of light pollution up in the mountains, just like they had in Salida.

But my eyes were itching and my thoughts were unsettled. Moira Amin was scared, and someone at that table had been oozing guilt, enough so I could taste it, but not enough to pinpoint who it was. As Alec piloted the Italian Job down the mountain, I stared out my window into the surrounding trees, wishing I knew better how to handle the current situation without anyone having to die.

I was still sorting through various scenarios when the faintest whisper of distress slid into my thoughts, a small voice, the hopelessness overwhelming. Scanning our surroundings, I leaned forward and asked Alec to turn into the housing development we were passing by and go slowly.

She did, no questions asked, and Guppy turned sideways in her seat to look at me but didn't speak.

Someone was here; someone who needed justice, but the call was so quiet, faded, I was having trouble pinpointing the source.

Alec wove up and down the residential streets, listening for directions from me. It was a bit like playing the hotter / colder game that we did when we were growing up, only back then I was usually looking for something of mine that Alec had hidden.

I leaned back in my seat and sent out one word: *Hello?*

For several long moments there was nothing, then: *I'm not supposed to talk to strangers.*

My heart dropped; it was a kid. I said as much to my family. Meg immediately got on her phone and began searching for clues about who we might be looking for in this area.

I refocused on my quarry: *That's a good rule to go by. My name's Tisi.*

The silence stretched again. Meg leaned over and showed me what she had found on her phone.

I tried again: *Are you Emily?*

As I waited, Meg gave her phone to Guppy who started giving Alec driving instructions.

The response was smaller now: *Yes.*

I tried to put a smile in my voice; dealing with kids is the hardest: *So now we aren't strangers, right?*

The delay was shorter this time: *I guess.*

Alec finally pulled over to the curb, parked, and shut off the engine.

Across the street from where we sat stood a large gray-brick colonial mansion with a lawn that, at one time, had probably been fit to be on the cover of a landscaping magazine. Now it seemed a bit overgrown in places, hedges and ivy threatening to hide the windows. The For Sale sign in the yard also looked as though it had been stuck there for some time, though the clear acrylic box on the side still held a few informational leaflets, protected by the box lid from the elements.

I slowly exited the car and approached the house, going to the sign first as though I was interested in taking one of the spec sheets in case the neighborhood Gladys Kravitz looked out her window. As I slipped one out, I caught a small figure duck back into the shadows on the front porch.

"Emily?" I said quietly as I moved closer to her, resisting the urge to hold out my hand like I was offering it to a stray animal to sniff.

She nodded, still sticking to the darker shadows close to the walls, but she didn't slip away completely.

"Why can you see me? Are you a ghost, too?" she asked, her eyes narrowing and the corners of her mouth turning down.

Normally at this point, I would give my rehearsed response of 'I'm a witch, blah blah blah,' but watching this little girl and seeing the fear and distrust in her eyes, I figured the second the word 'witch' left my lips she would vanish like smoke, and I'd never see her again.

"I'm a fury," I stated simply, knowing she probably hadn't seen the many paintings and drawings depicting the classical furies, at least I hoped not as many of those paintings are terrifying. She was also young enough that the word might not even register as anger or rage to her, though if she was looking for justice, someone had taken out some anger and rage on her at some point, which led to this whole scenario.

Her eyes darted around nervously, scanning the porch and the yard behind me. "I have to hide better this time; he'll be back soon. He always comes back." She turned to leave, already fading.

"Emily, wait, I can help you. Who's coming back?"

But by the time I finished speaking, she had vanished, and I was talking to empty air.

I stood there for a few seconds thinking over what she had said. Who was coming back? I turned and slowly made my way along the front walk to where the car waited, my eyes scanning the area around me for movement. The bitter taste in my mouth was fading. There was no one here but me.

Looking at my watch, I noted the time. There was nothing I could do for Emily tonight; I was going to have to come back here tomorrow with Kit around the same time. Maybe the two of us would have more luck winning Emily's trust and would be able to help her.

Before I returned to the car, I called out one last time. "Emily, I'm going to come back tomorrow with my kitten; she's great at playing hide and seek and can show you the best places to hide." I paused, hoping to hear a response, but the only sounds were the wind blowing through the leaves and the noise of traffic from a few streets over.

With a deep sigh, I returned to the car, hoping that tomorrow I would be more successful with both of the issues I was currently facing.

Chapter 20

O nce I was back in the car, Alec immediately headed for our lodgings, and Guppy started talking, half swiveled in her seat so I could hear her better.

"Emily Buchanan," she stated simply and waited for my reaction. The name did ring a bell, but not a very loud one. When the confusion didn't leave my face, she continued.

"I remember talking to Ike about this when it happened; it really set the town on edge for a bit. It happened in July about fifteen years ago, just a few years after Ike returned and took up her professor position. Emily was put down for a nap before the big fireworks show on July 4th, and when her mom went to wake her up, she was gone. There was a block party going on, kind of like what we used to do with the Cahill, Warlow, and Rodriguez families when you all were younger; in fact, we were probably having ours when all the chaos hit Boulder."

Alec cut in at that point. "I remember that; all the party goers started searching for her, both inside and outside the house. By the time the police were called and arrived, any useful evidence had been contaminated."

Guppy nodded and continued speaking after my sister finished. "Yes. It didn't help that the party was a big one, more than eight families, tons of kids, with games and grills and music—the works. Total chaos."

"But they found her, didn't they, that same night?" I asked. I had been seven when this happened and didn't really remember any of the details.

"Yes," Guppy continued, "After a couple of frantic hours of searching, some of the older teens found her underneath a big evergreen tree, one so large the neighborhood kids used it as a fort. The rock used to crush her skull was found within throwing distance of her body. She was only six years old."

We lapsed into silence as Alec pulled into our parking lot. As we got out and started walking back to the residence hall, Guppy suggested that I speak to Dr. K about what had transpired during the investigation as she would have better details. Considering I didn't have snakes on my head yet, I believed that Emily hadn't received justice because either her killer was now also dead or was so far away, the snakes couldn't make out the scent. My concern now was whether that person, her killer, was also the mysterious 'he' who could always find her when she hid or just a random spirit being obnoxious.

I headed straight to Carlos's room when we reached our floor. Hearing laughter within, I figured he and the usual card crew were playing poker. I hoped they hadn't roped Kit into their game somehow so that we could go back to our room, and I could tell her about Emily's problem.

I tried the door and found it unlocked, but knocked before entering and announced it was me. The sight that met my eyes was, indeed, the poker crew, but sitting at one corner of their makeshift table, was Kit, who barely looked up when I entered and instead tapped one of Carlos's cards and motioned to Asher, who served as dealer at the moment.

"Well, you haven't led me astray yet," the older man said, laughing as he pulled out the card and asked for a new one. When he picked it up and added it to his hand, his smile widened, and he pushed more than half of his chips into the center of the table. "I'll see and raise."

The other members of the game groaned.

"No way; you can't have that good of a hand every time. I think Kit's bluffing." Mike said, squinting his eyes at Kit suspiciously.

The cait sith turned her face toward Mike, and as is the case with most black cats, her expression was unreadable.

"I'm out," Cole sighed, setting his hand down and turning to smile at me. "How was dinner?"

I patted my stomach. "Delicious; and Meg wants to try making some of the tapas we had."

Asher also folded. "I'll be looking forward to that," he quipped, watching the stare-off Kit and Mike were having, Mike getting more fidgety by the second.

Carlos said nothing, letting his fluffy little partner handle the situation.

The stand off lasted only about thirty seconds more before Mike threw in his hand, sighing loudly. "I hope you're buying lunch tomorrow, Carlos."

"Full house, threes over sixes," Carlos grinned, setting his cards down and raising a fist for Kit to tap with her paw.

Mike sighed again. "I want Kit to be my partner next time; I'm in need of a little black cat luck."

Kit walked across the surface and head-bumped Mike before stopping in front of me and yawning widely. I scooped her up, grabbed the bag of her stuff, and bade everyone good night before heading back to our room.

Kit kept a running parade of images going through my head, all of which had to do with the poker game and the incredible streak of luck she and Carlos had experienced and how much fun it was. I was glad she enjoyed her evening considering she was out of sorts when she discovered she wasn't coming with us to dinner.

When we were inside our room, I told her a little about Azafrán, and that I needed to talk to her about something else after I brushed my teeth and washed my face, though judging from her reaction, I may have said brushed my face and washed my teeth; I was a little sleepy. As I gathered my stuff and ducked out, she set about bathing, performing her own bedtime routine.

Once I finished, I zipped back to the room, locked the door, and turned out the main light. Kit was curled up in her nest on one of the beds; I climbed into the other, already browsing for entries about Emily Buchanan on my phone.

"Tomorrow night, you and I have a little something to take care of," I started, watching Kit's ears perk up at the idea of a mission. I briefly explained to her the little I had learned about Emily both from the spirit herself and the items found on the internet.

"I have no idea exactly what is going to be there, who this 'he' is that always finds her; it might not even be her murderer."

Kit tilted her head at me, not understanding why that was a possibility. I didn't have the heart or the time to explain to her that sometimes, when people died, they didn't stop being asshats. The reasons varied, but some spirits seemed to enjoy sticking around and making themselves major pains in the ass. Poltergeists range from being nuisances who might hide car keys or checkbooks, to being violent, exercising a meaner streak and would start fires or smash household objects. Why one would be picking on the spirit of Emily Buchanan was beyond me, but it was always a possibility. The one thing they all have in common is that they are major jerks just for the fun of it. Chances are, however, it was her killer, who had managed to escape the legal system but not the Fates. In either case, Kit's skill set was the surest way to remove the problem, whichever it might be, permanently.

"Anyway," I continued, "tomorrow I'm going to ask Dr. K if she has any information she can share with us so we have a better idea of who or what we might be encountering. I'm hoping Meg and Alec will come along as well in case we need to pacify any nosy neighbors that might catch an eyeful."

Kit sent me an image of our skirmish with the rusalka when we were searching for Melanie Connors.

"I don't think so; Emily seemed to be the only spirit there at the moment. Rusalkas like to collect more than one for feeding purposes, and Emily didn't seem too faded, especially considering how long she's been there."

The next image she sent was of herself as a small kitten alone in a dark place. I could almost hear the word 'scared' echo faintly in my head as the image faded. Or was it 'lost'? Either translation would work for this situation.

"I imagine she is. I'm not sure why she hasn't moved forward after so many years, unless she doesn't know how or something is tying her to the area where she died." If she was stuck in that area, it was more than likely because she had never received justice for her murder. But it could also be that the other spirit was stronger than she was and wouldn't let her leave. Kit and I could hopefully solve that part of the problem tomorrow.

A few seconds passed, and just as I said his name aloud, Kit sent me an image of Richard.

"That's a good idea. Richard might have some idea on why she isn't leaving or could maybe help her figure out how to move on." But I needed Richard on Laurel duty; besides that, he doesn't really get on with kids, and according to his stories, this was true when he was alive as well.

"They're always sticky and shrieking about something; they make my skin crawl," he had said once at one of our breakfasts the day of a show back when he had first decided to join us.

Alec had raised an eyebrow at him, "Is that why you had your nephews murdered in the tower?"

He had paused then, glaring at my sister. He had spent several weeks before this moment trying to sell us on the idea that he was the ghost of Richard III, which none of us bought, especially because he didn't know French—middle or modern.

Kit snorted her little cat laugh at the tale. I was glad she was feeling better and didn't seem mad anymore.

"Also," I continued, "I wanted to apologize for not understanding the different levels of names cait sith use. In my defense, I've never met one before and figured I never would."

Kit slow-blinked at me, accepting my apology, but also sending me an image of me in a dunce cap, though the words I heard had something to do with it not being my fault as I didn't know, not that I was an idiot.

We stayed awake a little while longer, not really making a plan, just running through possible scenarios that might occur when we returned to help Emily. Our biggest concern was being caught out by the neighbors, either head on or through local law enforcement they might call.

I'm not sure when I dozed off, but the next thing I knew, my phone alarm was chiming and sunlight was streaming through our window. By the time Kit and I pulled ourselves together for the day, Meg showed up at our door, ready to head to Willow's as was our morning routine, a routine I was going to miss when we finally packed out of Boulder for our next gig.

As we sat and sipped our poisons of choice, Alec pulled a piece of paper out of her purse and, looking directly at Kit, started talking.

"So this is a draft of your bio, Kit. We have to get it to the print shop today if we want it in the program this weekend." She theatrically cleared her throat, and started reading.

"Fiona Kindley joined Mustardseed Productions earlier this spring. A Salida native, she discovered her love of acting while playing a witch's familiar in *Macbeth*. When she isn't rehearsing or sitting for costume fittings, she enjoys sharpening her hunting skills on her Kick-a-roo or chasing her catnip mouse."

Kit tilted her head at me.

"Well we can't really say we're witches or furies or that in our spare time we mete out justice and remove dangerous creatures from the world," I stated, but she shook her head at me and sent me an image of my family, the word 'Kindley' whispered through my brain.

"Oh," I said, getting a clearer picture of what she was trying to say. "You're part of our family now, Kit; of course you're a Kindley, if you want to be."

The small cait sith glanced around the table at each of us in turn. When her purr started up it was loud enough for the table nearby to hear. She sent the image of her alone in the dark, storm raging around her, then quickly replaced it with a series of pictures—the poker game last night, my family playing mahjong around the table in the Vista, the two of us inside Gravy's store looking at the toys and the collars, and finally, the whole troupe taking their final bows from our last performance of King Lear. These images were accompanied by first the fear and loneliness she felt before we found her, and then the more positive feelings of having shelter and safety and, best of all, friends she could count on who became family to her. Then she turned sideways and head butted Meg's arm so hard the caffe latte she was holding nearly spilled.

Alec and I, on the other side of the table, got paw bumps.

"I think she's happy to be a Kindley," I said quietly, not sure how much I should reveal about Kit's feelings as I didn't want to embarrass her.

"She fits right in," Alec shrugged one shoulder. "She's got magic, an aptitude for acting, and most importantly, she's a smart ass who gives as good as she gets. It's hard to get any more Kindley than that."

Meg ducked down so Kit could head butt her head this time instead of her arm. "We can be a little overbearing, but you won't be alone anymore, Kit. Even if you might wish you could be if only for a little while."

I smiled and took the travel lid off my affogato so I could dig out the chocolate chunks left behind by the sea salt caramel ice cream I had chosen today over the usual vanilla. "We should get going; if the campers are going off-book today, we might need to do a little magic to help them out."

As we stood, Meg scooped up Kit and handed her to me to put either in my satchel or on my shoulder, depending on where the cait sith wanted to ride. Both my sisters still had coffee left in their cups, so I grabbed what little was left of Kit's ice cream after she arranged herself in the bag, choosing to travel there instead of in the open.

Today was going to be a full day, between working with the campers to help them solidify their lines off book, then working with our own production, and finally returning to help Emily Buchanan escape the "he always finds me" creep, we had a full plate plus dessert.

Chapter 21

When we entered the theatre, we were met with high energy chaos, or what would appear to be chaos to someone unfamiliar with how productions come together. Small groups were everywhere: Guppy was working on altering a few of the costumes while the players were in them; Drs. K and Galloway were fine tuning a scene involving the Gloucester family; and off in one corner, Eliava was running lines with three of the actors who were struggling to remember not just the lines, but when to say them. There was definitely some magic occurring in that corner if Eliava had been tasked to work with them.

My sisters and I slipped in unnoticed, and immediately broke for the areas we thought we could help the most, which for me, was helping Madi not flinch in her costume while Guppy stuck pins in it.

Guppy started talking to me as soon as I got into hearing range. "I've only stuck her once, and it wasn't that bad," she said around a mouth full of pins.

I glanced at Madi for confirmation; her eyes were a bit wide and her voice shook a little when she said, "Not bad at all."

When Guppy looked up at her, surprised at her tone, Madi started laughing.

"Who doesn't get stuck at least once during a fitting?"

I smiled. She was right; fittings weren't really fittings if you didn't get jabbed at least once. It was after the fittings, when, say, someone's dearest siblings would chase said someone around while sing-songing 'I'm gonna pin you' that were more traumatic than the actual fittings themselves. And to be fair, it was only when I got older that I figured out no real pins were involved in the teasing, so they weren't really going to stick me; but six year old me didn't know that at the time. Six year old me also didn't realize how much water I could throw when in a panic, and that I should have waited for the backdoor to completely close before sending a wave of pool water at my tormentors. Live and learn, I guess, but that was the only time I saw regret on Guppy's face about having the pool installed.

While my mom continued to work on the costume, I started to throw some of Kent's lines to the Fool at Madi to see how quickly she could make the correct response. I gave her a head's up about the Act first, then started.

"How chance the King comes with so small a number?"

For a moment Madi just stared at me; I could almost see the gears turning in her head as she searched for the response, which came after just a moment's hesitation.

"An thou hadst been set i' th' stocks for that question, thou'dst well deserv'd it."

We continued on with that scene, Guppy coming in as Lear when he reappeared. Madi's timing was a little slow, but she soon caught up, the hesitation vanishing once her confidence took hold.

We finished the scene about the same time Guppy finished the pinning for Madi's Fool costume, and as we did, Kit, who had been watching us perform, sent me an image of Ember decked out in a replica Fool's outfit.

"Oh yeah, I forgot to ask you this earlier," I said to Madi. "Do you think Guppy could borrow Ember for a little bit. We want to make a costume for her as a gift for Laurel."

Guppy had set all her pins aside and was helping Madi ease out of the costume carefully so as not to undo the alterations she had put in place. "That had totally slipped my mind as well. I promise I'll be careful with her."

Madi flashed us a wide smile, her eyes almost looking like they were about to tear up. "That is so nice of you. I can bring her by the outdoor theatre tonight, if that would be okay. Dr. K has a full day lined up for us; I think she's even bringing in lunch again so we don't let any time go to waste."

Guppy motioned to her next victim, a young man playing several different roles, including the King of France and Goneril's servant Oswald, and shooed Madi and me away.

For the rest of the morning, Madi and I ran her lines, worked on her gesturing, and talked through how she wanted her Fool to come across to the audience. The student King Lear, a college sophomore named Michael, wasn't nearly as tall as Carlos, so Madi was debating whether she should play her Fool not as younger, which worked for Carlos and me because of the height and obvious age difference but older since she and Michael were closer in height and age.

"What if I played her as old, as old as Lear himself even, who's been through the whole family drama since day one?"

We mulled that over for a while, working on her inflection and gait, and by the time we hit the lunch break, she was comfortable with her choice. When she rushed off to talk to the student make-up artists about her idea for an older Fool, I glanced around the theatre looking for Dr. K, whom I found finishing up the transaction with the people who delivered today's lunch.

She saw me coming and started speaking as soon as I was close enough to hear her without her raising her voice.

"Guppy told me about your encounter last night. Emily Buchanan's murder might be in the past, but it is still a topic of intrigue and frustration here."

We moved further away from where the students were now sorting through the lunch offerings, laughing and chatting about their upcoming show. Once we were seated in the back of the house, she continued her tale, keeping her voice low.

"I can't even begin to explain what a fustercluck the whole situation was. True, the party goers on that block were just trying to help, and no one's thinking went immediately to 'murder'; they just thought she might have snuck out because all the other kids were still getting to play and she didn't want to miss anything. But then her body was found, and the entire city changed, almost overnight."

Out of the corner of my eye, I could see Kit making her way to us; Dr. K saw her as well, and waited for the cait sith to arrive before she went on with her telling.

"In the end, the house was covered in the fingerprints of half the block–door knobs, light switches, everything. You know how when you're frantically searching for something you've lost, you look in the same places over and over? That's what happened here: too many people checking the same places again and again. The people whose fingerprints weren't found in the house were the ones searching outside, mostly the teen-agers. The smaller children were gathered together and brought to the house across the street where one parent could watch all of them while the rest searched."

Kit sent me an image of Sherlock, which I translated for Dr. K.

She nodded at Kit. "Oh yes, there were dogs there; they had a kiddie pool set up just for them. A couple were even brought into the house to search before the police were called; so you can see how big of a mess this became. Any prints or fibers found in the house were useless for the most part. When the police finally did arrive, it was too late to set up any zones of no entry; people had been everywhere. Then some of the teens returned with the news they had found her. They took the officers back to the tree, and shortly thereafter, the murder weapon—a good sized rock—was discovered."

The information she shared fleshed out the story Guppy had related last night. I was more interested now in the possible suspects, and asked Dr. K if she could elaborate on that aspect.

"And that is where it gets interesting," she started. "Emily's parents were divorced. Her dad lived in the same area as the Monroes. He is the one person never suspected by the police because he had an airtight alibi for the time of the murder: He was hosting his own party for his company. He was quick to throw his ex-wife's boyfriend, Jason Mallec, under the proverbial bus and went so far as offering a substantial reward for information particularly damaging to him."

"No love lost then in that divorce," I sighed. "Did anyone collect this reward?"

Dr. K shook her head. "Several people tried, and that just added to the confusion in general. Were the tips coming in valid, or just 'hail Marys' by people wanting to get that money? As I said earlier, total fustercluck."

We sat in silence for a moment before she continued.

"It's all the local news could focus on, and then it went national, and shortly after, international; and Edward Buchanan, Emily's father, made sure it stayed there, no matter how much the attention affected the investigation. The entire police department came under scrutiny, and many of the officers and higher-ups lost their jobs or quit over accusations of covering up or contaminating evidence on purpose. And in the midst of this, Emily's mom Cora and Jason were hounded so much they turned on each other, with Cora eventually putting the house up for sale and moving to Seattle and Jason moving to the opposite coast, somewhere in Virginia, I think. For years, theories were batted around, but the ones that seemed most likely had Jason as the killer, though many believed he and Cora had planned the whole thing, including their volatile breakup and were secretly still living together; the other main theory was that Edward paid someone to murder his own daughter to punish his wife for her affair. Within a few years of Emily's murder, Cora drank herself to death, Jason died in a motorcycle accident, and Edward's type A personality and workaholic lifestyle delivered unto him a coronary event of epic proportions."

She paused again as Kit and I pondered over all she had said.

"So now, it's mostly just a story people trot out around the Fourth so they can expand on their ever-growing scenarios of what really happened, and the news will mention it briefly, usually in conjunction with new leads, which are nothing but rumors being used to build some internet personality or pod-caster's viewer subscriber numbers."

She shrugged then, "And that's the story. Nothing was proved, and probably never will be. For all we know, it could have been a stranger, which many people wanted to believe because it's hard to deal with your neighbors if you think they killed someone, much less if that someone was their own child."

I chewed on the inside of my lip, keeping my mouth closed about the horrific statistics of how many children are killed by their parents each year and that the chance of Emily being killed by someone outside the family was statistically lower than one of her two parents or the mother's boyfriend committing the crime. I try to keep up on these numbers because, strangely enough, they help keep me grounded when I'm working on racing the snakes in my hair to find solutions. The point being that the likelihood of finding a stranger killer is low versus accidentally rolling up to a murder victim's parents and going full fury in a matter of seconds and in front of an audience. I know better than to put myself in that situation.

"Anything else?" Dr. K finally asked. "You might be the only person in the world who will ever know the truth about who actually killed that poor girl."

I glanced up and sighed. "And that's only if this spirit is actually the one who killed her; it could just be a poltergeist or other entity that's chosen not to move on for who knows what reason. Either way, we're getting Emily out of that predicament tonight, I hope. Thanks for all the information."

She smiled and squeezed my knee as she stood up to check on how lunch was coming along, already switching back into director-mode. " But you will tell us if it is her killer, won't you?"

I nodded. I always debriefed the moments I freed spirits or laid out some justice on killers with Guppy, and oftentimes my sisters as well, mostly because it's not actually something I could go see a professional therapist about. I guess I could, but then I might be locked up for sanity reasons.

Glancing around the theatre, I caught sight of Guppy, now finished with her costume alterations and helping Eliava with a different couple of student actors who also must have needed a little more magic to help them slide into their roles more comfortably. I headed toward her, scanning the theatre to see where the rest of my family was so I could talk to them about tonight.

When Guppy saw me coming, she excused herself from the small group and headed my way. Once she was near enough that we wouldn't be overheard, I started speaking.

"Has Richard checked in today, yet? I need him to bring me either Lionel or Maxine for the job this evening."

She shook her head. "Not yet; he usually shows up when we move to the Rippon theatre as there are less people. What are you thinking?"

I described my plan for Emily to her, adding in some of the details that Dr. K had given me about the murder suspects, but that I wasn't even sure that's who this spirit was.

"What I need is a ghost who could be a bit more comforting to a child, versus Richard. I'm hoping that either Lionel or Maxine fit that description and will be able to help Emily get to a better place than hanging around and hiding at her murder site." I went on to explain how I wanted Alec and Meg to come along as well in case we had to do some damage control due to overly curious neighbors.

Guppy smiled a little, "Yeah, Richard isn't the ghost you need tonight. As far as your sisters go, we are working on some of their scenes this evening, so I'm going to need them at the theatre. However, I think you're right about needing some back up for possible Gladys Kravitz look-i-loos. How about if Eliava goes with you? She can either help with some memory spells or glamour the whole area you need long enough to get the job done."

I mulled that over for a moment. Eliava was a viable option, and if things went sideways, she was good in a fight as well. "That'll work."

With that matter settled, Guppy scoped out the theatre. Most of the crowd had finished with lunch, which meant it was time for us to head over to the outdoor stage for our own work. As she was finishing her survey, Dr. K's voice rang out, stilling the noise almost immediately.

"Break time is finished. Guppy, good luck to you and your crew today and thank you for this morning's work. My troupe, let's have a brief regrouping and move on to this afternoon's tasks."

I gathered up my satchel, found Kit, and made my way over to the outdoor theatre with my sisters and Saumia, gabbing about the camp and how their show was coming along. Meg mentioned that she had been working with the make-up artists that morning, helping them organize the products for each character.

"Madi's idea for an old Fool is a pretty cool one. Gives a whole new reason for why the character disappears at the end of Act III."

"Did you tell her that?" I asked, knowing that getting recognized for a good idea was a great shot in the arm for any actor, but goes a really long way with newbies.

"I did," Meg confirmed. "I also told her it's a nice contrast to Cordelia. She's also going to play her as an old woman fool as well, which I think adds to that dynamic."

For the rest of the afternoon, it was just the Mustardseed Productions crew, fine tuning some light and sound cues and running through various scenes that didn't have our outside guest actors involved. Dr. Galloway was not our only additional cast; the others had jobs they had to do before coming to work on the show, which was why many of our rehearsals ran into the later evening–it all depended on who could be there at what times.

Since I was going to be out of pocket later in the evening, Guppy had us working on Act III scenes ii and iv, the scenes where Lear devolves into madness on the heath. Eliava was filling in for Dr. Galloway and Bre was filling in for various other characters who had lines here and there. I didn't notice Richard show up until we finished scene iv and Guppy called me over to where she sat with him in the middle rows of the seating.

"I already explained to him what you need," Guppy stated as I neared them. Richard was looking a bit miffed.

"You know," he said as I sat down backwards in the row in front of them, "I could still help you with this kid; I'm not some kind of monster."

I was ready for this. Knowing Richard's mood and his need for drama had trained all of us to have explanations at the ready when we knew he would get crabby over some decision we made. "I know that, Richard, and I appreciate your willingness to put your discomfort aside and help me, but I need someone I trust implicitly to stay with Laurel. I know leaving her with the Stephenses is okay for short periods, like when you come to inform us of what's going on at the hospital. But tonight might take a while, and I would feel so much better knowing it is you sitting there making sure no one messes with Laurel. Maxine can't physically intervene, and Lionel might not realize how important it is to act quickly. I know you do."

I did not look over at Guppy as I spoke, and she pointedly did not look at me either, mostly because if she did, we both might start smiling. Buttering up Richard has become not just an art form but a bit of a game in our family, and it has to be done carefully so as not to hurt Richard's feelings.

The ghost considered what I said. "That is true; Maxine doesn't know how to interact with physical objects yet. I would feel better if Lionel were with you since he can manipulate things, if need be."

"That's a good point, Richard," Guppy joined in the conversation. "I hadn't thought of that. It would be better if it were Lionel just in case." She looked over to me then, her eyes sparkling a bit. "Do you think you need them both, Tisi? It's hard to fill Richard's shoes."

For a brief moment, I thought she had overdone it, and I held my breath, waiting for the scene to implode, but Richard had started nodding as she spoke.

"Yes," he said, thinking a little before he continued. "You might want both of them in case a scrap breaks out."

"Well that's settled then," I said, "I don't know anything about how y'all travel, but if you can get them to the Vista they can ride with me, unless you think sending them directly to the old Buchanan house would be better."

Richard pondered that for a moment. "They're both familiar with the area; I'll probably send them to the house."

"Just have them stay out of sight," I warned him. "Emily is already spooked enough by the creep that's keeping her there. Have them look for the Fiat. Once I get there, we can come up with a plan."

Richard threw me a mock salute and vanished abruptly.

"Impressive," Guppy said, smiling at me. "I wish I had that on video to use as a training tool."

I returned her grin. "I learned from the best."

Chapter 22

Night had fallen by the time Eliava, Kit, and I made our way to the neighborhood where Emily Buchanan used to live and her spirit still haunted. Things were quiet, which wasn't a surprise considering it was a Tuesday night; lights from living rooms, the occasional blue flickering of a television, were the only sources of illumination besides the few porch lights that pushed against the darkness.

The Buchanan house was dark—inside and out, and the overgrowth made the place look a bit like a haunted house from a horror movie, and in some ways it was, but I had no fear of a hockey-masked, knife-wielding psycho swooping down on us. Of course if one did, I wasn't too worried about it. None of those slasher movies ever had a fairy, a fury, or a cait sith glamping about in high heels, wearing revealing clothing, and doing stupid things that many times had me rooting for the psychopath.

We had parked right in front, using the For Sale sign and its free info pages as our first line of defense. Mostly, if you act like you know what you're doing, people tend to leave you alone, but if anyone got too concerned about us loitering, Eliava was already weaving a type of glamour around the area that would not exactly hide us, but give the watcher no reason to be overly curious about what we were doing.

While the fairy stood at the sign, pretending to peruse the info sheet, Kit and I wandered up to the front porch.

"Emily," I softly called, "I brought Fiona to meet you; she's very nice."

Instead of the young girl appearing, Maxine and Lionel slowly came into view.

After greeting them and introducing both Kit (as Fiona) and Eliava, I asked if they had seen Emily yet.

Lionel spoke first. "When we arrived, we saw a small spirit going around to the back of the house; we thought it best not to follow her if she's as skittish as Richard said."

"Did you see anyone else?" Eliava asked.

"No," Maxine responded. "Just the small one, but she was looking around very careful-like."

Kit mewed softly, her whiskers forward as she sniffed around the hedges and the porch itself. She flashed me an image of two spirits and headed around the side of the house to the backyard, her pace quickening as she rounded the corner.

I cast a look back at Eliava, who nodded at me, and all of us took off after the cait sith.

The game of hide and seek was on, and, thanks to Dr. K, I knew exactly where we needed to go: the big tree where Emily's body was found.

Eliava was bringing up the rear of our procession, holding the glamour on us as we trotted to keep up with Kit. The cait sith kept a running visual commentary in my head which featured the tree, and as we kept moving, that tree finally came into view.

I raised my hand, signaling to the parade behind me to slow down while Kit ran ahead. Before I followed her, I turned to the Stephenses. "Wait here. Let us calm Emily down a bit first, then I'll introduce you to her."

When I caught up, Kit had already slipped under the tree. The large branches of the evergreen draped downward, giving the area around the trunk a slight clearing, not enough for me to stand up in, but enough that I could see why the neighborhood kids had used this old tree as a fort or a base for the games they played.

I crawled in and sat down. Emily looked away from Kit to acknowledge me.

"You did come back; I like your kitten," she said, the faintest hint of a small smile on her lips.

Even though she was a spirit, I could see the haggardness in her eyes, the fear that lingered there as she sat in what was probably the exact spot she was in when she was murdered.

I smiled at her. "I told you I would. Her name is Fiona, and she's been waiting all day to meet you. We're also going to help you out of this situation so you can move forward into a better existence than this."

She looked at me skeptically and quietly stated, "He won't let me go."

"I'm pretty sure we can convince him to," I responded. "But I need you to do me a favor."

She tilted her head at me, questioning.

"I brought some people with me who can help you find your way after we take care of the guy bothering you. Maxine and Lionel are friends of mine. Can I invite them into your fort?" I waited for her answer, hoping I was doing this right.

Like Richard, I'm a bit uncomfortable around kids, but not nearly so awkward or dismissive as he is, at least I hope I'm not. The few times I've had to deal with kids, besides when I was one, I've always tried to talk to them like little adults, no baby-talking, or, as I've seen some parents do, talking to them like they were a larger, bit more sentient pet. It's worked for me so far on both the living and the dead, so I must be doing something right.

"Are they nice?" Emily asked, a little tremor in her voice. And who could blame her; the last adult she dealt with killed her.

"Very," I said confidently, "And Maxine was a marine, so she could probably beat up this guy that's trapping you here."

Emily's smile grew a little at that comment. "They can come in. Is Fiona going with you?"

I nodded. "Yeah she is; I need her help. Though she be but little, she is fierce." I doubted Emily would catch the Shakespeare reference, but it was fitting for this occasion. "What I need you to do is stay out of sight, no matter what you hear, okay? Lionel and Maxine will make sure he can't hurt you as long as you stay with them. Is that a deal?"

She blinked a few times before speaking. "Deal."

I clambered out from under the branches and motioned for the Stephenses to head into the tree. After a few moments, Kit came out, flashing me an image of the three ghosts sitting together and chatting.

While I brushed the dirt and needles off the seat of my shorts, my mouth suddenly filled with the cold coppery taste of guilt, and I felt a slight twitching on my head. The snakes were waking up, and with their stirring, I knew that whoever had been hounding this poor girl was the same monster that had purposefully ended her life. And I wanted to know why. I voiced as much to Kit, her fur beginning to spark as the void around her slowly grew in size.

From a trio of large trees further into the park, I heard the faintest call.

"Emily? Where are you?"

It was sung out, like kids do when they're playing games in the vein of hide and seek or ghost in the graveyard, games my sisters and I had played with the other kids on our block. We'd probably been playing those games the same night Emily had been. The coppery earth flavor intensified, and I felt a cold smile slide onto my face.

I could feel Eliava boost the glamour as Kit and I walked away from where Emily hid and toward the voice that had called to her.

"Ready or not," the voice called out again, and the spirit of a man in maybe his early forties stepped out, the smile that had been on his face immediately faltering before falling off completely when he saw me instead of the little girl he had been expecting.

"Who . . . what are . . . where's Emily?" Both his face and his voice went through several changing emotions, starting with confusion, cycling through that to reach suspicion, and finally landing hard on anger.

I had seen enough pictures of all the players in this drama to recognize the spirit standing in front of me, and I wasn't surprised.

"Jason Mallec, I presume?" My voice had changed with the arrival of the snakes, so I was doubly sure that this was the man who had ended Emily's life and was now haunting her, his guilt and anger keeping her from being able to move forward.

Jason tried to fade back into the trees, but the snakes had him. Some of those myths about Medusa have a little basis in reality. Seeing someone with snakes for hair can actually cause a bit of muscle paralysis, mostly through fear or shock. I wasn't actually turning the guy into stone—I'm a fury, after all, not a gorgon.

He glared at me once he figured out he couldn't move. "This has nothing to do with you," he snapped, his eyes going to the tree behind me, the tree where Emily currently sat safely with Maxine and Lionel, Eliava guarding them all.

"But it does," I hissed, the sibilance of my words drawing out the strangeness of the three voices now speaking for me. "Justice is kind of my thing. And Emily deserves justice."

Jason's eyes flashed anger. "She needs justice? What about me? You think this was my idea?"

Kit and I traded looks, the images she sent filled with question marks.

"Are you saying your motorcycle accident wasn't an accident?" I asked, growing a bit confused by his statement.

He snorted angrily. "No, that's not what I meant."

I waited for him to elaborate, the snakes twisting and stretching to get a better look at him, scenting him with their tongues. When he didn't oblige me, I spoke.

"You killed her, Jason. These snakes aren't some kind of party hat I wear for the hell of it. Why did you do it? Are you some kind of perv? Did you get tired of having to deal with another man's kid? What?"

Jason's face had changed when I called him out. "No! I'm not a pervert; that's just . . . that's just sick; you're a sick, sick person to think that."

I took a step closer to him. "So sorry; you're not a pervert, just a child murderer. Feel better now?"

He glared at me, but the fight was leaving him. "What about my justice? I only did this because it's what Cora wanted. It was her idea."

Kit and I exchanged glances again.

"Jason, I don't know how to break this to you, but it was your hand that brought the rock down on her head, a decision you made right before you did it. At any point, you could have decided the other way."

The spirit in front of me started wringing his hands, trying to conjure up tears that would never come and could never change the outcome of this moment even if they did arrive.

"But it was Cora's idea. She told Emily to go hide, but not let anyone see her." His voice had lost some of its anger and was instead filled with the whine of being confronted by a truth that he had long since buried.

I shrugged my shoulders. "It may have been Cora's plan, but it was your hand that held the rock, and your arm that brought it down."

Jason fidgeted a little more, waiting, I think, for me to say words I never could to him– that it wasn't his fault, that since it was all Cora's idea, he was absolved from all the blame, move along, sir, we were sadly mistaken, sorry for taking up your time, have a nice day.

When the silence became too uncomfortable for him, the spirit threw his hands up in frustration. "It worked perfectly, except Cora started drinking more and her guilt began to eat her alive. Our little 'fake' break up became a very real split; she said the sight of me made her sick. So I left her wallowing in a bottle. She knew she couldn't confess because I would spill that the whole idea was hers, all of it. Then she died, and I thought I was home free, went out to celebrate and the tire blew out on my cycle. Stupid way to die and just when I thought I could start living again."

I sighed a little. "She's not here, Jason; for what it's worth, she's probably off in her own personal hell due to her own guilt over starting this whole mess."

"It's not fair," he sulked. "If I apologize to Emily, will you let me go?"

I shook my head. "No can do, Jason. Emily should have been free to move on a long time ago, and again, you could have made the decision to let that happen. But you didn't, just like you didn't make the decision to not kill her."

As I finished speaking, Kit, the sparking void around her nearing the size of Sherlock, leapt forward and engulfed the spirit in front of us. He shrieked once, but didn't fight the cait sith as she absorbed him. With Jason not fighting, Kit was finished with him in about twenty seconds, and once he was gone, the void shrunk down and she started licking her fur back into order, dispersing all the remaining sparks.

We slowly walked back to the tree, allowing the snakes time to drop limply into locks of hair and my voice to become only mine once again. But my scalp still twitched, letting me know that while this particular issue was over, there was still something going on concerning Laurel, even if I couldn't figure out what it was.

Eliava raised her eyebrows in an unspoken question as we approached: Finished?

I nodded and called out to the spirits under the tree. "He's gone, Emily. You can come out now."

The trio of ghosts slowly emerged, Emily looking around nervously, searching for her tormentor who would never be visible to anyone again.

"You did it," she finally whispered when she was certain Jason was well and truly gone.

Lionel was smiling at me. "That was quite a show."

He caught the look I threw at him and continued on quickly. "I'm the only one who saw; the gals here were too busy gabbing about the merits of a good hiding spot."

Maxine grinned. "I was the hide and seek champion of my neighborhood when I was little. I wasn't afraid to hide where there might be critters and such."

I smiled back, then glanced over to Emily. "I think his guilt was trapping you here, Emily, but I also think you might be trapping yourself. You know about your mom's involvement, am I right?"

The little girl looked down at her feet. "Yes." She paused for a moment, trying to form her next question. "Why didn't she love me?"

And this right here is exactly why dealing with the spirits of children is not something I like doing. How do you explain to people so young the intricacies of emotions beyond their understanding? That the person or persons responsible for bringing them into the world had eschewed the responsibility of that decision to bring forth a life and so decided to remove it from this plane of existence because they no longer wanted that responsibility, or worse, that particular life essence was cramping their style. If Guppy were here, she would know what to say and how to deliver it. As I was searching for a response, my mouth opening and closing like a fish on land, Maxine, whose eyes had filled with sympathy at the question Emily had asked, turned to the girl, dropped to her knees to be on eye-level with her, and spoke softly.

"Some adults are just incapable of showing love the way they should, and it has nothing to do with you, sweetheart. There are people who can't feel past their own needs, and I think your mom was one of those people. They're incapable of loving anyone but themselves. But that was not, and never will be, your fault."

Emily looked at her, her smile quivering as she tried to cry, but like all ghosts, the tears couldn't come.

Maxine stood back up. "You should come with us back to the hospital, Emily. Lionel and I are helping protect a young woman who narrowly avoided being killed. Maybe you can help us. I sure would like your company; I'm a little new at being dead."

Emily's smile gained in strength. "How can you be new at being dead?"

I missed the answer as the three spirits took a few steps, fading as they did so, and reappearing, I presume, back at the hospital. I wish I had explained to Maxine about Richard's discomfort when around kids, but I think the former gunnery sergeant would be able to handle him.

Once they were gone, Eliava turned to Kit and started talking. "That was amazing. I've seen cait sith in action before, but none were quite as sparkly."

Kit jumped into my arms and scrambled onto my shoulder, yawning as she made herself comfortable. I tried to translate what I was both seeing and hearing to the fairy.

"I think she said she likes the added drama, but it might have been something about going for style points."

Eliava laughed and then started texting on her phone. She continued to do so as we headed back to the Fiat. As we neared the car, she said, "Guppy says to just go on to Baker Hall; the rehearsal is just about finished, and she wants to hear all about what happened."

"Check," I said, sliding in and helping Kit into the back seat as Eliava entered the passenger side. Once we were all in, I cast a final look back at the Buchanan house. It didn't seem as dark and foreboding as it had. Maybe the realty company would be able to sell it now.

As we drove on, I could hear a soft snoring coming from the backseat. Kit was already asleep. I guess the devouring of a soul was a bit taxing or maybe it was a kind of over-full stomach nap. Whatever it was, it was well deserved. Emily could move on now, and it had been another successful excursion for me and the cait sith. We were really becoming quite the team.

Chapter 23

The following morning, Kit and I slept in, per Guppy's orders. She had been waiting for us outside the door to our room. But instead of coming in and debriefing the evening's events, she asked me only two questions: 'Are you both okay,' and 'is Emily free'. I was able to answer 'yes' to both; it was then that she told us to sleep in the next day, and she would see us at the theatre closer to noon than to eight am.

It isn't often that I get to take a leisurely morning when we are involved in a workshop-type production. I think I made it to about nine-thirty before I started getting antsy about what was going on at the theatre; of course that also could have just been my bloodstream calling out for caffeine and ice cream all packaged up in one good-sized to-go cup of deliciousness.

As I stood to leave the room, I noticed that Kit was still snoozing, one paw curled up over her eyes, shielding them from the sunlight streaming into the room. I quickly grabbed my shower kit and headed off to prepare for the day. When I returned, Kit was taking her own bath, and only acknowledged my return by sending me an image of her sparkly collar.

I gave her a few more minutes to finish, then hooked the piece of jewelry around her neck. She spent a couple seconds checking out her image in the mirror, then headed to my satchel, the word 'Willow's' floated into my head.

"Already on the schedule, hep cat," I said, waiting to grab my bag as she finished securing herself inside.

Both of us were fighting yawns as we made our way out of Willow's and toward the theatre. I was half finished with my affogato, waiting for the caffeine to kick in and clear the cobwebs out of my head. Kit had finished most of her ice cream, knowing I would carry it for her and she could finish it at the theatre. The day was going to be beautiful again, weather-wise, which had been the norm since we got here.

We snuck quietly into the theatre, heading unobtrusively to the back to finish our breakfast treats. I could see Alec, Meg, and Saumia working with their understudies, helping them put the finishing touches on their costumes. Guppy was working with Madi since I hadn't been there early; I hoped she would let me know the reason she gave for my lateness before someone asked me. I was guessing she had whipped up a story about me having a headache of some sort the night before and that I had snuck up to my room without anyone noticing to sleep it off. But it would be nice to have confirmation before I opened my mouth and potentially stuck my foot in it.

Dr. K was currently circling the stage, making notes on her ever-present clipboard. Asher walked with her, taking pictures of the stage tape marks. The students were about to move out of the University Theatre and begin work on the outdoor stage. They would be using our blocking for the most part, but there had been a few changes. Asher, Mike, and the rest of our tech crew would spend some time setting up the differences to ensure that the campers made a smooth transition to a new space.

Madi noticed us first; she started waving, which sent Guppy's attention our way as well. The first thing my mom did when she saw me looking was tap the side of her head with a couple fingers. This gesture let me know that I, indeed, had been suffering from some sort of headache, probably a migraine as that type of pain also could explain away when I had to wear sunglasses to hide any growing blackness in my eyes. I had checked that in the bathroom mirror this morning when I got up to shower and came to the conclusion that I was okay without shades for the moment, but I did have them secure in my bag should the need arise.

After saying a few words to Madi, Guppy started to make her way to the back of the theatre where Kit and I were sitting, finishing our Willow's treats. Dr. K had also seen the exchange, made her excuses to Asher, and headed toward me as well.

Once they reached me, I started quietly answering the inevitable question of who had murdered Emily and what exactly had happened when we confronted the spirit.

Dr. K listened intently, shaking her head as I finished the tale.

"So the conspiracy of Cora and Jason working together was right. That one at least had more credibility than Edward hiring someone to kill his daughter, but still."

I shrugged. "Nothing really surprises me anymore when it comes to the motivations of murderers. I wish it did. The only surprise here is that Jason didn't sabotage Cora's car or poison her before he left, just to ensure she kept her mouth shut. She must have been really far down the neck of a bottle."

Guppy appeared to think that over for a minute before speaking. "Maybe she still loved him, or maybe he figured no one would believe her. Either way, Emily is free, and that is what matters."

"Exactly!" Dr. K said, clapping her hands together, a mannerism she shares with Guppy when they want to signal a change of direction. "Let's get this show over to the outdoor stage and see what we need to polish."

She stood and began walking toward the stage, clapping her hands again and calling out loud enough so everyone in the theatre could hear her. "Time to move, Poppets!"

At her command, the student cast, all decked out in their medieval finery, began the stroll over to the Mary Rippon Theatre. It wasn't a long walk, and there weren't many people lingering on the campus, but those who were out and about stopped to watch.

When the clapping and whistling started, the students, like the actors they were, slipped into character and began to wave, some stopping to curtsy or bow or to nod like royalty at the 'peasants' who had come to see a royal procession. Lear looked regally down his nose at the crowd that had moved closer, beginning to take their phones out for pictures; Lear's daughters followed his actions, except for Cordelia, who waved and smiled sweetly, blowing kisses; Edgar nodded regally, Edmund scowled, and the Fool flitted among them all, held bunny ear fingers over Lear's head, stuck her tongue out at Goneril, then turned an adoring gaze to Cordelia.

Dr. K allowed them their moment in the sun and took the opportunity to throw in an advertisement with her stage voice. "Please come see us perform *King Lear* on Saturday and Sunday afternoon at the Mary Rippon Theatre! Tickets available online. We would love to see you there."

The rest of us followed slowly, giving the cast distance so they could ham it up for the impromptu audience. I could see Guppy smiling at their antics. She had trained all of us to become our characters the second we were in costume, and it appeared that either she or Dr. K or both had instilled that skill into the students. Money could buy all kinds of advertising, but the best way to hype a show was to do what the students were doing now: flirting with a potential audience and piquing their curiosity. Whenever we performed in conjunction with a festival, we would perform little pieces in costume while on the festival grounds, as Derek and Saumia had done in Salida. Sometimes we were tipped, but the main reason we did it was to drum up business. The fuller the house, the better the performance; we feed off the energy of our audiences, as most actors do.

By the time we reached our destination, the students were riding high on being seen in character by strangers for the first time. It took a minute for Dr. K to regain control of them, but she did let them enjoy the moment for a bit, knowing they needed to get the energy out and that what had just occurred would be a great incentive to work hard for the rest of the afternoon and into the evening, which is just what we did.

Once the students were finished, we would begin our own practice, which wasn't nearly as rigorous as what the kids had done. We mostly discussed any changes that we wanted to include, worked through the more difficult scenes, like those including fist-fights or sword-play, or in this case, cat-kicking, which is a new one for all of us.

Before she left, Madi told me she was going to the hospital to sit with Laurel, which was pretty much what she did every night after practice, but tonight they were going to work on writing a personal note from Laurel that would go into the literature about the new trust, a sort of thank you for thinking about donating kind of thing.

"She still doesn't remember who pushed her; I don't think she ever will since it was so dark, but the police have started questioning everyone again. Ms. Faulkner doesn't want me going over to the house alone anymore. Not that she thinks I'm going to be attacked, but because she doesn't want the police to think I'm tampering with things. So now when I go to water and feed the wildlife, either she or Ms. Norris meet me there. It's weird, but I get it."

I watched her join the rest of her troupe as they set off for the theatre building to change and go about their lives, then turned my attention back to the stage where Alec, Meg, and Kit were working on the most physical scene for all of them. Kit was getting better at selling both getting booted and the pain that followed. By the time they finished and we all packed up for the night, I knew the cait sith was going to sleep like a rock.

When Guppy called it a night, she let us know that we would be meeting the students at the outdoor stage tomorrow, but not to rush. We were getting ready to start the run of our last four shows, and she wanted us well-rested and relaxed for Thursday's performance.

Nobody argued with her. It had been a whirlwind of action since we arrived, especially for me and all the extracurriculars I had been involved in when not with the camp or my own troupe. I planned on sleeping in, making sure Kit also slept in as well, having a leisurely affogato after a nice relaxing shower, and then sitting in the audience helping fine tune the students' performance until it was time to get ready for our own show.

And in a perfect world, that's exactly how the day should have gone, but the world is not perfect; it's not anywhere close to being perfect.

Granted, Thursday morning went great: Kit and I slept in; I took a nice long shower; my ice cream coffee was heavenly as always. Working with the student actors was easy, as mostly we sat as an audience and provided feedback for Dr. K on each scene as it unfolded. Most of the feedback was positive; the campers knew their lines, found their marks, and generally proved they were just about ready to do this for real for an audience full of family and friends and strangers.

At one point, I received a text from Officer Larkes informing me that Sherlock had passed his first series of trials, and he was hoping to come see the show Saturday, having already asked for the day off. I responded appropriately, congratulating them both and assuring him that I would have seats reserved on the aisle, as that's where service dogs sit. I know technically Sherlock is not a service dog, but he is a police dog, and exceptions can be made for him. I told Kit they were coming and she started purring.

Midway through the practice, Penelope Faulkner and Beth Norris arrived, the latter with her phone out, taking pictures of the actors and the set while her superior spoke with Dr. K, who began scanning the audience. When she caught sight of Guppy, she waved her up to the stage while continuing her conversation with the lawyer.

Once my mom had reached them, the trio moved off to the side to speak; Ms. Norris continued to take pictures, and Dr. Galloway took over the direction, dragging the performers' attention back to the task at hand.

Kit, long finished with her ice cream, but still working on getting her whiskers clean, sent me three letters: WTF?

I turned to her, surprised. "Who taught you that? It was Asher, wasn't it. What kind of manners are you learning when you're playing poker?"

She rolled her eyes at me. Instead of an image, I heard "Qué?"

My surprise went up a notch. "You know Spanish now?" She had been spending considerably more time with Carlos as the three of us had many scenes together. I guess I shouldn't be surprised. My own Spanish was rudimentary at best, and I suddenly wondered if Kit would pick up languages easier than I ever could. Not gonna lie, I think I was a bit jealous of her at that point.

She slow-blinked at me and twitched her tail, finally deciding that her face was clean enough to stop working on it, and sent me an image of the lawyers.

I looked back to the action occurring on the stage, including the action that had nothing to do with *King Lear*. "I don't know. Maybe they're getting pictures to help publicize the trust? I know Guppy has offered to help get the thing rolling at our Saturday show, right after the campers perform."

The cait sith appeared to think that over as she settled into a loaf position next to me, face pointed to the stage, eyes slowly narrowing to slits. We were nearing the time that the students would leave and we would fix any stage dressing for our own performance. That meant that it was nearly time for Kit to go take her pre-show nap, and as her roommate, it was my responsibility to make sure that she did.

Before I could stand up to go, Mike walked back to where we were sitting, holding a program in his hand.

"Thought Kit might want to see this," he smiled, handing me the booklet. "Dr K. has some great connections around here. I'm surprised they got it updated and printed so quickly."

Kit sat up, waiting for me to flip through to find her entry.

Once I found it, she crowded closer, nearly knocking the thing from my hand. The picture was adorable. She was facing the camera, head tilted just a little to the right, ears fully forward, eyes wide open, and rhinestone collar glimmering.

She looked back to me then, and head-bonked my arm, nearly making me drop the program again. When the bacon and eggs image hit, I knew she was happy.

So that part of the day went well, and so did Kit's pre-show nap, which allowed me time to go back and help with dressing the stage and learn why the lawyers had come out to speak with Dr. K and take pictures. They were, in fact, putting together not just an information sheet that would be made available at tonight's show and those that followed, but also a website, complete with pictures of the current production, that would allow patrons to learn about the trust, receive updates about upcoming shows and events, and make online donations.

I also learned that the trust board had decided to formally kick the whole shebang off during the time between the student show Saturday afternoon and ours later that evening, and that they would be attending our show, having already purchased tickets to give to certain community members they knew would want to be founding donors.

In other words, we needed to be at our best Saturday to woo these potential donors into writing hefty checks. I'm just going to add here that we always do our best at shows; we don't hold back. Mustardseed Productions goes all out every time we perform.

So, the afternoon and early evening part of the day went by swimmingly as well. We had a full house for a Thursday, which can be rare, but not really considering where we were. Boulder has a great appreciation for the arts, and our audiences for each performance had all been full.

We also nailed our performances. The abuse of Kit and her eventual death hit the audience hard, hard enough so that when Lear entered the stage with the dead Cordelia in his arms, no one was even attempting to hide the fact that they were weeping.

This included me. I just cannot get to the end of this play without crying. All tragedies have multiple characters dying or dead by the end, but for some reason, *Lear* just hits harder than the others.

We took our curtain calls, basking in the applause and love that our audience showed us. Carlos received a standing ovation for his portrayal of Lear, again, and Kit did as well. I wondered briefly if the applause was a reaction to her acting or to the fact that she was unhurt, as if cats can't be trained the same as dogs to perform. Of course, our cat was a cait sith, and if she could speak, she could probably pull off a major role.

For the first time that I can remember, more people wanted to get pictures with Carlos and Kit together instead of Saumia and our shifter brothers, although they still had plenty waiting to snap selfies with the unnaturally handsome entities they were.

It wasn't until the interaction between the cast and the audience had tapered down to just a few people chatting while the rest of us cleaned up that the day suddenly went south.

Dr. K had been present for our show, as she had for all our performances in Boulder. She helped us backstage, fixing costumes, adjusting the setting if needed—basically being a jack of all trades to make sure the show went smoothly. She had been on her phone for most of our interactions with the audience, furiously texting with someone right as all the curtain calls had finished.

The next time I noticed her, she was huddled up with Guppy discussing something, her phone still clutched in her hand. When she saw me watching them, she motioned me over, glancing around to see that no outsiders were still present, taking pictures or whatnot.

As I approached the two women, I could see that both of their faces were lined with concern, and Dr. K's mouth was turned down at the corners. Whatever she had been texting about was serious.

"Tell me," I said when I was close enough for only them to hear.

Guppy's face was solemn as she spoke. "Madi just texted from the hospital. Cal Garrett was just brought in. She's not sure what's going on, but from what she's overheard, he isn't expected to make it."

Chapter 24

The next morning as my sisters, Kit, and I made our way to Willow's, I realized that no one had gotten much sleep the previous night. I thought maybe it was just me, but my sisters were both yawning more than usual. More of our crew were also heading in that direction than the other mornings, and all of us would order the largest size available for whatever drink we were getting. Whatever event happened to Cal Garrett affected the whole troupe, and we were all hoping for a little more information this morning.

As we stood in line behind Carlos, Cole, and Derek, who had beaten us in the door, two words worked their way into my sleep-addled brain.

Mas grande.

I looked down at Kit and she blinked at me. "More Spanish? I guess it's good you're practicing." When I looked back up, Carlos quickly looked away, hiding a smirk.

"Are you teaching her Spanish?" I demanded.

"Moi?" he teased, reaching out a hand to Kit who pushed her head into it for scritchies.

I sighed. "I'm drawing the line at French; you know I'm bad at languages." And I am. I had to take two years of a language to graduate high school, and I was lucky to escape Señora Escobedo's Spanish I and II with a C, which she assured me was because I wasn't trying hard enough. The only reason I had managed to pass was because of Carlos, who would help me study if he was around, making up songs to help me remember things. I took so many tests humming weird little tunes to myself, that the señora would always sit me in the back of the room so I wouldn't bother anyone else. I suppose the humming was just one more quirk that the 'weird' Kindley sister had.

Instead of meeting up at the indoor theatre, everyone was meeting at the outdoor stage. While the student performers would still get ready inside the University Theatre Building, they wouldn't be spending much time there beyond prep work. Dr. K was going to run them through the show with no stops, taking notes as they progressed. This was an exciting moment for the kids, but also a nerve wracking one. It was also a study in staying quiet for Dr. K. Once they were finished with the performance, they would debrief everything, with the actors going first with what they thought had been done well and what hadn't, before the director would scan her notes and bring the hammer down, if need be.

When we arrived, Madi was already in costume and working on her slightly limping gait. I had suggested giving her a cane, which she could also use in various ways to accentuate things she was saying. I was happy to see that Dr. K liked my suggestion as Madi was clutching a gnarled wooden walking stick, which looked more like a wizard's staff than a cane, but it fit. The Fool is, after all, one of the wiser characters in the play, even if that wisdom is hidden in rhyme and song.

She smiled when she saw me coming, and started speaking immediately when I reached her side.

"Crazy about Mr. Garrett, isn't it? I'm still not sure what happened, but there were more police on Laurel's floor when I left last night."

"Was it an accident or something?" I asked, hoping she might know a little more than she thought was important.

She shook her head. "Nothing. Everyone is being very tight-lipped about it."

Before I could speak, Dr. K clapped her hands and called her students to her for a run-down on what they were about to undergo.

While she did that, Mustardseed Productions took seats in the audience in various places—the tech crew up front and the rest of us spread out to cover every zone. Our job this morning was to make sure we could hear everyone and understand what they were saying. We each focused on our understudy; Guppy, Eliava, and Bre focused on the other characters, juggling multiple clipboards so each actor would get their own feedback sheet.

Guppy had thrown me a look after Madi had left to join her fellow cast members on stage, and I responded by shaking my head and shrugging my shoulders. I had no news to share.

For the next three hours and odd minutes, we watched *The Tragedy of King Lear* slowly unfold, taking notes both for Dr. K and for the characters we were observing. Whatever magic had been employed, it was working, highlighting a very talented cast whose nervous energy slowly faded into a professionalism that was wonderful to see.

When they finished, we applauded heartily, only stopping when Dr.K motioned for silence. In the time we had left before noon, we debriefed with the cast, shared our notes with them and with Dr. K, and worked on the larger issues with the individuals who needed a little more help. Eliava worked with those cast members, strengthening whatever magic she had employed earlier.

Once my part in the critiquing was finished, Kit was ready to go take her pre-show nap, and to be honest, so was I. A few other members of our troupe were also returning to the dorms, looking to catch up on some missed sleep or just relax a bit before call time.

I wasn't sure I had even fallen asleep before a knock sounded on my door. Kit's ears twitched as I went to answer it, but she didn't fully wake up, which made me a bit jealous. I guess the giant affogato I'd had that morning wasn't ready to let me get some rest so easily.

When I answered the door, Eliava was there with Maxine in tow. A faint smile reached the fairy's lips, but her eyes held concern.

"She was looking for you or Guppy, but she found me instead. I think you'll want to hear what she has to say. Your mom is still at the theatre, so we need to take good notes."

I invited them in and sat next to Kit to leave room for our guests to make themselves comfortable. Eliava perched on the desk; Maxine opted to sit on my bed.

"First off, Richard sent me. I'm sorry I didn't find you right away; I'm new at this," she started, and both Eliava and I assured her it was fine. "I figured it would be better if I didn't go to the theatre."

We waited again for her to arrange her thoughts; when she was ready, she started speaking, keeping track of her points on her fingers.

"Cal Garrett apparently poisoned himself using the same drugs and type of Scotch that were used on Laurel, maybe even a bottle taken from the Monroe house; that was unclear. When he missed his evening shift and the opening of Cesare's the next morning, and no one at the restaurant could reach anything but his voice messages, one of them called the police."

She paused here, looking to see if we understood so far or had questions. When we didn't, she continued.

"The police went to his house and found him face down sitting at the kitchen table, the bottle of Scotch next to him as well as a handwritten note that read *I'm sorry*."

Eliava and I both raised our eyebrows at this information as the spirit rushed on with her points before she forgot.

"They pumped his stomach, but the damage to his organs was already done. They have him hooked up to a machine, but don't think there's a chance he's going to wake up. Richard didn't want to leave Laurel alone, so Lionel is in her room while Richard has moved to where they are keeping Garrett so he can listen in on what is going on." She stopped and looked at us in turn, her expression grim.

Eliava spoke first. "Thank you for filling us in; we've been on pins and needles all day over what had happened; I'm not sure any of us expected it to be this."

She was right. I had been expecting a car accident of some sort, not a suicide attempt. I noticed Kit had been listening, waking up when she heard Maxine's voice. She sent me an image of the very pregnant Mama

Matilda, only her image had the squirrel balancing a thick pair of glasses on her nose.

Curiouser and curiouser, I thought to myself and sighed, "Well, to give her credit, it was stormy that night, and it was late; she might have still been half asleep when she thinks she saw Laurel leave."

Kit yawned for an answer, stood for a second or two before turning around a few times and curling back up in a cinnamon-roll shape, one paw draped over her eyes.

Pushing herself slowly off the desk, Eliava also let out a sigh. "I guess the police reopening Laurel's case freaked him out a bit. From all you've said about him, he seems wound tight; I guess the stress of waiting to be interviewed again took its toll on his mental state."

I thanked Maxine again as she also stood to go. "If Richard hears anything else, let us know. Oh, and thank him for keeping an ear open to news about Garrett, and thank your husband for taking care of Laurel."

Before she could leave, Eliava asked one more question. "How's Emily?"

The spirit smiled. "She's hanging out in Laurel's room. Turns out they went to the same elementary school for a while before the divorce happened. I'll keep you posted. Maybe I won't get lost when I need to come back next time," she said, and with that vanished through the door, already on her way back to the hospital, or someplace thereabouts if she struggled with traveling again.

As Eliava opened the door, she turned back to me before stepping out. "You want to tell your mom or should I?"

I wanted to think about this information for a while, so I asked the fairy if she would spill the tea to Guppy; that should give me enough time to think through everything I'd heard while attempting to catch up on my sleep for tonight's performance.

Of course, I wasn't able to get a nap in because my head was working through all the moments Meg or Alec had picked up on Garrett's anger or on his jealousy, the rage he had felt while arguing with Moira in the coffee shop, or the throw away remarks on becoming the new owner of the restaurant he ran for the Monroe empire. His attitude toward his employees had set me off when we first went to Cesare's for lunch, had set off my sisters as well. The obvious disdain he had toward Laurel, toward anyone who stood higher on some metaphorical ladder than he did had painted him as the obvious suspect in her 'accident.'

Now it seemed he had confirmed that. With all the bluster he carried himself with, I guess the thought of being put on the hot seat at the police station had rattled him. I would have never taken him for the type to remove himself from a situation so permanently. I guess a fear of a life behind bars, because I'm sure Ms.

Faulkner would have pushed for that or worse, got into his head and messed with it a little, or really, quite a bit.

Because I couldn't sleep, I decided to text Officer Larkes the latest development in the Laurel situation and to let him know his ticket would be waiting at the will call box in the University Theatre Building. Then I tried to get a little shut eye, pushing the thoughts out of my head and letting the information just swirl around; I hoped if I left it alone, maybe it would start to put itself into some kind of order.

I must have finally drifted off because I jerked awake when my text message alert went off. For a brief moment, I thought I might have slept through call time, but it was only Ethan returning my text.

Are you free? Call me.

With no audience, this should be easy, I thought, though worried because apparently it was either too much information to type or sensitive information he didn't want a written record of floating around. I dialed immediately and he picked up just as quickly.

"Tisi," he said instead of hello. "I made a call to my academy friend, Julissa. She confirms what Richard passed on to you. She also confirmed that the bottle of Scotch is one taken from the Monroe house, but the amount of sedative in it was more than triple what Laurel consumed. So he apparently added more so as to not end up in intensive care. He was on the list to be re-interviewed today."

I sighed. "What about the note? Any news on its authenticity?"

"It appears to be his handwriting and not a forgery; the tablet and pen were found on the table with the Scotch; his prints were on all of it."

"Well crap," I huffed. "I guess I had an unreliable witness in Mama Matilda."

I heard him chortle a bit on the other end. "You'll find most witnesses are unreliable, but their information is still important. Your squirrel may have seen Garrett or she may have seen Laurel or she may have seen someone completely off your radar. Just because we have a note doesn't mean we have a killer, or attempted killer. The interviews will still go on; Boulder PD isn't closing this case just because of a note, or the Monroes' lawyer."

"But the Scotch is from the house? Maybe the same bottle Laurel was drinking," I countered.

"And you said it yourself days ago. Whoever pushed Ms. Monroe had a key; carrying out a bottle of liquor would be simple. It would fit in that bag you use to carry Kit around. From what I know about Boulder, everybody carries a backpack all the time. Keep your eyes and ears open. Julissa and the department are still investigating, dotting the i's and crossing the t's, if you will. We can talk more Saturday after the show. I gotta go. See you soon."

With that, he hung up, and I sat there with my mouth hanging open wondering, in the brain fog of having just woken up, if he had just asked me on a date or if he was referring to the meet and greet after the show. He probably meant that latter, but why had my brain even gone to the former?

"Get a grip, Tiss," I whispered, not that it mattered. Kit had woken up during our conversation, and now she flashed me a picture of the stage, suggesting we go ahead and leave for call time. Dr. K was providing us with some snack trays before the production so we weren't having a full meal, and Kit wanted to see what was available.

I slipped off her collar and grabbed my bag. All of this could wait until the show was finished tonight. After locking my door, we set off, my brain switching between the unfolding situation with Cal Garrett and the conversation with Ethan Larkes.

"Get a grip," I repeated as we exited the building. The show always comes first.

Friday's audience was as appreciative as Thursday's had been, and it took us a little longer to wrap things up after the show, but that might have been because we were too busy talking about the situation with Cal Garrett and Laurel Monroe.

I was not the only one who felt that something was off, just not quite right, as far as this latest suicide attempt went. After all someone had tried to convince the world that Laurel was also so despondent that she was looking for a way out, and that little plan had failed. And it had failed because of two things: there wasn't enough sedative in the Scotch, and Laurel may have drunk enough to make her not stiffen up for the fall, so it didn't kill her, sort of like how drunk drivers many times survive horrific accidents because they don't tense all their muscles when the crash happens.

Assuming Mama Matilda needs glasses, if Cal Garrett had tried to kill Laurel, he learned that more sedative was needed; he probably also learned to check for a pulse to make sure someone is actually dead before exiting the house. If he'd worn gloves, it wouldn't have left a print, so maybe he was rushed or nervous and now believed he couldn't keep up the charade through another police interrogation.

Or maybe it wasn't him.

Putting the squirrel back into the equation, whoever had drugged the Scotch also learned that the dosage wasn't enough, and so when they went to remove Garrett from the land of the living, they put that knowledge to use

When Meg caught me staring off into space instead of organizing my part of the costume storage for tomorrow, including the student costumes as they would be on stage first, I explained my conversation with Officer Larkes and how I wished I had a crime board to keep track of everything.

She nodded sympathetically. "It all hinges on that squirrel, which sounds ridiculous when you say it aloud. But Larkes is right about the note. Garrett could have been apologizing for taking the last plums out of the ice box for all we know."

I gave her a lopsided smile for the literary reference, which grew into a full smile when she offered to help me finish up my chores. Tomorrow would be hectic, what with getting the students prepared for their show and then resetting everything for our own performance in front of not just a usual audience, but an audience filled with potential donors to a fledgling trust.

We had just finished up my section when Guppy called for the lights to be shut down and for all of us to head home and get a good night's sleep so we would be well rested for tomorrow's full schedule.

After we entered the residence hall, we all split up to head to our rooms, and Meg hugged me suddenly. "I know your brain is working through all this information, but try to sleep. Sometimes the simplest solution is actually the right one."

Chapter 25

The circle up out of sight of the growing audience was electric as the nerves of the students were humming with both anxiety and excitement. Dr. K was leading them in some vocal exercises, trying to achieve that balance of nerves and energy that tends to produce the best shows. Too many nerves, lines often get dropped; too much energy, the timing can get botched. When the two are in harmony, a production flows naturally, drawing the audience in and holding them captive. Both Dr. K and Guppy are masters when it comes to prepping a cast for a first show. Most of the fidgeting had stopped, and from where I was standing, I could see the students cease to be themselves and slowly become the characters they had worked on so hard for the past two weeks.

Guppy and Meg were working at a table set up at the back of the house, talking to people about the trust, handing out the information brochure, complete with pictures taken by Ms. Norris, and waving anyone who looked interested over to them. Saumia, Cole, and Derek were handing out these same pamphlets as people entered the space, occasionally helping someone find their seats or manage a walker or cane.

Asher and the tech crew had finished testing all the lights long ago and were now in their positions for the show itself. Thirty minutes before showtime, Asher turned on the music, the first step to transporting an audience to a different time or place.

For *Lear*, we usually don't change the time period or setting like we do some of the others, mostly the comedies. When we do change the era, we play music to bring our audience into our interpretation before the show even starts. Guppy has created playlists highlighting music from various decades and cultures so that once she's decided on when and where to set a show, she has the music ready to go. The *Lear* playlist is music from the Renaissance era, which mostly features lutes, recorders, gambas, and harpsichords, and cannot be mistaken for anything modern.

As I glanced around the house looking for people who needed a helping hand, a couple around Guppy's age tentatively approached me, smiling, but unsure of themselves.

"Are you Tisi?" the woman asked, her voice quiet.

When I nodded, she continued. "We're Madi's parents. She's told us so much about you and your troupe, we feel like we know you."

I felt my breath escape me in an inaudible sigh of relief. Strangers make me nervous, especially when they know who I am. The introduction helped calm my anxiety.

"It's so good to meet you," I said, a smile sliding onto my face. I was calling up all my social interaction talents at once, hoping I didn't overdo any of them.

Her dad spoke next. His voice was gruff, but friendly. "This camp has been the best thing for her, next to Laurel recovering. I understand you're the one who talked her into staying."

"Guilty," I confirmed, "but Dr. K also had a hand in it; we sort of tag-teamed her."

Mrs. Drake reached out and placed her hand on my arm. "We just wanted to thank you for taking her under your wing, helping her with her lines, and just listening to her talk about Laurel, especially when it was touch and go there for a while."

I was proud of myself for not flinching or pulling back when she touched me, but I did glance around to help me refocus, noticing that the house was filling up and that the trio from the law firm had arrived—Faulkner, Norris, and Dandridge. "She's really good. I'm so glad she stayed with us. Do y'all need help finding your seats? That's my job right now."

Mr. Drake presented the tickets. "I think we're up front somewhere. Madi chose the seats."

I motioned with my free arm to the front, and began leading them toward the stage, her mom never releasing me. Once I had them safely seated, I turned to make my way back to the middle of the house, searching for anyone else who looked confused and lost.

It was then I noticed the cold and bitter taste of guilt resting on my tongue, and I cast a quick glance at the Drakes, noticing that Mrs. Drake also fit Mama Matilda's description. I chewed on the inside of my cheek, scanning the audience. Most of the women present could be described by the squirrel's testimony. More than half the people seated and wandering around fit it. Mama Matilda probably needed glasses, and Meg was right, sometimes the obvious solution is the right one.

I headed to the back of the house where Guppy and Meg were still handing out brochures to the rapidly growing crowd. A few people were confused about their seating, so I led them away, catching sight of Alec doing the same thing. We continued to help seat people, only pausing when Asher flashed the lights, cuing the audience that it was nearly time, and they needed to sit down.

The house was a little more than half full, which is great for a Saturday matinee student performance. Dr.

K came out on stage as Asher flashed the lights again and slowly reduced the volume of the music until it was gone, allowing her to welcome the audience, thank them for their support, and brag about the students they were about to see perform. She mentioned both the trust and Laurel's involvement, again thanking the crowd for their interest in the trust and inviting them to join.

After the obligatory reminder to shut off phones and not take pictures, she introduced the play, and disappeared off stage right. The audience applauded as the characters entered from multiple directions, and the students began the first performance ever by the newly minted Lucia and Paul Monroe Theatrical Trust, or LPMTT.

The name is cumbersome, but the Monroes had been active members of the Boulder community, not just the university, and it was important to the board of the trust to include their names in the camp, so LPMTT it was.

The first half of the show, for the most part, went great; there was a costume issue for Regan (the hem on her gown had gotten torn and she had nearly tripped on it) and the King of France had missed a cue, but was able to play it off by exaggerating how awestruck he was by Cordelia. Other than those things, it looked and sounded marvelous.

During intermission, while Guppy fixed Regan's costume, Dr. K gave a pep talk and expressed her pride in how the students were performing, bolstering them for the remainder of the show. I found Madi and told her I met her parents, which made her smile.

"I just wish Laurel could be here, but the doctor and Ms. Faulkner both said no," she said as I checked her costume for possible mishaps.

Asher was filming this production, as he would their second one as well, so Dr. K could start a library for the LPMTT. It was easier for Asher to do it because he records most of our shows rather than have Dr. K trying to figure that aspect out while teaching and coaching her actors. Once the camp expanded, their tech crew would be responsible for the filming and every other aspect Mustardseed Productions had covered this time around.

When the show ended, the audience rose to their feet during the curtain calls and applauded robustly. Granted, it was mostly friends, family, and various CU faculty members, but the enthusiasm was deserved; the students had done a fantastic job with a difficult play, and they earned the recognition.

Like our shows, the students had a meet and greet with opportunities for pictures, but, unlike our show, after this happened, the casts' family and friends were asked to stay a little longer to be questioned by Dr. K about the performance and what feedback they had for the actors. While this was happening, our crew began cleaning the house, picking up forgotten items for the lost and found, which would be the table in the back for now in case the owners realized their error and returned for them, gathering programs to be used for the next matinee, and setting out boxes of our own programs for our performance later today.

Guppy and Meg restocked the trust table with some of both programs and more information pamphlets while the rest of us began to redress the stage for our show.

Once Dr. K had finished the critique, we helped the students out of their costumes, checking for areas that might need repair to avoid another issue like Regan's, and reorganized the areas off stage as well, knowing it was one thing we wouldn't have to deal with later as we got closer to show time.

The performers had been given the rest of the day off so they could celebrate if they wanted, and after the crowd thinned out, the students disappeared in different directions with their families and friends while we headed back to Baker Hall and the food Dr. K had catered for us since we had been busy all morning and afternoon with the matinee.

Before I sidled up to the food, I retrieved Kit from our room. We had decided that the day's early events were going to be a bit chaotic, and that it would just be safer for her to stay in the dorm, catching up on her sleep. She was sitting on the desk when I opened the door and started meowing the second I entered.

I tried to decipher and answer her questions as accurately and quickly as I could.

"It went really well. Madi did great, especially when she 'dies' instead of leaving the shack. The audience was very appreciative. Yes, it's time for dinner, and yes I can put your necklace on but we'll probably need to leave rather quickly for the theatre, so you might not want to wear it tonight."

She pondered that for a moment and decided to go sans collar to dinner. I grabbed my bag, and we headed down to eat, my stomach already growling with the thought of food.

By the time we were fed, costumed, warmed up, and ready to go, the house was packed. Eliava had taken us through our vocal exercises because Dr. K was taking Guppy around to different parts of the audience to meet some of the potential big money donors, knowing that Guppy, with or without magical aid, can be very persuasive and engaging. They only stopped schmoozing with the audience when Asher flashed the lights, which is more noticeable during an evening show than a matinee, and stepped up to center stage to address the audience.

Dr. K began by thanking our viewers, and then continued to explain the purpose of the new trust and how it came to be. Laurel's story, of losing her parents and then nearly her own life, moved everyone, even though most everyone already knew it. As I said before, the people of Boulder were aware of the Monroes and their philanthropy. She introduced the board members and others involved in the trust, including Madi who had returned for the performance, and pointed to the general direction they were sitting, front and center, asking them to rise so they could be seen. The only person missing from the group was Cal Garrett, but Dr. K didn't address that situation. Instead, she moved on to how the trust was hoping the camp would grow to include all the aspects of a production, not just the acting part, and encouraged the audience to help support the endeavor, by either a one time donation, becoming a founding member, or sponsoring the project through monthly contributions.

When she was finished, she introduced Guppy who smiled broadly and began the speech that would start the performance.

"Tonight Mustardseed Productions is extremely honored to be part of the Lucia and Paul Monroe Theatrical Trust kick-off. We are dedicating tonight's show to Laurel Monroe, wishing her a speedy and strong recovery. And without any further ado, please enjoy tonight's performance of William Shakespeare's *The Tragedy of King Lear*."

As the lights went dark, everyone in the opening act moved to their places. Asher gave them a few seconds to get settled, then slowly brought the lights up, beginning the play.

I'm not on stage until the fourth scene, so Kit and I watched from the wings, hidden from the audience by portable partitions that allowed the actors to enter and exit unseen. Kit noticed Officer Larkes before I did, motioning with her paw to the general area where they were. Once I knew where to look, they were easy to find as they were on the outer edge of the orchestra section, stage left, and Sherlock looked to be the only dog present for the show. Ethan was dressed in street clothes, which might also explain why I hadn't seen him right away; for some reason I was looking for him to be in uniform.

The taste of guilt which had somewhat left my mouth when I returned to the dorms between shows, slowly slid back in, not strong enough to cause me issues, though my eyes were itching, but decidedly stronger than it had been earlier today.

I turned to Kit, opening my eyes wide. "Am I okay?"

She studied me for a couple seconds, raised a paw and then startled me by making a so-so gesture with it. Before I could ask her where she learned that, she flashed an image of Asher into my head. She then turned and headed toward Guppy; I followed her, knowing I needed to tell my mom about the guilt taste and let her judge my eyes. It wouldn't be a problem if the other character I had the most dialogue with besides Lear wasn't Dr. Galloway's Kent / Caius. The audience was too far away to see that small of a detail, but Dr. G and I had several moments of close contact.

Guppy gave me a thorough once over. "They do seem to be going dark; let me see what I can do with your hat."

I unpinned the coxcomb and handed it to her. She started diving through the various bags of costume repair items, surfacing with some black netting and a few colorful feathers. After quick-stitching the net so it would shade my eyes, she added the feathers, one of which she purposefully caused to fall forward.

"Now push it back into place," she commanded, watching as I did so. The feather stayed put for about fifteen seconds before falling again. "Perfect. We can use this as both cover for you and as a vehicle for some comedy. I can make it fall, you just push it back like it's an annoyance, but leave it down when you're close to Galloway. Now say something."

"Something," I obeyed, my voice still normal.

"Okay, you're good there and your hair is tied back. Let's pin this cap on a little tighter, and you should be good to go." She fussed with me a bit longer, then sent me back to wait until I would enter the stage.

As we finished Act I and slipped easily into Act II, the cold, earthy taste of guilt kept wavering, growing stronger for a while, then suddenly dropping off, but never disappearing completely. Carlos advised me to leave the feather down for the remainder of my role, and I had to resist the urge to rub my eyes, only managing to do so because my scalp had started twitching.

Just like in our previous shows, when both Goneril and Regan kick the Fool's Cat, a few gasps peppered the audience but this time there was one whine; I had forgotten to warn Ethan that Kit was in a fight scene, but Sherlock quieted down quickly when he saw Kit exit on her own four paws.

By the middle of Act III, with Asher's fake storm raging and Lear falling apart, the taste of guilt was growing more constant, as was the tingling on my head. Carlos had the audience in the palm of his hand as his Lear increasingly slipped into despair and madness, putting his absentee daughters on trial, using the Fool and Poor Tom as justicers, until Kent convinces him to finally rest. Kit had sent me one image, that of a small pale pink snake beginning to form on the back of my head.

We're almost done, I sent back as I helped Kent and Gloucester carry Lear off stage left.

But something was happening. I dared not turn my back to our supplemental actors, knowing what was happening was not preventable. I heard Cole finish Poor Tom's speech, and watched as Kit missed her jump to the bench.

As I slipped back on stage, tasting the intense bitter copper earth in my mouth, feeling my eyes darken and my hair shivering, I stumbled to where Kit waited, still playing dead. From the corner of my eye, I could see a red haze near center front but couldn't look because at that moment, I could feel the snakes beginning to twist through my hair. I had to finish this scene before all hell broke loose. When I knelt down to scoop Kit up, the cry of despair that left my lips was more of a discordant shriek, my voice no longer mine alone, as a jolt of pain rocketed through my skull.

I clutched Kit tightly, admirably still playing dead while I fell apart, and staggered blindly off stage right, running into Guppy who immediately threw a cloak over my head and pushed me into Alec's arms. "Eliava, go get Officer Larkes," she ordered, then slipped out on stage and announced intermission before returning to me.

"Tisi, I'm going to have Larkes take you back to the dorm," she said soothingly, assuring the rest of the cast I was just having a migraine and it had been threatening all day, but our troupe knew what was happening; this was just a little play within a play for our guest actors.

Kit started squirming, fighting to get down; when I let her go, she slipped onto the stage, watching the crowd shift around, stretch, and do all the things audiences do during intermission.

At that moment, Ethan and Sherlock arrived backstage, escorted by Eliava and Dr. K. Guppy quickly filled him in as we walked hastily toward the easiest way to get out of the theatre area without running into anyone.

Sherlock was firing questions at me, his front feet performing some kind of frenetic tap dance, his eyes wide and searching around for Kit.

"Someone died right? That's why the snakes are back. Where's Kit? Is she okay?" He continued to search for her even as we moved further from the stage and closer to the exit.

I stopped at his words. "Laurel." I whispered, although with the other voices joining it, the whisper sounded even creepier than my speaking voice.

Guppy stopped when she heard me, but made shooing motions at Larkes. "Get her out of here." Then she turned back to the area we had just left, calling out directions to the rest of the staff and acting like nothing untoward had happened and that me having a crippling headache was a common occurrence.

"Someone needs to check on Laurel," I said quietly, trying to manage the voices and succeeding a little bit, though the one that seems to talk while inhaling continued to breathe in for a couple seconds, like a weird sigh in reverse.

Sherlock suddenly took off, back toward the staging area, making a beeline for what I had to assume was Kit, who is rather hard to see in the dark. Ethan called after him, and to his credit, the big puppy did stop and throw a glance back at us. When he did so, his demeanor suddenly changed; he lowered his head, a low growl rumbling in his throat as his glance slid over us to something at our backs.

Larkes turned immediately to face whatever was approaching, just as Kit rounded the partitions and flew past Sherlock, leaping into my arms.

I dropped my hold on the cloak to catch her, and heard the sharp intake of breath from behind.

"What the fuuuuhh?" But the word never finished, stuck on the 'uh' because the speaker couldn't finish.

I turned to face Madi. It was not the first time someone has asked, or tried to ask, me that question, and I'm sure it won't be the last. Her face was filled with fear and something else, something bordering on revulsion, and one of her hands had crept up to cover her mouth. I was relieved to see she did not have a red haze around her; I could mark her off my list.

Kit pushed one image into my head: Madi, front and center, seated with the Trust, the space on her right occupied by a hazy figure, a disturbingly hazy, red figure.

"No time," the voices snapped, and Madi flinched hard, her eyes growing wider. "Call Laurel, now!"

My own voice was frantic, but the others were hard. They never asked; they always demanded.

She stood unmoving, still staring at my hair, mouth hanging open behind her hand. I tried again, forcing my own voice to be stronger. "Madi, please. Call Laurel, now. Please."

After what seemed ages, her hand dropped to her bag, and she pulled out her phone, her eyes never leaving my face, and the fear never leaving her eyes.

The image of the empty seat slammed into my head again, and to emphasize it, Kit yowled directly into my ear.

Madi's voice shook when she started speaking, "Hey Laurel, are you doing okay? There's a ton of people here tonight."

She paused, "I was just thinking about you and wanted to make sure you were okay." After another pause, she laughed a little nervously. "I'm sorry if I woke you up; should I stop by tomorrow with lunch? I can sneak in whatever you want."

My heart, which had been beating so furiously I thought it might burst from my chest, began to slow. Her conversation which could have been with an answering machine changed when she laughed and asked that last question. Laurel was alive; someone else had met their end tonight and their killer was in our audience. Kit yowled again, her claws beginning to dig into my shoulder.

When Madi wrapped up the call, she looked from Ethan to me and back, the fear still on her face when she dragged her gaze back to me.

"Madison," the voices began, "I need to know who you were sitting next to tonight."

Her voice was still trembling as she spoke. "Marcos Canelo and Beth Norris."

Ethan turned his gaze to me. "Your squirrel might not need glasses after all."

"Beth Norris was on your right," I stated, my eyes not leaving her face, the snakes having long since pushed my cap off, writhing and hissing in frustration.

Madi managed to nod; she was shivering now, her fear beginning to overwhelm her senses as she tried to make sense of what she was seeing.

Ethan noticed her panic growing and put his hands on her shoulders, turning her to face him, though it took a serious effort for her to tear her gaze from me and focus on him.

"Madison, please listen to me. Does Norris have a key to the Monroe house?"

She nodded again, still trembling, but her eyes locked onto Larkes now, holding them as a drowning swimmer clutches whatever is near them in hopes of surviving.

From where we were, I could see the flashing of the stage lights; the show was about to continue and there was no way we could let Madi return to her seat considering she was probably slipping into shock.

Ethan removed one hand from Madi, reached into his pocket, and pulled out his credentials, holding them in front of her eyes.

"Madi, I'm a police officer. I know you don't know me, but I need you to trust me right now." As he finished speaking, Sherlock walked slowly up and sat down, turning his big brown eyes to Madi and whining softly.

I took this opportunity to put the cloak back on, flipping the hood up to contain the snakes, though some of them fought to stick their heads out. I wanted to speak, but I knew my voices would only push Madi further into shock, so I stayed as still as possible, trying to minimize the threat I had become.

Larks threw a quick glance to me before continuing. "Tisi isn't here to hurt you; she's here to protect Laurel. You know what a fury is, right? Tisi is one of those, as are her sisters. They helped us close a case in Salida that would have remained open forever. I promise you she is trying to help Laurel."

Before Madi could respond, we were all startled by the sound of approaching footsteps. I half turned to see Guppy briskly walking to us, the faint shadow of Richard behind her, using her for cover.

"It's Garrett, Tisi. He died pretty much as Act III was happening; the doctors resuscitated him a couple times, but it wasn't to be. He's your murder victim." Her voice betrayed no shock at seeing Madi, but her eyes were darting from her and Larkes back to me, questioningly.

"It's Beth Norris," I said as calmly as I could, the voices wrecking the attempt. "She killed him, and I'm guessing she is who Mama Matilda saw leaving the house the night Laurel was pushed."

My mom nodded at my conclusions. "I don't know how all this ties together, but she's back in her seat, untouchable for the moment."

I slowly turned back to Madi, who had calmed down a little, but still looked like she could shatter into a million pieces if pushed.

"Madison," I said as softly as possible. "I don't know why Norris tried to kill Laurel and then pin it on Garrett, but I know she may try again. She needs to be . . ." I searched for a word for a few seconds. 'Taken care of' sounded too murderous, and 'corrected' didn't sound much better. I finally settled for ". . . stopped."

Madi took a deep breath then, her eyes never straying from Ethan's face, still afraid to look at me even though most of the snakes were undercover. Her face was slowly hardening, her fingers mindlessly flipping her phone around though her body and voice still shook slightly.

"What can I do to help?"

Chapter 26

The three of us and Sherlock made our way to the residence hall. I had sent Kit back with Guppy; I didn't want her to miss the curtain calls, and I wanted her to see if the red glow extended to any of the other members of the trust. She hadn't wanted to go at first, but after a brief conversation where only my side was audible, she jumped into Guppy's arms, making me promise I wouldn't do anything without her.

Sherlock and Ethan walked on either side of Madi, not so much to keep her from running away, but to keep a buffer around her, making me less noticeable. Ethan was questioning her about Ms. Norris, if she had ever noticed any behaviors that, in retrospect, seemed odd.

Madi kept her gaze away from me, but was doing her best to answer all of the questions asked. "When I was still allowed to go there without supervision, I found her coming out the front door with a banker's box. She told me Ms. Faulkner had sent her to retrieve some papers. It didn't seem strange at the time because they were in the middle of setting up the trust. Do you think she was stealing some of Mr. Monroe's Scotch? Is that what was in the box?"

"It's a good possibility," Ethan said, his voice calm and encouraging. "Though she may have taken it at any time after the initial investigation was over." He then smoothly changed the subject, leading Madi to a lighter place. "How is Laurel? Are the doctors happy with her progress?"

I was only half listening as she responded, my brain was circling ideas of how to get Norris away from any prying eyes so I could dish out some justice. Like with Keith Connors in Salida, I wanted to leave the lawyer with only her guilt so she would confess to everything she had done. The legal system could mete out the rest of the punishment on what was left of her.

Because I was tuned into my own thoughts, I missed the question Ethan asked me the first time, but caught it the second as he interrupted my thoughts with my name.

"Tisi, what do you think about that idea?"

I kept my voice low, hoping to minimize the impact on Madi. "I'm sorry I was zoned out; what idea?"

"Madi told me about the Monroe's house; it seems like that would be the most sheltered place to do what you . . . do," he finished, unsure of how to put my purpose into words. "Since she needs one of the lawyers there to ensure no tampering is happening, Madi thinks she can get Norris there. She can also call the police when it's over."

"Are you going to kill her?" Madi blurted out suddenly, her voice both scared and angry.

I shook my head. "No, that's not what I do; I'm not a murderer." I paused, a little unsure of how to explain this to Madi without further freaking her out. Of course when we were finished with all this, my sisters and I would need to wrap up these memories and replace them with something less traumatic. I really didn't need to tell her that right now, though. "I'm going to make her feel the guilt she has been wrestling with since the initial attempt on Laurel, guilt she might not even realize she is feeling; once that's in place, she'll start confessing, hoping that by telling someone, the pain of the guilt will go away."

I didn't add that it would never go away, that it was something she would be stuck with, agonizing over, until the Fates dealt with her in their own time.

The three of us were silent for a while, Sherlock sniffing ahead, then returning to walk by Madi's side.

I finally broke that silence. "Are you sure you want to help, Madi? I don't want you to feel pressured or put on the spot."

Sherlock stuck his nose in her hand and woofed quietly. "She's really nice and won't hurt you," he was saying, though the others only heard dog sounds.

Madi drew in a deep breath. "That woman tried to kill Laurel. I'm not going to let her get away with that or find another opportunity to try again. And you know she'll try to swindle Laurel somehow once Ms. Faulkner retires. I'll call her in the morning and set up something. I'll text you the time." She paused for a moment, and when she spoke again, there was the slightest hint of real fear in her voice. "Can I go home now?"

Ethan spoke before I could. "Of course. Let me get Tisi into the dorm, and I'll drop you off myself. She is no danger to you, Madi. And Laurel will be safe."

When we reached Baker Hall, Larkes turned to me and set his hand on my arm. "Had I known that all this was going to go down this evening, I would have asked for tomorrow off as well. As it is, I have to get back to Salida. I'll talk to Madi some more about tomorrow while I'm getting her home. Call me if you need to talk, but for sure tomorrow after it's all over. And tell your mom I'm sorry I missed the end of the play."

He squeezed my arm before letting it go, motioning for both Madi and Sherlock to follow him, then waved back at me from the top of the steps.

I watched them disappear from sight before heading inside. The dorm was dead—our crew was still working, and the students were still out with their parents and friends. I kept the cloak over my head anyway and scurried to my room, wanting to get a shower in before I tried to get some rest. Lucky for me, my snakes like water, so I stood in the spray for a while, letting them enjoy it.

When I returned to my room and crawled into my temporary bed hoping to get some rest—even though I was sure my thoughts would keep me up, spinning as they were—I noticed I had a voice message from Officer Larkes and a text from Madi. I opted to check the text first, breathing a sigh of relief when I saw it wasn't long: *Norris agreed to meet me at the Monroe's at 8:30 tomorrow morning; I'll be there at 8:15.*

My fingers hesitated to respond. I wanted to explain so many things and double check that she wasn't completely freaked out, but in the end I merely confirmed the time: *I'll be there at 8:15.*

After hitting send, I immediately regretted not saying more and added a brief apology and a thank you. Then I turned my attention to the voice message. Ethan's voice sounded concerned, the droning of the Jeep's engine forcing him to speak louder than his usual volume.

"Tisi, it's Ethan. I think Madi is a bit calmer now. I told her about the situation in Salida, and said she should just let you in the house, and then go about watering and doing stuff outside once Norris gets there as she doesn't need to be present when you and Kit do your thing. I'm sorry I missed the rest of the play; the first three acts were great! Please call me when you're finished and let me know how it went and if Madi is okay. She's just a bit overwhelmed and scared right now. Be careful and don't forget to call."

I set my alarm to give me plenty of time to wake up and walk over to the Monroe's house, then settled back onto my pillow, the snakes fidgeting a bit as they tried to avoid being smushed. And suddenly, I felt a heavy weight settle on me.

I don't have many friends, not the kind you can tell all your secrets to or count on to have your back no matter what, outside my family and troupe. There are too many things that can go sideways quickly and bring too many inquiring eyes into our lives. We let very few people into our hearts because inevitably, we have to let them go, removing ourselves from their memories for everyone's sake, not just ours.

Ethan Larkes was different. His ability to see ghosts, an ability he doesn't advertise, allowed him to understand us, and the way he handled what I did to Keith Connors demonstrated that he not only understood us and our dilemmas, but he trusted us as well. I'm sure most of that teaching came from his grandmother who also could see spirits, and she had probably early on taught him to not talk about his gift with people, who would more than likely either turn on him or call him crazy. Guppy had done the same with my sisters and me.

He had found in our troupe people who wouldn't look at him as if he had a third eye, people who understood what it was like to live with a secret. Of course our profession had us pretending to be other people on a daily basis; we were used to acting around people as it's what we do for a living. I imagine it was hard for Ethan growing up, made easier only through his relationship with his Nanna. With her gone, I think he enjoyed being with our troupe because he could be the guy who sees ghosts without being teased or doubted, something he couldn't do with his co-workers.

One of the snakes stretched out a bit, then relaxed, draping down over one of my eyes. Rather than move it, I just kept my eyes shut, hoping my brain would shut off so I could get some sleep. I sighed again into the dark, waiting for morning to come.

———————————

I don't usually sleep so hard, and when my alarm went off, I snapped awake like someone had thrown a bucket of cold water on me. I glanced over to the other bed. Kit was awake as well, washing her face while the sun streamed in, warming her.

"Hey," I croaked, clearing my throat to get better volume. "How'd the curtain calls go?"

She sent me the image of her entering the stage with Guppy, who gave a brief explanation of my absence before setting the cait sith down to receive her adulations. She also shared with me that she had sat for a few selfies with various board members, including Norris. What followed this tidbit of info was an image of a sparking Kit-Void and me draining out the lawyer's essence and leaving only the guilt followed by a question mark.

I smiled at her. "In fact, we're about to go do that now. I just need to brush my teeth and put on my best snake-hiding hoodie and we can be off."

When I returned from the bathroom, Guppy was sitting on my bed looking worried.

"You have a plan, I understand? Officer Larkes swung by the theatre before he headed out of town. He stayed to watch some of the play and let Sherlock and Kit catch up but then headed home."

I quickly outlined the plan we had come up with the night before, including that Ethan had taken Madi home and calmed her down a bit.

"We still have to take away some of these memories, you know," Guppy said solemnly, her eyes watching me for any reaction.

I only nodded, sliding my sunglasses onto my face, pulling up my hood, and tightening the drawstring. "I know. We'll be back soon." I looked over to Kit; she walked toward my satchel, waiting for me to pick it up and put her in it.

"Be careful," Guppy said as we slipped out the door.

I threw her a small smile. "Always am."

When I walked up the steps to the Monroe's front door, it swung open suddenly, and Madi rushed me inside, making an effort to not actually look at me.

"I'm not supposed to go inside by myself," she explained, looking out the door in both directions, and, finding nothing to be concerned about, closing it just as quickly as she had opened it. "Just hide, in the pantry or something. When we come in, I'll go out back to start watering. Let me know when to call the police."

She was nervous, her voice shaky and her eyes avoiding me at all costs. Before I could speak, she started up again.

"Did Mama Matilda really tell you she saw someone leave that night? Can you talk to squirrels?" She stopped abruptly, her eyes suddenly filling with tears.

"Am I losing my mind?"

"Madi," I said, trying to sound as normal as possible and failing miserably at it. I started to lift Kit out of my bag. "You aren't losing your mind. I can understand squirrels, dogs too, and certain magical cats."

Madi half stretched her hand out to pet Kit, a natural reaction as she had been doing it pretty much since the moment she met the cait sith, but drew it back awkwardly.

Kit tilted her head at Madi and meowed.

"I . . . I have to get outside. Hurry and hide," she said, withdrawing her hand completely and heading toward the door to exit. I could hear the tumblers turn as she locked us in so she could begin her 'I've been waiting outside for so long' act for Ms. Norris.

I moved into the pantry, Kit wondering why Madi wouldn't pet her; I could tell her feelings were hurt.

"Well," I started, wondering how to explain what Madi was going through at the moment, and knowing the cait sith probably wouldn't understand it anyway. "I'm afraid I've frightened her. Not everyone is like Officer Larkes and Sherlock. She'll be okay though, once we get through this."

I opened a few drawers in the old apothecary, remembering the stories Madi had told me about her friendship with Laurel. When Kit's ear pricked up, her head turning to the door, I stopped my snooping and listened. I could hear voices, which soon grew louder as the door opened, and the two women entered.

Madi's voice rose and fell in volume as she moved around the kitchen, giving me a running commentary as she did.

"I just don't want her to come home to a bunch of dead plants and angry squirrels," she was saying, the sound of the water faucet cutting off some of her words as she filled a pitcher to water the indoor plants.

I couldn't really hear Norris's reply, but whatever it was, it didn't impress Madi.

"Well, I'm so sorry you feel that way." Madi's voice was strained, rising as her temper did. What did the lawyer say to her that I missed?

Again, I could hear the other woman speaking but couldn't make out the words, but I could hear Madi clear as day; she must have planted herself in front of the pantry. I started willing her to go outside, but instead, she responded.

"Yeah? So why did you push her down the stairs? Lie all you want, but I know it was you."

At that point, everything went quiet. There was no response from Norris, and Madi offered no follow up to her initial argument. Kit glanced up at me, her eyes wide with worry.

When the noise picked up outside the pantry, I flipped my hood back, stuffed my sunglasses in my pouch pocket, and threw the door open, hoping to stop Madi from doing whatever it was she was thinking about doing.

My entrance brought everything to a screeching halt. Madi, her back to me, had the watering carafe poised to throw, and Norris, having grabbed one of the knives from the butcher block, was closing in, her eyes filled with anger.

"Bethany Norris," I stated, the voices rising in volume, forcing both women to freeze where they were.

Madi didn't turn to look at me. Her shoulders were shaking as she broke down crying. I set my hand on her shoulder, ignoring the slight flinch as I did so, and pulled her to one side and pushed her into the pantry, getting her out of the other woman's range.

Norris opened her mouth to speak, but at that moment both Kit and I reached for her, the voices already beginning to catalog her deeds and awaken the guilt inside her. Added to the three voices coming from me was Madi's own, damning the woman for trying to hurt Laurel, her words flowing as fast and freely as her tears.

Norris had dropped the knife, reaching for her head instead, the voices shrieking at her, words so fast and angry they were intelligible to everyone but me and the lawyer, whose wailing was growing in volume. The hissing of the snakes intensified as I stepped closer to the crumbling figure in front of me.

Unable to take her gaze from me, Norris began to collapse in on herself, dropping to the floor, her wailing turning into words, words of confession, words of regret, words that would send her to jail, and words that would soon become the only words she would be able to say as her guilt consumed her, swallowing the confidence she once had and reducing her to little more than a shell of her former self.

I turned to Madi, curled up on the floor crying, Kit standing in front of her, protecting her from any sudden moves that Norris might make, even though I knew she was incapable of doing anything at the moment except continue to admit her guilt as it burned its way out of her.

"Call the police now, Madison," the voices commanded as I shut the door to the pantry and turned back around to face the broken figure in front of me. With Madi safely ensconced, Kit and I reached for Norris's soul, beginning to draw it out, draw out the essence that made her who she was, leaving behind only enough to keep her aware of her guilt and compel her to confess the whole of her actions.

Once we stepped back, leaving just that tiny bit, I could hear Madi on the phone with the police. I knew we needed to get going before they arrived; our presence would only complicate matters.

I lightly rapped on the door. "Stay in there until they arrive. You have nothing to worry about; Norris will confess everything. Thank you, Madi, for helping me. I know it wasn't easy."

After a second's thought, I slid a chair under the knob, wanting to keep Madi in there and out of trouble should she decide to come out before the police arrived. I didn't need Alec there to know how much anger Madi was still feeling.

Kit leapt onto the counter and nudged my bag, already climbing in it as I picked it up and slung it over my shoulder. I could feel the snakes beginning to tire, their thrashing over now that their quarry was a sobbing mess on the floor. Soon they would disappear completely, but in the meantime, I flipped my hood up and slid my glasses back on before heading out the door and down the block. I wouldn't leave the area until I saw the police arrive, but of course that would be from a distance.

I was halfway down the block when I heard the first sirens. I turned and began walking back to the house. I knew they would pay me no mind, but just in case, I wanted to seem like I wasn't leaving a crime scene. A car raced by me, followed shortly by another. At that point, I turned onto a side street and began to make my way back to the theatre, my hand already reaching for my phone to call Larkes and let him know it was done.

Chapter 27

B y the time I reached the University Theatre Building, wishing I had stopped off at Willow's for an affogato but resisting, the student actors were crowded around Dr. K, their panic palpable to everyone in the room. I slid my hand under my hood. The snakes had stopped squirming halfway to the campus, and now they were completely gone. If the snakes were gone, my voice should be normal again as well, so I called out to Guppy the second I saw her.

She motioned me over, her eyes occasionally darting to the cluster of noise that was Dr. K and her students.

"Everything copacetic?" she asked, as I put down my hood and stowed my sunglasses back in the pouch.

Kit, who had jumped out of my satchel and was now sitting on the back of a chair, answered Guppy's question with the same so-so paw motion she had made to me earlier.

"She's right," I said. "It could've been smoother, but it's finished." I looked around the theatre and asked a question of my own. "What's going on here?"

Guppy followed my gaze, speaking as she did so.

"Dr. Galloway is down at the police station hoping to bring Madi back here in time for the matinee, and Dr. K is explaining to the cast why their Fool isn't here yet, hoping to calm them down. It might take a wee bit of magic to get through this last production."

I nodded, agreeing with her. "Madi didn't go outside; she provoked Norris into an argument. When I came out of hiding, they were getting ready to scrap, and Norris had a knife.

It was Guppy's turn to sigh. "While I admire her loyalty to her friend, we are going to have some serious cleaning up to do here before we go."

We both watched as Dr. K dismissed the students so they could begin their vocal warm-ups; a few hung back and she leaned in to hear their concerns better, her face a mask of encouragement and empathy. Jaime hugged her before joining the other cast members working with Eliava, who was handling the warm up since Dr. Galloway was unavailable. When she was finished with the few remaining students, she approached us.

By now my sisters had also worked their way over to Guppy, Meg giving me a quick side hug and Alec raising her fist just a bit for a subtle fist bump. With her other hand, she handed me what could only be a large affogato from Willow's.

Kit meowed in protest, and Meg produced a cup of ice cream she had concealed behind her back.

"Chill, kitten; we didn't forget you," she smiled as Kit jumped from her seat, honing in on the ice cream like she was starving. "Don't forget the possibility of brain freeze."

"So," Dr. K began, "We find ourselves in a bit of a pickle if Mathew can't spring Madi in time." She checked her phone again, something she had been doing off and on since Kit and I arrived. "I asked him to text me the second they left the station. Now I'm just trying not to freak out."

Guppy reached out and rested her hand on Dr. K's arm. "Why don't you take the cast and Eliava into the changing rooms; getting into costume might help them relax. We'll wait here for Madi's return. There's some things we have to do." Her voice trailed off; there was no need to say more.

As Dr. K made her way to the vocal practice group, calling out her intentions as she went, my family settled in to wait; Kit and I focused on finishing our treats. I didn't want to think about what we had to do next.

It was nearly an hour later that Dr. Galloway walked in with Madi, whose eyes were still red from crying. They both scanned the empty theatre, their eyes finally coming to rest on the only living things waiting for them. Mathew broke into a smile at seeing us and headed our way; Madi's glance started skating around, the look on her face suggesting she was caught in a trap with nowhere to run.

Guppy was on her feet immediately, waving them over, her hands continuing to fidget even as they approached us, weaving a web of serenity which stretched out into the theatre. Once they were within talking distance versus shouting distance, she began speaking, her voice adding to the aura of peace.

"Dr. K and Eliava have taken everyone to get changed; she asked that Madi stay with us to get a little bit of her vocal warm-up in before she enters the chaos of the changing rooms."

The lie slipped from Guppy's lips easily, and Dr. Galloway threw her a mock salute and headed that direction, giving Madi's hand a brief squeeze before leaving her in our care.

For a few moments, no one spoke. Madi's eyes were large with fear, and she refused to look in my direction, focusing instead on my mom, who continued to weave her spell.

"I won't tell anyone," Madi finally said, her voice breaking and the tears starting up again, her hand furiously wiping them away.

Guppy reached out and took Madi's hands in her own. "Relax, Madi; we know that. You are a true and loyal friend to Laurel. We really are here to get your warm-up in."

As she finished speaking, Alec began the spell that would take away the memories of me, of my snakes, of my voice, removing the fury she had seen, both directly after last night's encounter and this morning's adventure. Meg's voice chimed in next, spinning a new narrative of how Bethany Norris was apprehended and Madi's role in it, removing my involvement and Kit's presence completely, And finally, I joined, my voice shaking a little, as I removed any trace of friendship or affection Madi might have felt for me once, knowing that if she picked at the memory of me too much, she could unravel the whole thing. It would be best if I were just another actor in the troupe who came to help Dr. K.

Guppy reached out to steady me as I removed myself from another possible friend's memory. This wasn't the first time I had done this, and I knew it wouldn't be the last.

As we finished up, there was a beat of silence before Madi blinked and looked around, embarrassment on her face.

"I'm sorry, what was I saying? I feel like such a fool for being late, but I had no idea that Ms. Norris was going to go off the deep end like that."

Alec laughed, "Well feeling like a fool is a good thing for someone about to go be a fool on stage. Head on over to the dressing rooms, the rest of the cast is waiting."

Madi smiled at her, "Right-o; one fool coming up!" And without a backward glance, she headed out of the theatre and into the arms of her friends and fellow cast members.

Later that evening when we were doing our own vocal warm-ups for our last performance at the Mary Rippon Theatre, Dr. Galloway filled us in on what had occurred and what he had overheard at the police station.

"So that lawyer apparently had a total meltdown. Freaked out Madi so much she hid in the pantry and then the crazy lady put a chair in front of the door to lock her in. And at that point, was screaming about why she had tried to kill Laurel and had actually succeeded in killing Garrett. Madi was in shock and wouldn't talk at all; she just kept asking me if she was safe. Poor kid, she's really shook up. I'm not sure what you said to her, but she seems much calmer now, not so haunted."

We had all merely smiled, Guppy finally responding with some comment about Madi just needing a mother figure at that point so she had stepped in to fill that role as needed.

"Anyway," Galloway had continued, a conspiratorial tone in his voice, "Scuttlebutt is that she and Garrett were in cahoots, trying to get Cesare's away from the fold as it is the most profitable of the three establishments. When they couldn't get the other managers on board to also break away, they decided to remove Laurel, thinking with the last Monroe gone, the restaurants could be easily taken. That didn't work out, but then the trust idea came about and Ms. Norris realized she would soon have control of a lot of money once Ms. Faulkner retired."

He had paused then, his eyes going a little unfocused as his memory traveled back to the police station. "She was just screaming out what she had done; everyone in the building could hear her. It was more than a little disturbing. She killed Garrett because she was afraid he would crack, but also because she didn't need him anymore and didn't want to share the money she was planning on siphoning out of the trust once she was the Monroe Estate's attorney. All of this at the top of her lungs, like it was exploding from her. And when she finished, she just started right back up again at the beginning. I couldn't get Madi out of there fast enough."

Alec was the first one to respond. "Sounds like she had a little mental breakdown caused by her guilt. Many people don't realize how heavy guilt is and how it never goes away, just gets heavier and heavier."

I nodded in agreement but didn't speak. Bethany Norris had done what neither Cora Buchanan nor Jason Mallec could do, or at least didn't have time to do before they died: she killed her co-conspirator, and all for the idea of getting a larger payout for herself. I'm sure it had been a long time in planning, starting when the Monroes were conveniently removed from the land of living by a petty little spirit working her way toward becoming a local legend. I wish I could say I was surprised, but greed, next to love, is one of the top contributors to murder, dollar signs shining brighter than any light and singing a siren song many cannot refuse, even if it means killing someone.

"I worry about Laurel," Dr. Galloway continued. "How is she ever going to trust anyone who isn't Penelope Faulkner again?"

"Madi," I said simply, my voice quiet. "Madi will help her; she's a good friend and has proved over and over she isn't around for the Monroe money."

Meg threw her opinion in as well. "Not to mention, when she finds out that both Moira and the Canelos told Norris and Garrett to kick rocks, I think her restaurant kingdom is going to become stronger. She has a good network; I'm sure Ms. Faulkner will stick around a while longer to vet another candidate to take over, maybe even Jeremy from Cesare's."

The conversation stopped when Dr. K approached us, smiling. "The cast is coming back for your last performance, except for Madi. I gave her Ember in the costume, and she is going to the hospital tonight to give it to Laurel. She said to thank you and to break a leg."

She threw a glance at Mathew then before speaking again. "Has he coerced you into spending some of your time off in Denver?"

Dr. Galloway blushed at our looks of confusion.

"Oopsie," Dr. K smiled and winked, heading out into the house to help Asher run a last light check before the crowd entered.

We all turned to Dr. G, who fidgeted with his costume for a moment before speaking.

"I'm hoping you might come and speak to the Richard III Society; we're having our annual meeting in Denver, and I think they would love to pick your brains about the Shakespeare text and historical inaccuracies." He smiled sheepishly, glancing at each of us in turn until his gaze came to rest on Guppy.

I could tell from her expression that we would be going to Denver and to this Society convention; I could also tell she was debating how to break that news to our Richard, worried that he would start up his campaign of proving he was, in fact, *the* Richard III.

"Well," she finally said, hands on her hips, "I think some of us can arrange that. We can't do a full performance because it is a break for my crew and we need a lot of extra characters, but I know a few cast members who would love to be there. Find us a place to call home for a week, and we'll see what we can do."

Galloway's face broke into a huge smile. "Done! Thank you a million times over." He rushed away, probably going to text someone that he had gotten the go-ahead from us.

Later that evening, in our circle up before the show began, Guppy gave a heartfelt thank you to our guest performers, acknowledging that we couldn't have been successful without them. She also thanked Dr. K, asking her to pass on our gratitude to the university. As she dismissed us to our starting places, she stopped me, setting her hand gently on my shoulder.

"Are you okay, Tisi?" she asked, her eyes worried.

I inhaled deeply and nodded. "Yeah, I'm okay. I don't have to go to the Richard III thing, do I?"

She laughed, "No. I want you and your sisters to have fun this next week; go to the museums, go hiking, go out and have a nice dinner and some drinks." She paused then, and I could see her brain working through what she wanted to say next.

"I'm sorry things turned out the way they did. I know you're hurting, and nothing I can say can take that away, but I want you to know . . ."

The flashing of the lights cut her off–her cue to step on stage and introduce the show. She cast a look at me, knowing she couldn't finish because she had to go be Madam Producer. So instead of talking, she quickly threw her arms around me and pulled me into a tight hug.

"You are a wonder," she finally whispered before pulling away and stepping into the single spotlight on stage.

I looked down when I felt something touch my leg, finding Kit sitting there, her eyes wide and staring at me. When she bunched up to jump, I instinctively caught her, helping her onto my shoulder.

"What's up, hep cat?" I asked quietly, watching as the play began, feeling the familiar need to be on stage pulling at me.

Instead of an image, I heard words, loud and clear, in a tiny voice inside my head.

"I'll always be your friend. Always, always, always."

I tipped my head sideways, and Kit threw herself into the strongest head butt, nearly tumbling from her perch.

I felt a heaviness begin to lift from my heart. I had my family; I had my troupe; and I had people who understood and accepted that I was a witch and a fury to boot. In the end, I also had saved a life; Laurel and her estate would be safer now that Norris was gone from the picture.

"Back at you, Void Kitty," I smiled. "Let's go break our legs."

Acknowledgments

The book you are holding in your hands now was started in the spring of my last year as a public school teacher. By the time it was finished, I had retired, and my first readers suddenly were not in my life five days a week. So I am eternally grateful that Rebekah and Rhonda still found the time to look over my drafts, point out my errors, and give me feedback on the direction I was heading. I am also thankful that we are still meeting for coffee or brunch when our schedules align and that our friendship has survived the major changes in our lives. I am lucky to have you both in my life.

The same goes for my editor, Joyce, who still finds time to scour the text and offer suggestions, even when she's busy with Grammy Camp or exploring her different artistic talents. I am so happy that we are both pursuing our creative sides, and that we still meet for Spontaneous Lunches which often involve margaritas. If there are typos in here, that is all on me.

I wish people could have heard or read some of the conversations I had with my mom, Bunny, during the process of figuring out the plot. If the powers that be were listening in, they probably put a tracker on my phone after all the times she would ask or text "Have you killed anyone yet?" I am grateful that Bunny, and my two sisters—Lori and Amy—continue to serve as role models both in my books and in my life.

Many thanks also to Lindi, Travis, and Erin Van Wander-the-Halls, who continue to help me navigate my way through modern publicity. I think I'm a bad student as I can't seem to think of things to post on social media. I appreciate your patience with me as I continue to stumble along.

I would also like to thank my junior and senior English teachers when I was in high school—Rena and Dixie; though you are both gone now, I will never forget how you supported my creative writing in serious assignments and encouraged me to continue playing with language. Both of you helped me become the teacher I was and the writer I am.

Once again, my imaginative niece Sophie has designed a cover that matches the first in both creativity and understatement. The books now remind me of Arden Shakespeare covers. Please check out what she can do when she lets her mind run wild on Insta: @straydogpress.

And as always, to my husband, Aaron, who continues to support me and all my crazy ideas, including talking squirrels, and never even looks at me like I've lost my mind. I love you.

About the Author

M A Dershem spent 27 years teaching English Language Arts in a public high school. When she wasn't grading or planning, she was dreaming up plots and outlining novels she hoped to write in her spare time, which was non-existent during her years in the classroom. When she retired, all the spare time in the world showed up at once, and *Something Wicked*, her debut novel, was the result. When not writing or reading cozy mysteries, she enjoys spending time with family and friends, taking long walks if it isn't 100 degrees outside, fighting with figuring out how to make macarons, and sampling new varieties of bourbon. She currently lives in north Texas with her husband and their two incredibly spoiled cats.

About the Artist

Sophie Walton is an illustrator and printmaker. Originally from Colorado, she received her BA in Classical Studies from the University of British Columbia and her MFA in Fine Arts from the University of Montana. Her work has been shown at the Cawein Gallery in Forest Grove, OR, the Brinton Museum in Big Horn, WY, and the Montana Museum of Art & Culture, Allez! Missoula, ZACC Gallery, and Radius Gallery in Missoula, MT, among others. She has also been featured in I Like Your Work's 2023 MFA Catalog, the Spring 2023 edition of Camas Magazine, and provided the cover design of Cutbank Literary Magazine, volume 95. She resides in Missoula, MT with her partner Alexandra and cat Sam.

Coming Soon

Join Tisi, Kit, and the rest of the *Mustardseed Production* players as they return to Salida and the mountains for their next mystery, *So Far in Blood*.

Made in United States
Orlando, FL
15 December 2024

55708968R00202